DESIGNATED DISRUPTER

TROY ANDERSON

FRONT
LINE

We are at the inception of the next Great Awakening. With all the chaos, evil, and vile murder of key voices, a rise is coming. There is a sound, a holy roar, which has been stirred. Those who once stood by and cowered to the threats of society have the choice to awaken and return to the One who called them to stand and take back what has been stolen—souls. Troy Anderson has written a vital piece for his move to take place. *Designated Disrupter* delivers a message of hope in a time when we need it most. He says, "God may yet save America—not because of our merit, but for the sake of the faithful remnant who still serve Him." Well done, Troy, thank you for this call to action. This is a call to the apex of our time. Let's rise!

—Joseph Z
Author, Broadcaster
JosephZ.com

In *Designated Disrupter*, Troy Anderson provides a compelling and eye-opening perspective on how God often uses the most unexpected people to accomplish His purposes. Much like Jonah's message to Nineveh, America is at a crossroads—facing either judgment or revival. Anderson skillfully blends biblical truth and cultural analysis to demonstrate how figures such as Donald Trump, Jordan Peterson, and others may serve as catalysts for a spiritual awakening in our time. This book is both a wake-up call and a roadmap for Christians who long to see God's hand move mightily once again in our nation. I highly recommend *Designated Disrupter* to all who desire to understand the times we are living in and their role in advancing God's kingdom.

—Dr. Robert Jeffress
Senior Pastor, First Baptist Church, Dallas

America is standing at a Nineveh moment. Will we turn back to God or plunge into darkness? In *Designated Disrupter*, Troy Anderson unveils how God is raising up surprising voices—leaders, influencers, President Trump, and truth-tellers—to shake our culture and prepare the way for revival. This message is timely, prophetic, and desperately needed for such a time as this.

—Paul Begley
Evangelist; Author, *Revelation 911*

With prophetic urgency, Troy Anderson shows that America's destiny hangs in the balance. *Designated Disrupter* is both a wake-up call and a roadmap for revival—and a reminder that our nation must stand with Israel to secure God's blessing.

—Rabbi Jonathan Bernis
President, CEO, Jewish Voice Ministries International

This is a fascinating book. It is certainly clear that God is doing something spectacular in our nation, as Troy Anderson documents in this masterpiece like only he can. As usual, Anderson hits a home run. Don't miss *Designated Disrupter*.

—Alex Newman
Senior Editor, *The New American*

I have known Troy Anderson for seven years. We first met when I worked with *Movieguide* and attended his graduation from Dr. Ted Baehr's class. From that day on, we have shared a friendship rooted in faith, prayer, and the power of the Holy Spirit. Together, we have witnessed many miracles—answers to prayers when we prayed in agreement. As he was writing *The Trump Code*, we saw God's hand spare President Trump's life and raise him up as a leader for this pivotal hour. Every morning at 8 a.m., we pray, and we have marveled at how the Lord has moved in our lives.

Throughout history, God has raised up "designated disrupters"—men and women who confront darkness, call a nation to repentance, and change the course of history. America has been spared again and again through the obedience of these disrupters who answered God's call. We have recently said goodbye to our dear brother Charlie Kirk, who is now in heaven, but Trump remains, and I believe God still has work for him to do. The church in America needs to awaken, to rise up, and to march in step with the Holy Spirit. Jesus is coming soon. We must be ready, and we must be bold. I encourage every reader to place your hand on this book, *Designated Disrupter*, and pray for God to keep raising up disrupters—leaders who will stand for truth, resist evil, and point our nation back to Jesus Christ.

—JERRY MOSES
FORMER MEGACHURCH PASTOR
FORMER ASSISTANT TO THE PRESIDENT, *MOVIEGUIDE*, CBN, BENNY HINN
MINISTRIES

I am so thankful for Troy Anderson. I know him personally, and he is an outstanding researcher and writer. My hope is that this new book will be a huge hit. We live in a time when revival is desperately needed. Needless to say, revival almost always comes from unlikely sources. We have seen this pattern occur throughout history over and over again. In our time God is moving in very unusual ways. Just like during so many other times throughout history, institutional churches have been slow to understand what is happening because it doesn't fit their existing paradigms. I encourage you to get this book. It will cause you to think. We are truly living in one of the most important times in human history, and what is coming next is going to shock the entire globe.

—MICHAEL SNYDER
FOUNDER, *THE ECONOMIC COLLAPSE* BLOG

In these pages the author provides timely insight into what many of us are witnessing: God stirring hearts across our nation and our world. Across society, cultural shifts, political turning points, and even tragic events are awakening a new spiritual hunger. As a Christian podcast host, I hear the longing for truth daily and the signs of revival rising in unexpected places. This book is more than a commentary—it is a testimony that people from everywhere are seeking Christ again. Readers will come away not only informed but encouraged that the Spirit is moving powerfully today. I gladly endorse this important and hope-filled book.

—BRUCE OLIVER, DDIV
HOST, *TALKS FOR CHRIST*

Cataloging-in-Publication Data is on file with the Library of Congress.
International Standard Book Number: 978-1-63641-547-5
E-book ISBN: 978-1-63641-548-2

1 2025
Printed in the United States of America

Most Charisma Media products are available at special quantity discounts
for bulk purchase for sales promotions, premiums, fund-raising, and
educational needs. For details, call us at (407) 333-0600 or visit our website at
charismamedia.com.

DEDICATION

I DEDICATE THIS BOOK to my Lord and Savior, Jesus Christ—the original designated disrupter without whom there is no hope, revival, or eternal salvation.

I also dedicate this book to President Donald J. Trump, whose incredible courage and resilience amid unrelenting attacks—even assassination attempts—embodies the spirit of the designated disrupter of our time.

I further dedicate this book to Charlie Kirk, a modern-day martyr for truth whose life and death echo the story of Stephen, the first Christian martyr, who also bore witness to Christ with unshakable faith. Kirk lived with the same unwavering conviction that the gospel is worth the cost, even life itself.

And to Charlie's wife, Erika Kirk, who in her grief has stepped forward with remarkable courage, carrying an Esther-like mantle—just as the late prophet Kim Clement foresaw when he declared that an Esther would arise to pour out the "oil of gladness" and healing, helping turn a nation back to God. Her forgiveness of her husband's alleged assassin and her "yes" are multiplying the seed of Charlie's sacrifice into a rising generation who loves Jesus.

In addition, I dedicate this book to renowned faith leaders Billy Graham, Reinhard Bonkke, and Sid Roth, who foresaw the revival now unfolding in America and globally, mostly among young people.

This book is also dedicated to Jordan Peterson, Tucker Carlson, Joe Rogan, Megyn Kelly, Mel Gibson, Sylvester Stallone, Paul McGuire, Pastor Paul Begley, Rabbi Jonathan Bernis, Pastor Greg Laurie, Pastor Mark Francey, Sean Feucht, Joseph Z, and to all the modern-day watchmen and unlikely agents God has raised up—thank you for standing in the gap, for speaking truth when it costs everything, and for igniting sparks of awakening the Holy Spirit is spreading around the world. I also dedicate this book to the young generation rising with holy boldness—may you carry the flame of revival, disrupt the darkness, and lead countless souls into the light of Christ.

Finally, this book is dedicated to you—the designated disrupters of our time—who, by God's providence, are helping usher in the great end-times revival now breaking forth upon the earth.

CONTENTS

THE CHARLIE KIRK EFFECT

HAVING PENNED THE foreword to his previous book, *The Trump Code*, I am honored that my longtime friend and coauthor, Troy Anderson, asked me to write the foreword to his providentially timed new book—*Designated Disrupter: Trump and Other Unlikely Agents of Revival.*

As I write these words, our nation and the world are still reeling from the shocking assassination of Charlie Kirk, a man rightly profiled in these pages as a "designated disrupter." Charlie's tragic death at the age of thirty-one—struck down by a sniper's bullet while speaking in Utah—has become more than an unspeakable loss.

While myriad questions surround his untimely death, it has become a prophetic moment: a hinge in history. Charlie's ministry is called Turning Point USA. In a way that no one could have anticipated, his death on September 10, 2025, became exactly that—a turning point in the flow of history.

His assassination, which was televised globally, is helping ignite a global revival of Christianity and a new Great Awakening.

Throughout history, God has raised up certain men and women to disrupt the status quo. They are often unlikely figures: imperfect, sometimes controversial, but appointed to challenge the forces of darkness and awaken God's people. Their mission is often costly. For some, like Charlie, it costs them their lives. Yet their sacrifice often inspires what their words and labors alone could not: a movement that changes the world.

As gut-wrenching as it was, Charlie's death—as I believe history will show—will energize a global movement for God that will be unstoppable, as it sweeps through America and the world on a scale Charlie could never have achieved while alive.

THE ROLE OF THE DESIGNATED DISRUPTER

A designated disrupter, as defined in this book, is an unlikely person whom God raises up to confront entrenched powers and help catalyze revival. Such people rarely fit the mold that religious institutions or political establishments prefer. They provoke controversy, upset comfort zones, and often face fierce opposition.

The Bible itself is filled with such figures: Joseph in Pharaoh's court, Daniel in Babylon, Deborah leading Israel in war, John the Baptist crying out in the wilderness. And consider the courage of the prophets—Elijah confronting Ahab, Nathan confronting David, Amos calling the nation to justice.

In our time, we have seen a wide range of disrupters: 1) Donald Trump, who defied political norms to defend America's Judeo-Christian heritage; 2) Charlie Kirk, whose passion for evangelism infused a new generation of young leaders with courage; 3) Tucker Carlson, who has become a surprisingly outspoken voice of faith in God and repentance; 4) Joe Rogan, whose candid conversations have opened millions of skeptical minds to discussions of meaning, morality, and even biblical wisdom; and 5) Jordan Peterson, the Canadian psychologist who warns against the dangers of ideological tyranny and is reawakening audiences to the moral foundations of Western civilization.

None of these individuals would be the obvious choice to lead a revival movement. Yet, as in biblical history, God often uses the unexpected.

THE SPIRITUAL WAR BEHIND THE HEADLINES

To understand why designated disrupters are needed, we must grasp the nature of the massive spiritual conflict we're in. For more than seventy years, powerful globalist elites have worked to replace America's Judeo-Christian worldview with a secular, technocratic, and increasingly transhumanist vision of humanity.

The reality is that most people in America and many more around the world have been under a kind of mass delusion. Writers like Aldous Huxley, author of *Brave New World*, warned of a future scientific dictatorship that would enslave humanity not by chains but by mass conditioning. The classic 1932 novel is a "darkly satiric vision of a 'utopian' future—where humans are genetically bred and pharmaceutically anesthetized to passively serve a ruling order."

Today we see its tools at work: censorship, surveillance, narrative-shaping algorithms, corporate capture of institutions, and engineered crises that keep the populace compliant. Many sense that something is "off," but they cannot always identify it.

The result is a kind of mass delusion— a psychological fog that dims one's vision. When people no longer know who they are, what the truth is, or where to place their hope, society becomes malleable in the hands of those hungry for global control.

That is why the call to biblical repentance and truth is so explosive. It cuts through this fog. It reveals that rights come from God, not from the state; that human beings are created in the image of God, not programmable units of production; and that freedom is a stewardship, not a governmental gift.

A NEW PARADIGM OF REVIVAL

Traditionally, believers expected revival to come through pastors and evangelists preaching at large gatherings. That still happens. But in our time, God is moving through an array of unconventional messengers—media personalities, entrepreneurs, even former skeptics and critics of the faith.

Designated Disrupter shines a light on this paradigm shift. It calls us to recognize the hand of God at work in unlikely vessels, and to understand that revival is not confined to pulpits or church buildings. It can break out in podcasts, boardrooms, universities, and even political rallies—wherever truth confronts deception and the Spirit of God touches hearts.

The people you are going to read about in *Designated Disrupter* are not the people that most Christian groups would choose to lead a ministry or movement. In these pages, you are going to discover the energizing force behind all these men and women that God is using as highly unlikely disrupters, helping inspire revival.

On July 4, 2012, during a time of prayer for America, I experienced a vision of a coming Great Awakening in our land—one that would hinge on the repentance and intercession of God's people. I believe the current turmoil—the assassinations, the crises, the surprising conversions of public figures—is part of God's way of preparing the soil for a historic outpouring of His Spirit.

A CALL TO DISCERNMENT, COURAGE, AND HOPE

You hold in your hands a book that is not merely about politics or personalities. *Designated Disrupter* is about recognizing what God is doing in our time—sometimes in ways that surprise us, sometimes through people we might not have chosen.

It is a call to discernment: to see through the fog of propaganda and to recognize the larger spiritual battle beneath the headlines. It is a call to courage: to resist the temptation to withdraw in despair and instead take a stand for truth. It is a call to hope: to believe that God is not finished with America or with His church.

The story is still being written. The outcome is not yet determined. But if history teaches us anything, it is that God often uses the least likely instruments to accomplish His greatest works.

The message of *Designated Disrupter* is both unsettling and profoundly encouraging: The Holy Spirit is on the move. The question is whether we will recognize His hand, join His mission, and play our part in the revival and awakening He desires to bring.

Designated Disrupter reveals the paradigm shift in revival we are now experiencing. Troy is asking us to observe something entirely new in what God is doing in our time.

In this book you will discover why this is happening, how this will dramatically change the course of the future of America and the world, and the role God has planned for you since the "foundation of the world" (Eph. 1:4).

—Paul McGuire

Author; Speaker; Coauthor, *The Babylon Code* and

Trumpocalypse; Paulmcguire.us

A HOLY DISRUPTION

But God chose the foolish things of the world to shame the wise;
God chose the weak things of the world to shame the strong.
—1 CORINTHIANS 1:27

SOMETHING ASTONISHING, MIRACULOUS, and life-changing is unfolding today—something foreseen by renowned faith leaders Billy Graham, Reinhard Bonnke, and Sid Roth. It is flooding America and the rest of the world, and it is most powerful among young people.

President Donald Trump survived two assassination attempts and countless, relentless attacks by the media, the globalist elite, and even factions within his own country and yet returned for a stunning reelection on November 5, 2024.

Then, on September 10, 2025, Charlie Kirk was killed in the most high-profile political assassination in a generation while speaking at a Turning Point USA event at a university in Utah. Two days later his widow, Erika Kirk, spoke to the nation, saying, "They killed Charlie because he preached a message of patriotism, faith, and of God's merciful love. They should all know this: If you thought that my husband's mission was powerful before, you have no idea. You have no idea what you just have unleashed across this entire country, in this world—you have no idea. You have no idea the fire that you have ignited within this wife. The cries of this widow will echo around the world like a battle cry."[1]

Erika's remarks were followed by 54,000 new inquiries from students wanting to start Turning Point USA chapters on high school and college campuses, massive marches and gatherings worldwide, and packed-out churches nationwide. CBN News noted: "Charlie Kirk's martyrdom is igniting an undeniable Jesus revival, a Holy Spirit awakening that's shaking the very foundations of the church."[2]

A holy disruption is sweeping the planet.

The election, followed by Kirk's tragic martyrdom, was a prophetic earthquake that shook the globe, signaling the beginning of a spiritual turnaround and youth-led revival in the United States and the world.

Rabbi Jonathan Bernis, founder of Jewish Voice Ministries International and host of the syndicated television show *Jewish Voice with Jonathan Bernis*, said he realized during the Republican National Convention that America was at a pivotal "turning point." Prayer was not only an accepted but a welcome part of that convention, which clearly communicated that "God needed to be brought back into our nation."

As Bernis described it, "And I said, 'If Donald Trump is reelected, this marks a turning point for America.' It was at the convention that I felt the Holy Spirit saying to me, 'This is the beginning of a radical change and an opportunity to turn America around.' Is it the last opportunity for us as a country to turn back to God? It may very well be."[3]

It's as if God has pushed the pause button on the world's headlong rush into the apocalypse. Now, all around us, the Deep State and globalist systems that seemed so powerful not long ago are in retreat.

Big Tech billionaires—including Mark Zuckerberg, who suspended Trump from Facebook following the January 6, 2021, insurrection at the US Capitol—were invited to the Presidential Inauguration, signaling an end to the un-American social media censorship instigated by the Biden administration.[4]

Now, governments worldwide are making tariff deals with the Trump administration, helping America regain its financial footing.

All around us, the old systems are crumbling. But the battle is far from over, and powerful behind-the-scenes forces are not relenting in their crusade to destroy Trump, weaken his base of support, and regain power in Washington, D.C.

Yet in the midst of the chaos, a sound is rising. A cry. A revival. Hope. Across America and around the world, especially among young people, God is moving in unprecedented ways. On college campuses once known for atheism and apathy, hundreds of thousands are getting baptized. Stadiums are filling with worship. Voices once considered secular or even hostile to the church are asking questions. A generation once dismissed is being ignited by the miraculous power of the Holy Spirit.

And who is God using? Not the polished. Not the perfect. But the most unlikely. He always has.

He used Noah, a man who got drunk after surviving the flood.

He used Moses, a murderer with a stutter.

He used David, an adulterer who arranged a murder to cover his sin.

He used Paul, formerly Saul, the violent persecutor of Christians.

He used Peter, the hotheaded fisherman who denied Jesus three times.

And now, in our time, He is using men and women the world rejected, ridiculed, or tried to cancel, and even assassinated.

He is using Donald Trump, a man with a checkered past and a divine calling—not because he is flawless, but because he is willing. Willing to be a wrecking ball to globalist tyranny. A defender of faith, freedom, and the unborn. An imperfect vessel chosen to restrain the spirit of antichrist and realign America with its prophetic destiny. He is using Jordan Peterson, Tucker Carlson, Joe Rogan, Megyn Kelly, Ben Shapiro, Chris Pratt, Justin Bieber, Mel Gibson, Denzel Washington, Sylvester Stallone, Eric Metaxas, Tim Tebow, Deion Sanders, Sean Feucht, Joseph Z, and countless others. These cultural influencers are now pointing millions toward truth and something greater than themselves. They are not theologians, but they are asking the right questions. They are lighting the spark.

They are designated disrupters.

This book is not about idolizing personalities. It's about recognizing the fingerprints of God in the least expected places. It's about understanding how heaven's strategies often offend religious minds yet fulfill God's purposes.

Designated Disrupter: Trump and Other Unlikely Agents of Revival will take you on a prophetic, counterintuitive journey through the headlines, the historical patterns of revival, and the raw reality of our broken world. It will show you how God is raising up a remnant—an imperfect, battle-worn, fearless remnant—to turn the tide.

This is not just America's moment. The entire world is on the brink of God's judgment—the catastrophic events described in the Book of Revelation. And yet, God is not done. In fact, He's just getting started.

In a 2013 interview for a seven-part WND.com series of stories on the possibility of an end-times revival, world-renowned evangelist Billy Graham told me he foresaw a "great spiritual awakening" coming to America.[5]

In the same series, I spoke with international evangelist Reinhard Bonnke, whose ministry recorded 100 million people responding to the call of salvation in Africa and other nations. He said that God told him the time has come for "a mighty wave of salvation to sweep the USA," declaring, "All America shall be saved!"[6]

Meanwhile, as former executive editor of *Charisma* magazine and Charisma Media, I have often spoken with Sid Roth, host of the popular television show *Sid Roth's It's Supernatural!* And over the last decade, Sid has told me many times that God's greater glory is coming.[7]

Revival is messy. So are the people God uses. But when heaven invades earth, nothing stays the same.

It's time to recognize the call. It's time to rise up. It's time to believe that the Spirit of God is still choosing the unlikely to shake the nations.

Let the broken be bold. Let the disrupters disrupt.

And may we all be part of a revival that changes history before Jesus Christ's glorious return to earth with the armies of heaven.

GOD'S GREATER GLORY

Very truly I tell you, unless a kernel of wheat falls to the ground and dies, it remains only a single seed. But if it dies, it produces many seeds.
—JOHN 12:24

THE NEWS BROKE like a massive thunderbolt across America and the world: Charlie Kirk, founder of Turning Point USA, was assassinated September 10, 2025, at a university in Utah. For millions of young people, the voice that had called them to truth, courage, and faith suddenly went silent. Or so it seemed.

But heaven tells a different story. Like Stephen in the Book of Acts, who as he was being stoned to death saw Jesus standing at the right hand of the Father, welcoming him home, I believe Jesus received Kirk with the same grace.

What the enemy meant to silence, God has turned into seeds of revival. In the days that followed, a groundswell erupted. Churches were packed. People gathered and marched worldwide. And Turning Point USA was flooded with more than 54,000 new requests for campus chapters. At the time, the organization had 900 college chapters and approximately 1,200 high school chapters. It was as if a generation had decided all at once: We will carry Charlie Kirk's mission forward.[1]

Then came Erika Kirk. Standing before the nation in her grief, Kirk's young widow lifted her voice—not in anger, but in courage. Years earlier, she had been crowned Miss Arizona. Now she stood crowned in another sense, clothed with Esther's mantle "for such a time as this." She declared that her husband's work would not die but would live on, that America would see revival, and that Generation Alpha, Generation Z, and Millennials would not be lost to the darkness.

"To everyone listening tonight across America, the movement my husband built will not die. It won't, I refuse to let that happen…All of us will refuse to let that happen," she said. "No one will ever forget my husband's name, and I will make sure of it."[2]

Erika's emotional words pierced the hearts of people worldwide. Students wept.

Pastors preached with renewed fire. And across the United States people asked, Could Charlie Kirk's martyrdom be the beginning of a new Great Awakening?

THE MARTYRDOM OF CHARLIE KIRK AND A GENERATION ON FIRE FOR JESUS

Kirk embodied what I call the spirit of a designated disrupter—a man who puts obedience to God and the truth above his own comfort and well-being. In Acts 6 and 7 we read the story of Stephen, the first Christian martyr. His courageous witness helped spark revival in the early church.

Just as Stephen's death helped inspire the early church, Kirk's life and sacrifice are now bearing fruit in this generation, igniting new courage and spiritual hunger. Generations Alpha and Z—the very generations Kirk poured into—are awakening with a passion for Jesus like never before.

When we look at Scripture, we see how God often raised up unlikely but powerful figures to change history—Moses to bring Israel out of Egypt, Cyrus to release God's people from captivity, Jehu to tear down Jezebel's altars, David to face down Goliath, and Joseph to rise to power to preserve his nation. In our time, President Trump has carried aspects of those mantles. But when I consider Kirk, I see something different. He carried a John the Baptist–like mantle.

Kirk was a voice crying in the wilderness—the wilderness of high school and college campuses, the wilderness of cultural confusion—calling a generation to repent, turn back to God, and prepare the way of the Lord. He confronted sin, but he did it with love. He listened and engaged in honest debate. That's why students flocked to him; not because he condemned them, but because they knew he genuinely cared.

After Kirk's death, Vice President JD Vance hosted *The Charlie Kirk Show*, interviewing Kirk's friends, including Tucker Carlson, Robert F. Kennedy Jr., White House Chief of Staff Susie Wiles, and White House Press Spokeswoman Karoline Leavitt, who said, "The President's massive gains with young Americans across the country was in no small part because of the efforts of Charlie Kirk and Turning Point USA." Kennedy remarked, "The thing that united us was his total commitment to free speech." Carlson said, "You just never forgot there was a person behind the views, and that inspired me, and God commands that of us." Susie Wiles commented, "He evangelized. He was on every college campus in every part of the country."[3]

Kirk understood that revival and reformation require prayer and participation—that faith must not retreat from public life, but rise up to bring truth and righteousness into every sphere, including government.

And just as Esther rose in her generation to pour out healing oil and preserve God's people, Erika Kirk called the church to unity, vowing to see Generations Alpha and Z and Millennials grounded in biblical truth. Her "yes" is an answer to the "Esther, Arise" prophecy of Kim Clement.

"As the beginning of the restoration, as it begins, there shall be a woman that shall rise up," Clement prophesied on March 25, 2011. "A woman that shall be strong in faith, virtuous, beautiful in eyes, and her eyes shall be so beautiful. Eyes shall be round and big. I have crowned her, says the Lord. As I crowned Esther.... For she shall have the oil of gladness for the pain and the mourning that has taken place. And she shall pour out the oil....Healing shall begin and then it shall flow rapidly. Schools will be free from potential damage and danger, shootings and murder, drug addiction. Cartels shall be afraid of a woman. A woman anointed by God. A woman set aside."[4]

> REVIVAL AND REFORMATION REQUIRE PRAYER AND PARTICIPATION.

This is the cornerstone of *Designated Disrupter: Trump and Other Unlikely Agents of Revival*. God is using unlikely servants—modern-day Moseses, Esthers, Daniels, Josephs, Davids, and modern campus evangelists—to disrupt society and prepare people to meet His Son. To put it simply: A designated disrupter is someone God raises up to turn the world upside down for His glory.

Disruption is biblical. The English word *disrupter* doesn't appear in the Bible, but the concept is weaved throughout Scripture. God often raised up people to disrupt evil, injustice, and idolatry in order to bring revival.

Jesus Himself was the ultimate disrupter. In Acts 17:6 (NKJV), the early believers were accused of turning "the world upside down." Jesus disrupted religious hypocrisy (Matt. 23), disrupted the money changers in the temple (John 2:15), and through the cross disrupted the power of sin and death.

Prophets were holy disrupters. Elijah disrupted Ahab and Jezebel's Baal worship (1 Kings 18). Jeremiah disrupted false prophets with God's truth. John the Baptist disrupted spiritual complacency by calling people to repent and prepare the way for the Messiah (Matt. 3:1–3).

Moses disrupted Pharaoh's tyranny to free God's people. Esther disrupted Haman's genocidal plan. And Daniel disrupted Babylon's culture by refusing to bow to idols.

Paul was a gospel disrupter. Everywhere he preached, he stirred revival—and riots (Acts 16–19). The gospel disrupted pagan economies and belief systems.

Kirk's martyrdom, Erika's rise, and the prophetic stirring in Generations Alpha and Z and Millennials all testify that disruption is painful but purposeful.

God is not finished with America. He is raising up designated disrupters in politics, media, education, and the church to lead us into what I believe will be the greatest revival in our nation's history.

Kirk's death was not the end. It was a trumpet blast from heaven declaring that God is not finished with America, and that His greater glory is about to be revealed.

GOD'S GREATER GLORY

If the United States of America could speak, the sound we'd hear today would be a sigh of hope. Over the last several years, our nation has walked through chaos, violence, and division. Inflation, addiction, corruption, and fear of tyranny amid the COVID-19 pandemic have weighed heavily on the American people. Many wondered if the American story was over.

But then came disruption. President Trump's historic return to the White House on November 5, 2024, was one kind of disruption—political, cultural, and global in impact. The martyrdom of Kirk was another kind—spiritual, prophetic, and eternal. Together, they signal what I believe is the threshold of America's greatest revival.

The prophet Haggai declared that a glory is coming greater than anything the world has ever seen (Hag. 2:9). That promise still stands. God's greater glory is breaking out, led not by one figure alone but by an army of ordinary believers who are carrying the message with extraordinary courage.

This is what *Designated Disrupter* is about. It's about how God is using unlikely men and women—Trump in the halls of power, Charlie and Erika Kirk among Generations Alpha and Z, pastors in pulpits, prophets in the wilderness—to reset the world. Disruption is uncomfortable. It shakes us. But it is also God's tool to awaken His people and prepare the way for His glory.

That's why we cannot retreat in fear. This is the hour to rise in faith and courage. A new Great Awakening is beginning.

"The Prophet Haggai said there is a glory coming that will be greater than any glory the world has ever seen," said Sid Roth, host of *It's Supernatural!* and founder of Messianic Vision. "Here's my spin, but I believe I'm right. We are on the end of the last move of God's Spirit. There's something coming. Many people say...there is a greater glory coming. 'Greater,' by definition, is something bigger than anything the world has ever seen before.

"And I've been praying the prayer of Moses. Moses said, 'Give me Your glory, God.' And you know what God did. He redefined the word 'glory.' He added a synonym. And God said, 'I will let My goodness be displayed before you.'...I just think the breath of fresh air that President Trump is releasing now is even greater because of what the previous administration had done, and this greater glory is going to be different than what anyone has ever even thought of because we've never seen it before....The timing is God. The question is, are we going to be ready when God says, "This is it"? I might add that I personally believe any second this greater glory could be released."[5]

This outpouring of the Holy Spirit is available to every believer.

With that in mind, let's get ready by praying each day: "Show me Your glory, Lord. Let this be the day. Use me."

I urge you to read on to find out what this revival means not only for America and the world, but for your role in this great move of the Holy Spirit.

To view my interviews with various leaders quoted in this book, scan the QR code or visit TroyAndersonBooks.com/resources.

PART I

THE JESUS REVIVAL

CHAPTER 1
JESUS REVOLUTION 2.0

WANTED: JESUS CHRIST

ALIAS: THE MESSIAH, THE SON OF GOD, KING OF KINGS, LORD OF LORDS, PRINCE OF PEACE, ETC.

Notorious leader of an underground liberation movement...

WARNING: HE IS STILL AT LARGE!

He is indeed. As the words of this Wanted poster from a Christian underground newspaper demonstrate, Jesus is alive and well and living in the radical spiritual fervor of a growing number of young Americans who have proclaimed an extraordinary religious revolution in his name.[1]
—*TIME* MAGAZINE, "THE JESUS REVOLUTION," JUNE 21, 1971

"THE JESUS REVOLUTION" surprised America and the world in the early 1970s—a faith renaissance among young people that captured cover stories in *TIME*, *Life*, *Look*, and other iconic publications. Now, a similar movement is stirring. But this time, it's emerging in unexpected ways and unlikely places.

On February 21, 2025, my wife, Irene, and I attended a pivotal event at Saddleback Church in Lake Forest, California: "The Return Gathering."

We first heard about it a month earlier when Stacie Wood preached a sermon that caught our attention. Wood is the teaching pastor at Saddleback—the megachurch made famous by Pastor Rick Warren, author of *The Purpose Driven Life*. Warren's book has sold over 50 million copies, making him one of the most influential Christian leaders of modern times.[2]

IT WAS A CALL TO RETURN TO GOD.

Saddleback Church is globally known for pioneering the seeker-sensitive movement, focused on making services accessible to the unchurched. But this sermon wasn't about church growth or strategy. It wasn't about programs or outreach.

Wood urged the congregation to pray, fast, and repent. She announced "The Return Gathering," a sacred assembly modeled after ancient Israelite convocations during national crises.

This was extraordinary. It was a call to return to God.

Wood cited 2 Chronicles 7:14, God's message to King Solomon and the

Israelites. They, like America today, were trapped in a cycle of sin, rebellion, and looming judgment. Wood told the congregation:

> Church, this is a word for us in this moment...because we are in an *even now* kind of moment culturally in this day and age—*even now*, folks, when 50 million people are being trafficked as slaves, *even now* when 26 million human beings are living as refugees, *even now* when political polarization is reaching dangerous levels...*even now* as the porn industry banks up to 100 billion dollars a year and is robbing a generation of their dignity and their destiny, *even now* as Millennials and Generation Z are leaving the church and religion altogether in droves...*even now* when it feels like we're in this Joel 1 kind of moment, and destruction is about to take us over, and there's this invading army that's ready to destroy everything we've ever known to be good and holy and pure.
>
> We are in an *even now* kind of moment and God is looking for a people who will return to Him, who will say, "God, we're sorry. We're sorry for our sins, we're sorry for the sins of our generation, and God, we will return to You with fasting and weeping and mourning because we know that You are a good God and You are kind and You are compassionate and You are gracious and You would so much rather send a blessing than destruction, and so, God, we're returning to You with all of our hearts."[3]

"40 DAYS TO SAVE AMERICA" AND "77 DAYS TO TAKE BACK AMERICA: IGNITING THE FINAL GREAT AWAKENING"

The fact that Saddleback Church held "The Return Gathering" stunned Irene and me. We had just completed our "40 Days to Save America"[4] and "77 Days to Take Back America: Igniting the Final Great Awakening"[5] campaigns, urging people to pray, fast, and repent during the forty days leading up to President Trump's reelection on November 5, 2024, and the seventy-seven days between his reelection and his inauguration on January 20, 2025.[6]

Graciously joining us in promoting these campaigns were Charisma Media; Pastor Paul Begley, host of a popular YouTube show and my coauthor of *Revelation 911*; Paul McGuire, former host of *The Paul McGuire Show* and my coauthor of *The Babylon Code* and *Trumpocalypse*; Bruce Oliver, host of the Top 100 Christian podcast *Talks for Christ*; Rev. Kevin Jessip, cofounder of The Return International; and Larry Keefauver, author of *Prayers of the Presidents*.

Buoyed by Charisma Media, these friends, and many others inspired by the Holy Spirit, millions joined us in prayer, fasting, and repentance, interceding for America and the world. At one point, someone sent us a video of hundreds of schoolchildren in India praying for Trump and America. We were amazed.

These campaigns and Trump's reelection came four years after The Return: National and Global Day of Prayer and Repentance on September 26, 2020, at the National Mall in Washington, D.C. This remarkable gathering was led by our friends Rabbi Jonathan Cahn and Rev. Jessip, alongside prominent faith leaders and politicians concerned about America's downward trajectory.[7]

BILLY GRAHAM: IS THIS AMERICA'S "NINEVEH MOMENT"?

The Return 2020 came about after a 2013 interview with evangelist Billy Graham for a seven-part series on the possibility of an end-times revival. Paul McGuire and I were inspired by Graham to call for a national day of repentance in our 2018 bestseller *Trumpocalypse*.[8]

In the interview, Graham warned of America's "Nineveh moment"—a chance to save the nation by turning back to God through collective repentance, intercession, and fasting.[9] He spoke of the prophetic parallels between America and Nineveh, the ancient city spared from destruction after the people heeded Jonah's warning.

Jonah 3:1–10 tells the story: Jonah proclaimed, "Forty more days and Nineveh will be overthrown" (v. 4). The Ninevites believed God, declared a fast, and turned from their evil ways. In response, God relented and withheld judgment.

Graham told me he believed the same thing could happen in America—a nation at a similar crossroads, facing the choice between judgment or revival.

The final chapter of *Trumpocalypse* included an interview with Rev. Jessip, whom I met in 2015 while serving as executive editor of Charisma Media. As a descendant of Pilgrim Fathers pastor John Robinson, Jessip believed it was his destiny to lead a national repentance movement. The Mayflower Compact of 1620 dedicated America to "the glory of God, and advancement of the Christian faith."[10]

After *Trumpocalypse* released, Jessip gave copies to Ben Carson and others in the Trump administration. He invited me to join him and a dozen leaders at the Billy Graham Training Center at The Cove to pray for national repentance. He later asked McGuire and me to write the White House executive summary for the event, and he persuaded Rabbi Cahn to serve as spokesman. By what we believe was a miracle of the Holy Spirit, The Return took place.

About 250,000 people gathered on the National Mall, and 42 million watched by television or simulcast. That day, President Trump flew over in Marine One and issued a proclamation for a "Day of Prayer and Return"—the first president to do so since Abraham Lincoln.[11]

Graham had asked every president from Dwight D. Eisenhower to George W. Bush to call for a national day of repentance, but none did—until Trump. Historically, George Washington credited national repentance with helping the colonial forces defeat the British in the Revolutionary War. Lincoln credited it with preserving the Union and ending slavery.

Interestingly, Lincoln often quoted my great-grandfather-plus Friedrich von Schiller, the playwright and poet who wrote "Ode to Joy," which Ludwig van Beethoven set to music in the Ninth Symphony. Schiller's drama *Wilhelm Tell*, about Swiss resistance to tyranny, was widely performed in nineteenth-century America, helping inspire about 250,000 German Americans, including several generals, to fight on Lincoln's side. Here are a couple of famous lines from the play, recently turned into a riveting movie, *William Tell*, available on Amazon Prime: "We shall be free, just as our fathers were." "The man of courage thinks not of himself. Help the oppressed and put thy trust in God." African American abolitionist Frederick Douglass called Schiller the "poet of freedom" and "prophet of liberty."[12]

Corné J. Bekker, dean of the School of Divinity at Regent University, finds the parallels between Lincoln and Trump intriguing, believing America is once again facing a "Nineveh moment."

> I do believe that we are standing in the moment of a reprieve. I think we are standing in a moment where God has relented of His judgment. When we think of…[how] America's the largest producer of pornography, when we think of the slaughter of millions and millions of unborn children, how could God not bring judgment on that? But I believe that people have prayed for decades and have prayed that ancient prayer of asking God to have mercy on this country….I believe we have leaders in place that have cried out to the Lord, and we are seeing the beginning of a movement of national repentance that could spark not only this reformation, this renewal, this awakening, but even beyond this, a revival back to the original call that's been placed on this country.[13]

To hear my interview with Corné J. Bekker, scan the QR code or visit TroyAndersonBooks.com/bekker.

Trump's return to the White House has reignited hope within millions of Americans, especially followers of Jesus who see his leadership as a divine catalyst, uniquely positioned to inspire both political renewal and a great awakening.

"Over the past eight years, I have been tested and challenged more than any president in our 250-year history, and I've learned a lot along the way," Trump said in his Inaugural Address on January 20, 2025. "The journey to reclaim our republic has not been an easy one—that, I can tell you. Those who wish to stop our cause have tried to take my freedom and, indeed, to take my life. Just a few months ago, in a beautiful Pennsylvania field, an assassin's bullet ripped through my ear. But I felt then and believe even more so now that my life was saved for a reason. I was saved by God to make America great again."[14]

TIME: "IS GOD DEAD?" TO "THE JESUS REVOLUTION"

Saddleback Church, February 21, 2025. Jon Tyson, senior pastor at Church of the City New York, took the podium, and Irene and I sat in awe. The Holy Spirit was moving in a way we hadn't seen in years.

Tyson began by showing the audience a 1966 *TIME* magazine cover with its iconic headline in bold red letters on a black background: "Is God Dead?"[15]

"This is the question they were asking," Tyson said. "In 1966, the U.S. was in a place of genuine decline. Post–World War II, you had a lot of the kids who were growing up who were rebelling against traditional values. The hippie movement was in its earliest stages. There was a growing disillusionment about the war in Vietnam. A lot of kids were throwing off their faith. A vision of sexuality was radically changing. A lot of the church's denominations were beginning to shrink, and so people were asking the question: Are we done with God? 1966—this was the cover. America was asking the question: 'Is God Dead?'"

Next, the church's big screens displayed the June 21, 1971 *TIME* cover: "The Jesus Revolution."[16]

"Apparently, God was not dead," Tyson continued. "Christ rose from the dead, and this is what was on the cover. The hippie movement had become the Jesus movement; worship was birthed out of churches right here in Southern California that has transformed the way that church is done. In fact, church has been fundamentally reinvented, and Jesus and God and the Spirit—who they thought were dead and done in the nation—made the front cover news that an entire generation was now following Jesus. That was a five-year period. How do you go from 'Is God Dead?' to 'Boy, Jesus is back' in five years?"

So how did this happen?

"A group of young people determined in their hearts that they would return to the Lord," Tyson said. "All it took—collectively—was a group of people to turn their attention and their hearts away from the culture, away from the world, and to take all of that passion, all of that vision, and turn it back to the Lord. That was called 'The Jesus Movement,' and it was one of the last great moves of God here in the U.S." [17]

REVIVAL SPREADING LIKE WILDFIRE

Since the release of Pastor Greg Laurie's hit movie *Jesus Revolution* in early 2023—chronicling what some scholars call America's "Fourth Great Awakening" of the late 1960s and '70s—revival has been breaking out across the nation. What began as isolated moments has become a wildfire of spiritual awakening. From the Asbury Revival to mass baptisms of young people on beaches and campuses, from tent revivals led by Mario Murillo and Todd Coconato to worship gatherings by Sean Feucht and other young revivalists, a new movement of faith is sweeping America. In his article "Is America on Brink of Jesus Revolution 2.0?" Laurie wrote:

> There's a new wind blowing across America. It's a wind of freedom, optimism, hope, and yes, patriotism. What's even more remarkable is that this movement isn't just being carried by the older generation—it's gaining momentum among the young. I haven't seen anything like this in decades. The last time I felt such cultural stirring was during the Jesus Movement when an entire generation found hope and transformation through a personal relationship with Jesus Christ.[18]

A Barna Group report titled "New Research: Belief in Jesus Rises, Fueled by Younger Adults" confirms this spiritual resurgence. Now, 66 percent of American adults say they have made a personal commitment to Jesus that remains important to them—a 12-point increase since 2021, when commitment hit its lowest in more than three decades.

"This shift is not only statistically significant—it may be the clearest indication of meaningful spiritual renewal in the United States," according to Barna.

In 2021 and 2022, commitment to Jesus hit a record low at 54 percent. Since then, there has been a steady increase each year, amounting to nearly 30 million more US adults who now claim to follow Jesus.

"Undeniably, there is renewed interest in Jesus," said David Kinnaman, CEO of Barna. "Many people have predicted the growing irrelevance of Christianity. However, this data shows that spiritual trends have a dynamism and can, indeed, change. This is the clearest trend we've seen in more than a decade pointing to spiritual renewal—and it's the first time Barna has recorded such spiritual interest being led by younger generations."

The "Jesus resurgence" is largely driven by Generation Z and Millennials, who have shown dramatic increases in commitment to Jesus since the pandemic. A surprising trend has also emerged: Younger men are now more likely to be Jesus followers than younger women. For example, Generation Z men saw a 15-point increase between 2019 and 2025, while Millennial men experienced a 19-point jump.[19]

"I believe that we are standing at the forefront of a monumental reformation, renewal, and revival in America," Bekker said. "I believe that the signs of this have been evident for the last…eight to ten years. We've started to see small signs of this, but I am very optimistic about the future, not only of America, but that this might be the beginning of a new great awakening back to God, to morality, and to holiness."[20]

UNLIKELY AGENTS OF THE "JESUS RESURGENCE"

From church pulpits to global stages, today's revival is being amplified by unconventional voices—the late Charlie Kirk, Jordan Peterson, Russell Brand, Tucker Carlson, Joe Rogan, President Trump, and many others who have emerged as unlikely agents of this faith revolution.

The Bible is filled with unconventional figures whom God used in unexpected ways —not unlike Trump, Kirk, Peterson, Rogan, and Carlson.

In my interview with Bekker, he commented, "It's a fascinating topic…the pages [of Scripture] are replete with examples of unusual figures used by God. And I think the reason why God often makes use of these unusual figures is so that none of us can take the credit for any of the things that God will do. That's the Psalmist who cries out and says, 'Not unto us, not unto us, but to Your name, give glory in the same way.' [See Psalm 115:1.]

TODAY'S REVIVAL IS BEING AMPLIFIED BY UNCONVENTIONAL VOICES.

"It's tremendously important for us that when we see God make use of people that we would not have chosen, that we would not have said, 'This is an instrument by God or a messenger of God,' we have to be ready to be surprised by God, and not only surprised by the Lord, but we should have our eyes open to see His hand is working on people."[21]

A prime example is the apostle Paul, originally Saul, once the chief "enemy of the church."

As Bekker discussed, "Luke, when he writes the Book of Acts, describes Saul in the following way: He said that this man was breathing threats and murders against the church. …This enemy of the church is transformed into the apostle to the Gentiles within one encounter with God. And I think it's tremendously important for the church to have our eyes open. I always say this to people: 'Be careful when you look at the enemies of the church; in that enemy might be a future Paul.' God is able to take people like this and transform them into His servants and instruments."[22]

A PIVOTAL MOMENT IN AMERICAN HISTORY

The rise of these designated disrupters and the spiritual awakening breaking out comes at a pivotal moment in America's history.

We are taught in America that there is a constitutional separation between government and religion. Each operates in its own sphere—religion guides belief, relationships, and morality, while government provides a safe and fair environment for social and economic life.

But as our second president John Adams warned, there is a vital connection between the two. He said, "Our Constitution was made only for a moral and religious People. It is wholly inadequate to the government of any other."[23]

Adams made clear that while government should not control religion, religion and morality must influence government. When faith recedes, society unravels.

In recent decades, secularism has surged while religion has declined. A Gallup poll before the 2024 election found that only 44 percent of American Protestants attended church weekly.[24]

Pollster George Barna reported an even more troubling trend. According to research from the Cultural Research Center at Arizona Christian University, although two-thirds of Americans identify as Christians, only 4 percent hold a biblical worldview. The vast majority, 92 percent, have embraced syncretism, blending biblical faith with conflicting worldviews. As Barna notes, this shift has contributed to "widespread worldview confusion and a significant shift away from the God of the Bible."[25]

WHAT HAPPENS TO GOVERNMENT WHEN A NATION ABANDONS BIBLICAL MORALITY?

The COVID-19 pandemic accelerated this decline. During the 2020 lockdowns, churches closed their doors, and many never fully recovered. As online church services became the norm, countless believers drifted away from the discipline of weekly worship.

Belief and behavior are inseparable. When faith declines, morality declines with it. When faith weakens, immorality and deception seep into the culture and truth becomes fluid. People redefine right and wrong according to personal preference. It's like the era described in the Book of Judges: "In those days there was no king in Israel; everyone did what was right in his own eyes" (Judg. 17:6, NKJV). When moral leadership fails, anarchy ensues.

What happens to government when a nation abandons biblical morality? We elect leaders who promise maximum personal freedom and minimum restraint—a weakness that Alexis de Tocqueville identified as democracy's Achilles' heel. In recent decades, America has experienced this reality. We drifted from the Judeo-Christian foundations that made us a moral people, and in turn, we elected officials who reflected our cultural decline.

We all want a better government—more open, honest, and constitutional. But we will only get a better government when we become a better people—a moral and religious people again. This requires revival on two levels: a return to authentic Christianity and, flowing from that, a revival of constitutional government.

THE FIRST NECESSITY: A RELIGIOUS REVIVAL

In her history, America has experienced four major revivals, often called "awakenings." The First Great Awakening, led by evangelists Jonathan Edwards and George Whitefield, began around 1734 and lasted until 1760, bringing about 25,000 to 50,000 people into New England churches.[26]

The Second Great Awakening began in the 1790s and lasted about three decades. It spread across the then-western frontier—Ohio, Kentucky, and Tennessee—with evangelists preaching in tent meetings and open-air venues.[27]

The Third Great Awakening began in New York City in 1857 after a stock market crash. Initiated by businessman Jeremiah Lanphier, the revival led to about one million conversions over the next few years.[28]

The Fourth Great Awakening, often called "The Jesus movement," began in the late 1960s—following the Azusa Street Revival of 1906–1909, post–World War II campus revivals, the rise of world-renowned evangelist Billy Graham, and the Charismatic Movement of the 1960s and '70s. Chronicled in Pastor Greg Laurie's 2023 movie *Jesus Revolution*, the movement started in California's counterculture centers and spread across the nation and the world.[29]

IS A FIFTH GREAT AWAKENING BEGINNING?

Do we see evidence that a fifth great revival may be arising in America?

The signs are there. One of the clearest is that by October 2024, Bible sales in America rose 22 percent compared to the same period the previous year. By contrast, total print book sales rose by less than 1 percent.[30]

Publishers credited the boom in Bible sales to fresh designs, new marketing, and a surge of young, first-time buyers. "It feels like a real revival is happening," said Alex Jones, CEO of the prayer app Hallow. He noted the surge includes young people exploring faith for the first time and older people returning after years of neglect.[31]

Opinions vary as to why this uptick occurred, but the timing is telling. The rise in Bible sales came just months before the November 2024 election, when the nation was deeply anxious and pessimistic about the future.

Anxiety and uncertainty prompt people to seek hope and stability. When the storm rocks everyone's boats, they look for a safe harbor. Their search often leads them to God. These signs suggest that a major revival is either underway or on the verge of happening again.

WE CAN BE THE SALT THAT PRESERVES OUR ENTIRE COUNTRY.

Yet given the depths of America's moral decline, many wonder if we've passed the point of no return. Is the road back to authentic Christianity too long and too steep?

When these doubts arise, we must remember Nineveh, the corrupt and godless city in Jonah's story. Nineveh seemed beyond redemption, yet after Jonah's brief campaign of preaching repentance, the people turned to God. It remains one of history's most dramatic moral turnarounds. If it could happen in Nineveh, it can happen in America.

That's what Billy Graham believed, and it inspired me to call for national repentance, leading to The Return, the greatest miracle of my life.

We also find hope in Genesis 18 and 19. There, the key element wasn't repentance but the steadfastness of a faithful remnant. At Abraham's request, God would have spared Sodom and Gomorrah if even ten righteous people had been found.

This reminds us that God may yet save America—not because of our merit as a nation, but for the sake of the faithful remnant who still serve Him. We can be the salt that preserves our entire country.

THE SECOND NECESSITY: A GOVERNMENTAL REVIVAL

All signs from the November 2024 election give good reason to hope that America's "Jesus resurgence" may spill over into government. As we become a moral and religious people again, constitutional government can recover its effectiveness.

Shortly after Trump's reelection, journalist Eric Mack wrote: "In appealing to voters of faith, President-elect Donald Trump vowed a religious revival in America."[32]

Here we have the man elected to the highest office in the land affirming our need for revival—and pledging to help bring it about.

Of course, one flower does not make spring. We must admit that Trump's personal history does not make him a paragon of religious virtue. Yet despite past moral failures, he has shown signs of real change. After his narrow escape from death in the first of two assassination attempts in 2024, many detected a new sense of destiny and purpose in him.

Moreover, his previous administration reflected evangelical values—especially in his opposition to abortion and his appointment of conservative constitutionalist judges and Supreme Court justices.

As Mack noted:

> Throughout the presidential election, Trump made an appeal to American voters to listen to God's word even if for the first time and for voters of faith to get to the ballot box like never before.[33]

Trump has forged a clear connection with evangelical Christians.

If you're skeptical about Trump's transformation, remember that God often uses flawed people to accomplish His purposes. King David, an adulterer and murderer, was called "a man after [God's] own heart" (1 Sam. 13:14). Even a ruler like Cyrus of Persia, who had no direct knowledge of God, was called "his anointed" (Isa. 45:1) because he fulfilled God's mission.

Whether Trump's move toward faith is authentic or not, he has shown enormous capacity for effective leadership. He has persevered through relentless lawfare, slander, assassination attempts, and obstacles that would have crushed less resilient men.

Judging by both his words and actions, it's easy to believe that Trump may have been placed here for such a time as this—to help bring about a revival of not just constitutional government, but authentic Christianity.

We can be sure that God is willing to do for repentant America what He did for His people in ancient times. Let's not forget the promise He gave to Israel when King Solomon dedicated the temple in Jerusalem:

> If My people who are called by My name will humble themselves, and pray and seek My face, and turn from their wicked ways, then I will hear from heaven, and will forgive their sin and heal their land.
>
> —2 Chronicles 7:14, NKJV

CHAPTER 2

AMERICA STANDS AT A CROSSROADS

I hope this is going to raise up an army of young people who will take a stand for Jesus Christ, who are not afraid to speak out and not afraid that they're going to be attacked or accused. We have to take a stand and be open to the truth and not be afraid to speak the truth.[1]
—Franklin Graham, president, Billy Graham Evangelistic Association, in remarks about Charlie Kirk's assassination

The revolution has begun. Inspired by the original revolutionary, millions of followers of Jesus Christ are returning to the radical Christianity of the first century.

As counterintuitive as it may seem, this movement is prophetically connected to November 5, 2024, a day that shook America and world, and September 10, 2025, the day conservative activist Charlie Kirk was assassinated.

On those days, to many Americans it felt as though the earth moved under their feet. But this was more than a stunning political comeback and a tragic assassination. It was a global spiritual shift and turning point in history.

For millions of people, Trump's reelection felt like God's intervention—a miraculous pause in a downward spiral they feared would end in national ruin. I interviewed and spoke to pastors, prophetic voices, and military leaders across the nation who described it as a reprieve from judgment—a window of time granted by God.

One person I spoke to was Paul McGuire, an internationally recognized prophecy expert and former CNN, Fox News, and History Channel commentator. He said, "If America was going to continue in the way that it was going before Trump got elected, we...would be very quickly morphing into a full-blown totalitarian state, a mixture of the communist Chinese social credit score system [with] Russia and Cuba."[2]

To watch my interview with Paul McGuire, scan the QR code or visit TroyAndersonBooks.com/mcguire.

McGuire warned that Deep State scientific mind control, social programming, and psychological operations (PSYOPs)—modern forms of tyranny that Nazi Germany employed before and during World War II—have been "playing out in America for the last 50 years."

> We were headed for an inescapable dictatorship....God answered the prayers of His people—the remnant church—and He roadblocked this path to totalitarianism using unlikely heroes like Trump and Elon Musk. Imperfect people became heroic, and heroism—like fear—can be contagious. Boldness is rising now where fear once ruled. That's really good news.[3]

But to Trump's detractors, it felt like the sky was falling. In the lead-up to the election, critics portrayed him as a modern-day dictator.

Anthony D. Romero, executive director of the ACLU, declared, "A second Trump Administration represents a clear and present danger to our democratic norms, processes, and institutions."[4]

To many Americans, Trump's victory wasn't just disappointing. It was devastating. A YouGov poll taken after the election captured the emotional toll. One voter described "tears of frustration, anger, extreme sadness and hopelessness." Some reported feeling physically ill. One said, "I suddenly became so ashamed to be an American and ashamed to be associated with the Americans who voted for this monster."[5]

Regardless of where you stand, November 5, 2024, changed everything.

Trump's reelection wasn't just improbable; it was nearly impossible. As a journalist who has covered national politics and prophetic trends for decades, I've never seen anything quite like it. He survived assassination attempts, multiple convictions, relentless media attacks, and unprecedented political opposition. Yet in the early hours of Wednesday morning, he emerged victorious, sweeping key battleground states that once seemed beyond reach.

As the BBC reported, "Donald Trump wins 2024 US

TRUMP'S REELECTION WASN'T JUST IMPROBABLE; IT WAS NEARLY IMPOSSIBLE.

election in historic comeback." He won the Electoral College 312 to 226 and defeated Kamala Harris in the popular vote 77 million (50 percent) to 75 million (48 percent), making him the first Republican to win the popular vote since George W. Bush in 2004.

Standing before a cheering crowd, Trump declared that the American people had given him "an unprecedented and powerful mandate."[6]

Throughout history, when nations approached a tipping point, God often raised up a disrupter. Sometimes it was a prophet. Sometimes it was a warrior. Sometimes, like King Jehu or Cyrus the Great, it was a flawed but chosen leader, lifted up to break demonic strongholds and confront corruption.

"I think God is obviously using [Trump] in massive ways," worship leader Sean Feucht said. "God is very unconventional. He doesn't follow man's plans, plot line, or trajectory—He has His own ways. His ways are higher than ours. He's chosen to use [Trump]...for a higher purpose....We don't get to say who He can and can't use. That's one of the beauties of following Jesus is that it's a journey of trusting Him. And so yeah, I'm real excited to see what's coming from his second term. And we've already seen some incredible things."[7]

To view my conversation with Sean Feucht, scan the QR code or visit TroyAndersonBooks.com/feucht.

Whether you love or loathe Trump, we must ask the question that cannot be ignored: How does Trump's presidency intersect with unfolding biblical prophecies?

Has he been positioned by God to lead America through one of the most perilous periods in modern history, a time possibly preceding the catastrophic events foretold in the Book of Revelation?

That is the question this book seeks to answer.

If God has indeed hit the pause button, granting humanity an extension of time, what happens next will determine not only the future of the United States but the fate of the world.

TRUMP, JEHU, AND AMERICA'S CRITICAL HOUR

In the aftermath of Trump's reelection, I reflected on the magnitude of what had happened. I wondered if we had moved into a "Jehu moment"—a time in which God, in His mercy, grants us more time to help bring as many to faith in Jesus as possible.

One person offering clarity on this question is my friend Rabbi Jonathan Cahn, the *New York Times* best-selling author of *The Harbinger* and other books. Cahn believes Trump's comeback has profound implications for America and the world.

> God saved his life, and God doesn't do anything without a purpose. The moment now is too important for us to miss. The political door has opened. But it's opened so that...the presence of God, the work of God, the will of God, the Word of God, the salvation of God, the Spirit of God, the redemption of God can enter through that door. This election is not the end of the story; it's the beginning.[8]

A MODERN DISRUPTER

To understand what is happening today, we must turn to the Bible. In the Old Testament we find the story of Jehu, a military commander called by God during a national crisis. About 3,000 years ago, Israel was ruled by King Ahab and Queen Jezebel, whose reign was characterized by idol worship, corruption, and the silencing of God's prophets. Truth was scorned. Evil was celebrated. The nation was divided and spiritually bankrupt.

Then, in 2 Kings 9, the prophet Elisha sent a young prophet to anoint Jehu as king. Jehu wasn't a priest or a politician; he was a warrior, chosen by God to restore righteousness.

Jehu didn't tiptoe into power; he rode "furiously" against the evil king (2 Kings 9:20, KJV). He toppled Jezebel, executed judgment on Ahab's dynasty (2 Kings 10:1–17), and eradicated Baal worship (2 Kings 10:18–28). He was courageous, tough, and unpolished, but he was obedient. Through him, God restored the nation.

Now fast-forward to today. Trump may not fit the mold of a traditional leader. Like Jehu, he came from outside the system. He didn't speak the language of diplomacy; he spoke the language of disruption. From the moment he stepped onto the world stage, he shook the foundations of the establishment. He confronted the media elite and defied powerful globalists, exposing widespread corruption. He faced off against progressive and globalist policies that threatened not only the sovereignty of America but its heritage as a Judeo-Christian nation.

Trump has emerged as a modern-day disrupter, not sent to maintain tradition, but to tear down what defies God's truth as laid out in the Bible.

The parallels are remarkable:

- Jehu was an outsider, not groomed by religious or political elites. "Thus says the LORD: 'I have anointed you king over Israel'" (2 Kings 9:3, NKJV). So is Trump.

- Jehu confronted systemic evil. So has Trump, challenging entrenched powers, media strongholds, and corruption.

- Jehu rose suddenly and unexpectedly: "I have a message for you, commander" (2 Kings 9:5). So did Trump.

- Jehu was known for driving furiously: "The driving is like the driving of Jehu…for he drives furiously!" (2 Kings 9:20, NKJV). Likewise, Trump is relentless and courageous.

- Jehu faced fierce resistance from the establishment. So does Trump.

- Jehu's mission wasn't about ambition; it was about God's mission for him. So is Trump's.

- Jehu toppled Jezebel's reign—a powerful woman who represented political and ideological strongholds. Like him, Trump has been called to confront powerful political women—first former Secretary of State Hillary Clinton, and more recently former Vice President Kamala Harris.

- Jehu's reign was imperfect, but he fulfilled the mission God gave him. Trump, likewise, is flawed but chosen by God because of his unique skills, talents, and tough personality.

- Jehu brought a temporary reprieve to Israel (2 Kings 10:30). Trump's second term may be America's window for repentance and revival.

JEHU WAS NOT CHOSEN BECAUSE HE WAS FLAWLESS

Jehu was not chosen because he was flawless. He was chosen because he was fit for the assignment.

Likewise, God has prepared Trump in the crucible of business, high-stakes negotiations, and relentless conflict. From the boardrooms of Manhattan to the political battlegrounds of Washington, D.C., he has been forged in the fire of adversity.

As Paul McGuire and I explored in our 2018 book *Trumpocalypse,* Trump's first presidency exposed the sheer depths of Deep State corruption—the rot embedded in government, media, and even parts of the church. The following years tested him enormously. They were marked by impeachment trials, media witch hunts, betrayals, and two assassination attempts. But instead of breaking him, those trials strengthened his resolve.

He returned to the White House, not wounded, but wiser and humbled, coming to understand God's assignment for him.

Now he knows who his enemies are. He knows who truly stands with him. And perhaps most importantly, he is beginning to grasp the prophetic weight of his return to the presidency.

This is not just a political comeback. It's a mission from God. Trump is not just governing; he's confronting deep spiritual darkness. The demonic forces of hell are seeking to destroy America. Trump's mission is to tackle these strongholds to make way for something bigger: a revival and return to God.

Like King David, he has been forged in fierce opposition—hunted, misunderstood, but never abandoned by God. Like Cyrus, he doesn't fit the mold of a spiritual leader, but he's been chosen for God's purposes.

And like Jehu, he has returned—not to maintain the status quo, but to tear down demonic strongholds, confront evil, and clear the way for revival.

IS THIS OUR JEHU MOMENT?

This moment isn't just about one person. It's about all of us.

Throughout history, God has raised up unlikely leaders, but He always holds His people accountable. Jehu confronted the altars of Baal, but it was Israel's response that determined her destiny. Today, Trump is confronting Deep State corruption and the globalists who seek control of the world, but it will be the followers of Jesus who help determine the outcome of this monumental battle. It will be determined by prayer, and it will be determined by our response.

THE CHURCH MUST RISE.

America stands at the precipice. In His mercy, God has extended another reprieve—an opportunity to repent and return to Him. But this window will not stay open forever. It is conditional. The idols must be broken. The altars of self and secularism must be torn down. Faith must replace fear. Courage must overcome apathy. And the church must rise.

If we miss this moment, the consequences will be catastrophic. Will we go forward in prayer, repentance, and holy resolve? Or will we shrink back, become complacent again, and watch God's window of mercy close?

I urge you—don't wait. Open the Bible to 2 Kings 9–10 and read Jehu's story. Ask the Holy Spirit to reveal what this historical account means for your life, your church, and your nation. Seek discernment. Ask God what role you are called to play.

Like Jehu, we must ride "furiously" to clear the way for the Holy Spirit to move again.

PROPHETS CONFIRM THE MISSION

Trump's return to the White House mirrors the biblical pattern of exile and restoration. Like Israel in the days of Jehu or the exiles under Cyrus, we are watching a similar pattern unfold.

Trump now leads with clarity forged in continual crisis. In his second term, he has become a man on a mission to fulfill God's calling to not only "Make America Great Again" but help ignite a spiritual turnaround in the United States and the world.

This is a presidency of action, not popularity. Christ's followers absolutely must shift with him—from spectators to intercessors, from critics to collaborators.

Trump's life has been a training ground. He has moved from real estate to casinos, from international negotiations to *The Apprentice* reality TV show. As a businessman, he learned to lead under pressure. In the casino world, he mastered risk and negotiation. As president, he disrupted the globalist machine, protected American sovereignty, and championed the Constitution.

In 2015, Paul McGuire and I published *The Babylon Code*—an investigative exposé of globalism and exploration of "Mystery, Babylon" in the Book of Revelation. In 2016, a prominent pastor shared *The Babylon Code* with the Trump team. Two months later, Trump announced, "Americanism, not globalism, will be our credo," as his platform for president.[9]

Since then, despite constant media attacks and legal persecution, Trump has fought "furiously" for America. He's become a man the world can't ignore because heaven has not released him from his assignment. Like Cyrus, Trump is a vessel in the hands of God: "I have even called you by your name; I have named you, though you have not known Me" (Isa. 45:4, NKJV).

Love him or loathe him, Trump has become a mirror to the nation and a catalyst for the church. Through him, as unlikely as it may seem, God is calling people to return to Him.

Trump's survival of two assassination attempts is not an accident. His mission is far from over. I'm not alone in saying this. Several prophetic voices have confirmed this.

JOSEPH Z: A TRAIL OF PROPHETIC CLARITY

International prophetic voice Joseph Z has been remarkably accurate in his insights regarding Trump.

Over the past several years, Joseph Z has released a series of prophecies about Trump, many of which now appear to be linked to current events. During live broadcasts between 2019 and 2024, he detailed prophetic declarations that outlined Trump's political journey, emphasizing his return to the White House, his survival of life-threatening challenges, and his role in fulfilling God's purposes.[10]

Here are highlights of Joseph Z's prophetic timeline:

December 31, 2019—Joseph Z prophesied that Trump had been fighting with one hand tied behind his back but would soon be "untied." He also said the White House would become a lighthouse, guiding America and the world.

September 8 and November 14, 2022—He warned of a four-year window to push back against globalist and anti-Christian forces and gave Trump an 80 percent chance of returning to the White House.

February 2, 2024—He declared 2024 a "do-over year."

June 3, 2024—He prophesied, "The attack will turn to a comeback," which many now interpret as predicting Trump's survival of two assassination attempts and his return as the 47th president.

June 7, 2024—He released a word about a "shot heard around the world," which was later linked to the July 13, 2024, assassination attempt on Trump in Butler, Pennsylvania.

July 13, 2024—On the very day of the attempted assassination, Joseph Z spoke of a coming storm in America and a "shelter in the middle"—a prophetic call for reform and national repentance.

As I neared completion of my second book about Trump, *The Trump Code*, my wife played me Joseph Z's video about the "shot heard around the world."[11] Amazed, I rewrote the book's preface:

> In what was described beforehand as the "shot heard around the world" by international prophetic voice Joseph Z, President Donald J. Trump survived an assassination attempt on July 13, 2024—sending shock waves around the globe. Later, he credited God for His miraculous hand of protection that saved his life.[12]

DUTCH SHEETS: MESSENGER OF HOPE FOR AMERICA

Dutch Sheets has been described as a "messenger of hope for America, boldly proclaiming she will experience a Third Great Awakening and return to her God-given destiny." He has been calling on the nation to hear God's heart regarding Trump since at least 2016.[13]

After the assassination attempt on Trump's life, Sheets said he was as shocked as anyone by what he witnessed live:

> Like so many in our nation, the trauma of watching the attempt live left it indelibly imprinted in my mind. I have since watched it replayed dozens of times—I didn't leave my spot in front of the TV for the next eight hours. I rarely watch Trump's rallies; I'm very busy and know his positions on the main issues. But for some reason, I was drawn to watch this one. Because of this, I, along with thousands of others, was praying immediately.[14]

Sheets believes Trump is now fully aware of the supernatural protection he experienced.

In a Truth Social post, Trump thanked the nation for their prayers and said: "It was God alone who prevented the unthinkable from happening." He stood up from the stage floor with a bloody face, shaking his fist and shouting, "Fight!" In his post he added, "We will FEAR NOT, but instead remain resilient in our faith and defiant in the face of wickedness." Trump also expressed love and prayers for the wounded and condolences for the man who lost his life.[15]

Sheets emphasized:

> If Trump ever questioned God's hand and destiny on him, he should now be fully assured of it! I have no doubt in my heart that prayer is why Trump is alive today. The Holy Spirit warned many of us, including myself, about an attempt on his life, and God responded to those prayers in a mighty way.[16]

In a post on GiveHim15.com, Sheets compared this moment to the role of John the Baptist, who prepared the way for the Messiah by clearing rough paths. Significant change often starts with disruption, and Sheets said this is where Trump comes in. Like a bulldozer, Trump's temperament is suited to clear the debris of corruption and dysfunction.

Sheets also drew parallels to President Ronald Reagan, who was known as a truth-teller. Reagan also brought healing to America following the rebellious 1960s and '70s, the counterculture movement, and the Vietnam War.

Sheets concluded with a call to prayer, asking God to guide Trump with wisdom, humility, and a heart for healing America so he can lead the nation in revival.[17]

SID ROTH: THE "GREATER GLORY" IS COMING

In August 2024, during a morning bike ride, I received a call from Sid Roth, host of *It's Supernatural!* Roth often reached out to me when I was executive editor of *Charisma* magazine, and he graciously endorsed my books *The Babylon Code* and *The Military Guide to Armageddon.*

That morning, he was excited. He told me there were prophetic parallels between Trump's assassination attempt and the ancient consecration rites of Hebrew priests in Leviticus 8.

The bullet narrowly missed Trump's head, grazing his ear and leaving him stained with blood. In the Old Testament consecration rite, the blood of a sacrifice was placed on the right ear, thumb, and big toe of the priest. During the attack, Trump instinctively raised his right hand to his bloodied ear, and the removal of his shoes mirrored the priestly act of ministering barefoot on holy ground.

Roth told me he believed Trump would be reelected and that the "greater glory" is coming. He said:

> [The "greater glory"] means by definition something greater than we've had before. And I'm preposterously believing that if we take all the revivals that have ever hit the world and combine them, it won't be as much as what's coming. That's where my hope is because it looks like a football game, and the devil is winning, especially in the US. So unless we have what I just said, there is no hope for the world, no hope for America, no hope for this generation. But I'm filled with hope. I have a scripture of the day on a calendar…[and] today's scripture is, "The horse is prepared against the day of battle, but safety is of the LORD" [Prov. 21:31]. In other words, you prepare, but it's all contingent on God—everything.[18]

To watch my interview with Sid Roth, scan the QR code or visit TroyAndersonBooks.com/roth.

The "shot heard around the world" prophecy from Joseph Z and Roth's message about the "greater glory" confirmed what the Holy Spirit was revealing to me in 2024. Despite the appearance that the devil was winning, God was about to confound the wise (1 Cor. 1:27, MEV). Trump would be reelected, and his return would usher in an unexpected spiritual awakening.

VIDEO: AN OPEN LETTER TO PRESIDENT TRUMP

Shortly before the election, following the release of my book *The Trump Code* and during our "40 Days to Save America" campaign of prayer, fasting, and repentance, I released a video on our Revelation Watchers' YouTube channel titled, "An Open Letter to President Trump, Urging Him to Lead America in Prayer, Repentance and Revival!"[19]

To view my open letters, scan the QR code or visit TroyAndersonBooks.com/open-letters.

I sent the video to Larry Keefauver's publicist, Jackie Monaghan, founder of Morningstar PR, and she sent the video to one of Trump's golfing partners, who I understand showed the video to Trump. A few days later, I asked Charisma House to send a copy of *The Trump Code,* along with a letter summarizing what I said in the video, to Trump at his Mar-a-Lago Club.

About a week later, Chad Dunlap, the Chief Operations Officer at Charisma Media, texted me a picture of a letter from President Trump to me, thanking me for writing *The Trump Code.* It was one of the greatest honors of my life. This is what President Trump's letter said:

> Dear Troy,
>
> Thank you for your very thoughtful letter and for sharing a copy of your book. Your continued support and prayers mean a great deal to me and my family.
>
> Our Nation is strong because of hard-working patriots like you who believe in—and defend—the great American ideals of faith, family, community, and country first. Know that I will never stop fighting for the America you and I cherish.
>
> May God continue to bless you.
>
> Sincerely,
> Donald J. Trump

COUNTERING THE GLOBALIST AGENDA

Before we examine the serious existential threats facing America today, it's essential to understand what God is doing through Trump and why both of his presidencies have become ground zero in a larger spiritual battle for the future of the United States and the world.

To millions of followers of Jesus, Trump's policies are spiritual barricades against evil. They serve as defenses against the encroaching tide of globalist and anti-biblical ideologies that seek to undermine and ultimately destroy the United States.

At the heart of this assignment is Trump's commitment to protect religious liberty, not just in America, but globally.

I witnessed a level of resolve during Trump's first term that few presidents have shown in recent decades. From the moment he took office, it was clear: this fight is about the survival of freedom and liberty in a world that is unknowingly opening the door in countless ways to the coming Antichrist system that the apostle John warned us about in the Book of Revelation.

MAJOR ACTIONS TO DEFEND RELIGIOUS FREEDOM

The following are some of the ways that Trump has worked to protect religious freedom and liberty.

Executive order on religious liberty

Early in his presidency, Trump signed a sweeping executive order directing federal agencies to enforce laws protecting religious freedom.[20]

Support for religious organizations

Trump's efforts to roll back the Johnson Amendment marked a pivotal moment. For decades, pastors and churches feared losing their tax-exempt status for engaging in political speech. Trump's push to repeal it restored the church's voice in the public square.

THIS FIGHT IS ABOUT THE SURVIVAL OF FREEDOM.

Health care protections

His administration expanded religious and moral exemptions under the Affordable Care Act, allowing Christian businesses and ministries to opt out of mandates that violated their beliefs, such as providing abortion-inducing drugs.

Defense of religious speech

Under Trump's Justice Department, there was a renewed defense of religious expression in schools, public institutions, and online platforms. I watched case after case where Christian students, organizations, and even government employees were finally given the legal support to live out their faith.

Global religious freedom advocacy

Perhaps most significantly, Trump made international religious liberty a top diplomatic priority. He formed the International Religious Freedom Alliance and hosted the first-ever Ministerial to Advance Religious Freedom, shining a spotlight on atrocities committed against believers in China, Iran, North Korea, and other nations.[21]

ONE OF THE MOST PRO-LIFE PRESIDENTS OF THE MODERN ERA

Trump's defense of religious liberty is part of a broader spiritual assignment. He's also emerged as one of the most pro-life presidents in modern history.

Unlike previous presidents who only offered lip service about the sanctity of life, Trump used his power to protect the unborn. Just look at the array of key actions he has taken in defense of unborn life:

Supreme Court appointments

Trump reshaped the judiciary when he appointed three constitutionalist justices to the US Supreme Court—Neil Gorsuch, Brett Kavanaugh, and Amy Coney Barrett.

The result? One of the most consequential legal reversals in American jurisprudence: the overturning of Roe v. Wade, the 1973 Supreme Court decision that legalized abortion.

After nearly fifty years of abortion-on-demand, the Supreme Court struck down Roe v. Wade on June 24, 2022. It was a historic moment. A demonic stronghold that resulted in over 63 million abortions in the United States fell because one man stood firm in his convictions.[22]

Expanded Mexico City Policy

Trump also reinstated and aggressively expanded the Mexico City Policy, cutting off federal funds to international groups that promote or provide abortions. Domestically, he redirected Title X funds away from abortion providers, ensuring taxpayer dollars would no longer underwrite the destruction of innocent life.[23]

Support for state-level abortion restrictions

Trump gave moral and legal backing to state efforts to restrict or outlaw abortion. From heartbeat bills in Georgia to bans in Alabama and Louisiana, his administration stood with governors and lawmakers defending life.

March for Life participation

In a historic first, Trump became the only sitting American president to attend and speak in person at the March for Life in Washington, D.C. Before a sea of pro-life advocates he declared:

> All of us here today understand an eternal truth: Every child is a precious and sacred gift from God. Together, we must protect, cherish, and defend the dignity and sanctity of every human life.[24]

Opposition to late-term abortion

Trump took an unflinching stand against late-term abortion. He advocated for laws protecting babies after viability and used his platform to expose the horrors of infanticide, challenging lawmakers to choose life over death.

For decades, believers prayed for a president who would not compromise on this issue. Trump became the vessel through whom those prayers were answered.

TRUMP'S WAR ON GLOBALISM

Trump's calling extends beyond defending life. He vowed to fight globalism.

From the beginning he made it clear that America would not bow to foreign interests, unelected bureaucrats, or elite globalist agendas. The old order opened America's borders, weakened our religious freedom, and promoted immorality. That order was about to be challenged.

Key anti-globalist actions and policies

America First Agenda

At the heart of Trump's philosophy is a conviction that America's sovereignty must never be surrendered. His "America First" platform is a line in the sand. Trump has argued that international alliances and global agreements often subvert the will of the American people, weakening the nation's ability to defend its citizens, values, and freedoms.

Trade protectionism

Trump moved decisively to rebuild America's industrial base and reduce dependence on adversarial nations. He replaced the North American Free

Trade Agreement (NAFTA) with the United States-Mexico-Canada Agreement (USMCA), imposed tariffs on China, and launched a trade war to expose the Chinese Communist Party's manipulative practices, including intellectual property theft, currency manipulation, and economic espionage.

Withdrawal from harmful international agreements

Trump withdrew from the Paris Climate Accord, the Iran Nuclear Deal, and the Trans-Pacific Partnership, recognizing that these agreements placed America's interests beneath those of the international elite.

Immigration reform and border security

Trump prioritized immigration reform and border security. He began construction on a southern border wall, and he implemented strict vetting and reduced refugee admissions.

Challenging global institutions

Trump openly questioned the power of the United Nations (UN), World Trade Organization (WTO), and North Atlantic Treaty Organization (NATO), demanding fairness and accountability. He also urged NATO allies to meet their financial commitments for defense.

National security and defense

From trade to military readiness, Trump prioritized national defense over global appeasement. His administration decoupled from Chinese markets, increased defense budgets, and launched the US Space Force.

To many Christian leaders, these policies represent prophetic resistance—a stand for sovereignty in a world hurtling toward global control. In the Book of Revelation, the apostle John warned of a coming one-world system. Many believe Trump became an unlikely vessel to disrupt the rise of globalism in our generation.

Despite lawsuits, investigations, and political sabotage, his resolve has only deepened. In a world marching toward the Antichrist system, Trump chose to confront the globalist elite because he understands what's happening and he's not going to let it unfold on his watch.

As Trump's second term continues, the battle between national sovereignty and global dominion continues. The question confronting America is urgent: Will we remain a nation under God? Or will we surrender to a system designed to erase our godly heritage and merge us into the "mark of the beast" system foretold in Revelation?

THE HEZEKIAH MOMENT

America's crisis is not just cultural or political—it is spiritual in nature. No leader or election can restore this nation without the Holy Spirit's intervention. Our hearts must return to God in humble repentance.

Trump's call to "Make America Great Again" resonated with millions. But true greatness cannot be reclaimed through politics. Without repentance, revival, and a return to biblical values, America cannot endure.

The Pilgrims and Puritans foresaw America being a "city on a hill" (Matt. 5:14). To fulfill that vision, we need revival.

Right now, we are living in a window of mercy extended to a wayward nation. This is a Hezekiah moment—a prophetic turning point in which time is being stretched to give God's people one last opportunity to turn the tide.

After decades of visions about America's future, prophetic voice and author Chuck Pierce sought the Lord for insight beyond 2026. The word he received was simple: "Extend time, Hezekiah."[25]

WITHOUT REPENTANCE, REVIVAL, AND A RETURN TO BIBLICAL VALUES, AMERICA CANNOT ENDURE.

That phrase became the foundation of a prophetic message rooted in King Hezekiah's story, when God granted him fifteen more years of life (2 Kings 20).

Pierce saw a pattern in 2 Kings 19:29–31 in which Israel experienced a three-year recovery process. Pierce believes this biblical passage aligns with what God wants to do from 2025 to 2027.

The key isn't merely the fifteen-year extension of Hezekiah's life, but it's what he did with the time:

- Year One—Eat what grows of itself.

- Year Two—Eat what springs from the same.

- Year Three—Sow and reap.

Pierce believes this mirrors God's blueprint for America from 2025 to 2027: a supernatural reset, a time of recovery and preparation for the coming harvest—the "greater glory" that Sid Roth has foreseen.

"And the Lord said, 'I want to show you that if you will progress through the next two years, you'll have new fruit in 2027,'" Pierce said. "What the Lord was saying was, 'I'm bringing you a three-year turnaround period.'"[26]

Thanks to my many conversations and interviews with faith and prophetic leaders across the nation, I agree that we are in a time of revival. But this will not happen automatically. It requires:

- Intercessory prayer

- Authentic repentance

- Obedient and courageous leadership

Pierce warned that the enemy will use this time to sow confusion, despair, and division. We're already seeing this happen. Satan will try to distract us from hope. But those who stand on God's Word and expect miracles will see them happen.

"You have to know and be motivated to press into your land that has a new fruitfulness," Pierce said. "Land in the Word of God is linked not just with promise, but is linked with your heart also."[27]

JUDGMENT OR REVIVAL?

This prophetic moment comes as America is teetering on the brink of what experts call a "classic, textbook civilizational collapse."[28]

At the same time, our culture has become post-Christian and secularized to a large degree. Postmodernism declares there is no God, no transcendent truth. In its place, society invents its own "truth," embracing immorality, rebellion against authority, family disintegration, and social disorder.

Truth, morality, and religious belief have broken down across every institution—education, government, media, health care, business, entertainment, and even parts of the church. If this trajectory continues, collapse is inevitable.

We've already seen the signs: lawlessness, riots, cancel culture, economic instability, open borders, fake news, rampant drug use, sexual anarchy, mental health crises, and suicide epidemics—all accelerated by COVID-19, which killed over 7 million people globally and marked the beginning of what geopolitical experts describe as an asymmetrical Third World War.[29]

Disaster looms from every direction. Will it be economic collapse igniting chaos in the streets? A foreign attack crippling our power grid and internet? A nuclear strike from Russia, North Korea, or Iran? Will China invade Taiwan, sparking World War III? Or will catastrophic natural disasters continue, like the wildfires in Pacific Palisades and Altadena in California?

The dangers are real—record levels of debt, global instability, and rising threats of war and other disasters. Meanwhile, the church is under siege and being pushed to the margins. Yet the recent wave of revival sweeping the nation gives us hope that this trend can be reversed.

International missionary and futurist Fred Markert points to Jeremiah 18:8 as the "bulletproof Scripture" that gives him hope that America can be saved: "And if that nation I warned repents of its evil, then I will relent and not inflict on it the disaster I had planned."

> I believe we can see revival and we can see [America] turn around. This is why I speak...[on] what they call the seven deadly scenarios. [Scholars] can only see seven ways the near future can go, and it's all deadly: world war, collapse of America....But I have the eighth scenario: The Jesus scenario, the revival scenario.[30]

EXTEND TIME, HEZEKIAH

The prophetic word Pierce received is key: "Extend time, Hezekiah."[31]

Despite the gathering storm, Trump's reelection has opened a window of mercy. God has pushed the pause button, but America has not yet fully repented.

As described above, the challenges are vast. Worst of all, however, is that the church is fractured and sleeping at the hour of its greatest peril.

America is a nation in crisis, but we're not beyond redemption. We stand at the edge of a prophetic cliff. The question is no longer if America will awaken, but when, how, and who will respond to the call? This is not just about survival. It's also about God's destiny for America.

Pierce said he received a prophetic word from the Lord in 1986 that the United States would be in a desperate place by 2026—unless there was an intervention—and would go into "deep, deep decline starting in 2026." The Lord later told him the only way America would survive is to "play the Trump card"—that Trump's reelection was necessary to prevent America's collapse.

WE STAND AT THE EDGE OF A PROPHETIC CLIFF.

"I just consider it a miracle that we are in a place now to see a turnaround in this nation over the next three years," Pierce told Charisma Media Founder Stephen Strang on the *Strang Report*. "I mean it is great hope, great conflict, great chaos. Our nation is almost completely divided...[2025] and 2026, it will be a lot of the same type of warfare. But in 2027 we can see a shift occur completely that brings us back into a prominence worldwide that we have not had over the last 10 years."[32]

CHAPTER 3

THE REVIVAL BLUEPRINT

We're a failing nation. We're a nation that's in serious decline....We have wars going on in the Middle East. We have wars going on with Russia and Ukraine. We're going to end up in a third World War. And it will be a war like no other because of nuclear weapons....What these people have done to our country...allowing millions of people to come into our country, many of them are criminals, and they're destroying our country. The worst president, the worst vice president in the history of our country.[1]
—PRESIDENT DONALD TRUMP IN A DEBATE WITH
FORMER VICE PRESIDENT KAMALA HARRIS

CIVILIZATIONS DON'T RISE and fall by happenstance. They follow predictable patterns—what scholars call civilizational cycles.

From Babylon to Rome, the British Empire to modern-day America, the same trajectory holds true: nations go through a series of stages.

Over the last five thousand years, historians estimate twenty-seven major civilizations have risen to world power only to fall in inglorious ignominy. The average lifespan of these empires and nations was 238 years. With America's 250th anniversary in 2026, we're beyond the historical median. Statistically, we're on borrowed time.[2]

Existential risk experts say the United States is in the last of seven stages that civilizations undergo before collapse. The stages are outburst, conquest, commerce, affluence, intellect, decadence, and collapse. America is well into the decadence stage when the fragile systems that hold society together—government, the economy, education, religion, and morality—are breaking down.

The next stage is civilizational collapse.

Futurist Fred Markert calls America "a classic, textbook civilizational collapse."[3] He goes on to explain the seven stages of civilization. The first stage, outburst, is when a new civilization is born. In America's case, this was 1776. The next stage is conquest, where the civilization exerts military power for the first time. Markert says America did this in World Wars I and II. The next stage, commerce, involves the civilization doing business on an international level because no one else is in a position to trade on that scale. Much of Europe was devastated by the world wars, leaving America in this type of position.

The next stage, affluence, comes as a direct result of commerce. Markert says that America was in this stage in the 1950s and '60s. Affluence leads directly into intellect, when as Markert says, "your academics lose their minds and go crazy." This results in systems breaking down: government, education, the economy, and moral values. That's the final stage, decadence. Markert concludes, "We're in late decadence. We're at the very end. So we are on the verge of civilizational collapse. No scholar believes America can be saved, but I do believe America can be saved."[4]

By nearly every measurement—cultural, economic, educational, and moral—we are entrenched in decadence. But history offers a choice. Collapse is not set in stone. In the Bible, when the Israelites faced destruction and humbly repented of their sins, God responded not with judgment but with mercy.

Faith leaders I've interviewed say only a massive spiritual awakening can save America. Encouragingly, they not only see signs that this is beginning but also believe the United States and the world are on the verge of one of the greatest revivals in history.

"It's going to be turbulent the next few months and into 2025, but I promise you this, God is going to win," Dutch Sheets, internationally recognized author and the founder of Dutch Sheets Ministries, said in the spring of 2024. "The harvest is coming, and this nation is going to turn around."[5]

HISTORY OFFERS A CHOICE. COLLAPSE IS NOT SET IN STONE.

Following President Trump's reelection in November 2024, Robert Jeffress, senior pastor at First Baptist Church, Dallas, said most Evangelicals, conservative Catholics, and conservative Jews greeted Trump's reelection with relief and gratitude to God.

> There's a very real sense that our country has been in a downward spiral the last four years, and mainly because of our departure from the Judeo-Christian foundation of our nation. To many people, I believe President Trump's reelection represents God giving America another chance—perhaps her last chance—to reverse this downward trajectory.[6]

HOW GREAT AWAKENINGS RESHAPED AMERICA

In my years of studying the possibility of an end-times revival,[7] I learned that when nations reach a point of potential destruction or collapse, God doesn't always respond with judgment. When corruption, complacency, and wickedness flourish, He often responds with revival. He did it for ancient Israel, and He has done it for America as well.

These disruptions, known as Great Awakenings, are not anomalies. They are part of a biblical pattern. From the fire of Jonathan Edwards's preaching to the influence of George Whitefield and Charles Finney, revival has proven to be the only force strong enough to save a dying nation.

As I see it, we are now entering another such time. Understanding what happened in prior awakenings is not just history; it's the revival blueprint of what the Holy Spirit is doing again.

THE FIRST GREAT AWAKENING (1725–1760)

The First Great Awakening was America's original spiritual earthquake. Between 1725 and 1760, revival fires spread across the colonies, culminating in a surge between 1740 and 1742 that shook the order of the day.

At the same time in England, the Wesleyan revival transformed that country. By the time clergyman and evangelist John Wesley died in 1791, his movement had birthed over 79,000 Methodists in England and 40,000 in America. It was a transatlantic move of the Holy Spirit.[8]

In the colonies, Jonathan Edwards became the unexpected spark. He wasn't a charismatic speaker, but when he preached his now-famous sermon, "Sinners in the Hands of an Angry God," in 1741, the effect was explosive. Eyewitnesses described people weeping, wailing, even clutching pews in fear of God's judgment. His preaching inspired not only an emotional reaction but the fear of the Lord that broke through people's apathy.

"It is everlasting wrath," Edwards preached in his sermon. "It would be dreadful to suffer this fierceness and wrath of Almighty God one moment; but you must suffer it to all eternity. There will be no end to this exquisite horrible misery.... Oh, who can express what the state of a soul in such circumstances is! All that we can possibly say about it, gives but a very feeble, faint representation of it; it is inexpressible and inconceivable: For 'Who knows the power of God's anger?'"[9]

Yet, Edwards also proclaimed God's mercy:

> And now you have an extraordinary opportunity, a day wherein Christ has thrown the door of mercy wide open, and stands in calling and crying with a loud voice to poor sinners; a day wherein many are flocking to him, and pressing into the kingdom of God. Many are daily coming from the east, west, north and south; many that were very lately

in the same miserable condition that you are in, are now in a happy state, with their hearts filled with love to him who has loved them, and washed them from their sins in his own blood, and rejoicing in the hope of the glory of God.[10]

As pastor of the Northampton Church in Massachusetts, Edwards confronted a spiritually asleep generation, especially young people. His message was powerful: God is holy, judgment awaits the unrepentant, yet Christ's sacrifice on the cross paid the price for our sins and His grace is available to those who ask for forgiveness. Hundreds were converted, and the region experienced revival.

While Edwards inspired people with theological persuasion, George Whitefield, an Anglican evangelist and close friend of the Wesley brothers, set the colonies ablaze with his zeal.[11]

Between 1738 and 1770, Whitefield crossed the Atlantic seven times, preaching with such fire that crowds of 30,000 gathered in open fields. His "loud, commanding, and pleasant voice" was said to carry for miles, and wherever he went, repentance often followed. During his life, he preached about 18,000 sermons.[12]

Denied access to pulpits by ministers who feared his influence, Whitefield went to the streets, courthouses, and docks. The rich and poor stood side by side, convicted of sin, crying out for salvation. Even Benjamin Franklin, although not a professing Christian, admired Whitefield, marveling at the moral reforms his preaching helped inspire.

Whitefield wasn't just a gifted orator. Like many revivalists, he likely learned how to make every thought "obedient to Christ" (2 Cor. 10:5), allowing God to use him strategically as an architect of the awakening. His preaching transcended denominations, forging a shared Christian bond throughout the colonies. In many ways, he laid the groundwork for the unity that would later fuel the American Revolution.

The First Great Awakening wasn't just a revival. It was a cultural reformation. And it began with two men—one a scholar, the other a firebrand—fully yielded to God.

THE SECOND GREAT AWAKENING (1801–1840)

In my research into these amazing movements of the Holy Spirit, few moments are more instructive than the Second Great Awakening. If the First Great Awakening prepared the nation for the Revolutionary War, the second reshaped its moral compass and prepared the world for the end of the scourge of slavery.

This revival fire was ignited on the American frontier, in a rugged outpost called Cane Ridge in Bourbon County, Kentucky. In 1801, 10,000 to 25,000 people—nearly a tenth of Kentucky's population—gathered for what became a supernatural encounter. Under the preaching of Presbyterian minister James McGready and revivalist Barton W. Stone, the Spirit moved with such power that 1,000 to 3,000 conversions to Christ took place at a single event.[13]

Eyewitnesses described spontaneous weeping, trembling, and physical manifestations of repentance. One observer reported eight hundred people "were struck down," lying unresponsive from fifteen minutes to ten hours. James Finley, later a circuit rider, described the sound as "like the roar of Niagara" as he witnessed at least five hundred people slain in the Spirit with shouts and shrieks.[14]

From Cane Ridge, the fires of revival leapt across the nation through camp meetings—outdoor gatherings where thousands worshipped, repented, and recommitted their lives to Jesus. By 1811, an estimated one-third of all Americans had attended a camp meeting.[15]

This same revival reached Williams College in Massachusetts. There, in 1806, five students caught in a thunderstorm took shelter under a haystack and prayed for the world. That incident, now known as the Haystack Prayer Meeting, sparked the American foreign missions movement, sending waves of missionaries throughout the world.[16]

Key figures of the Second Great Awakening

The Second Great Awakening marked a major theological shift. Unlike the more Calvinist framework of the First Great Awakening, this revival emphasized free will and personal responsibility.

Instead of the belief that God chooses certain individuals for salvation before they are born (the doctrine of predestination), salvation was now seen as a gift God offers those who ask for forgiveness of their sins. It inspired the belief that individuals could change not only themselves, but society too.

The revival birthed powerful voices and movements:

- Charles Finney was a lawyer-turned-preacher known as the "Father of Modern Revivalism" and forerunner of evangelists like Dwight L. Moody, Billy Sunday, and Billy Graham. He pioneered "new measures" such as the altar call and public prayers of repentance. Under Finney's fiery preaching, more than a quarter of a million people were converted. "When there is a [lack] of brotherly love and Christian confidence among believers, then revival is needed," Finney wrote in *How to*

Experience Revival. "When the church finds its members falling into gross and scandalous sins, then it is time to wake up and cry to God for a revival of religion."[17]

- Lyman Beecher, a Presbyterian minister, led efforts in New England to channel revival energy into action, birthing organizations dedicated to social reform and evangelism, including the American Bible Society, American Sunday School Union, and American Tract Society.[18]

- Timothy Dwight, president of Yale College, preached a series of famous sermons at the college chapel, including "The Nature and Danger of Infidel Philosophy," inspiring twenty-six students to found the Moral Society of Yale College. The society discouraged immorality, profanity, and excessive drinking. By 1800, it included one-third to one-half of the students at the college, laying the foundation for four revivals at Yale.[19]

Revival built America

In studying the long-term impact of the Second Great Awakening, it becomes clear that revival played a significant role in shaping the young republic.

Churches exploded in size. Methodists and Baptists swept the countryside with circuit-riding preachers whose gospel message was raw, emotional, and easily understood by the masses.

Revival inspired reform. The movement against slavery was fueled by prayer meetings and fiery sermons. So were temperance and prison reform.

Education became a mission field. By 1860, many US colleges had been founded by denominations birthed in revival. Institutions like the American Bible Society and the American Sunday School Union spread literacy and biblical truth from frontier cabins to distant continents.

The revival also democratized the church. The majority of converts were women, who then stepped into prayer leadership, organized reform efforts, and pioneered missionary societies. African Americans birthed historic institutions like the African Methodist Episcopal Church, connecting revival to the fight for freedom.

Revival helped define what it meant to be American, not just as citizens of the republic, but as stewards of God's plan for the United States. National identity was reimagined through the lens of Scripture.

The Second Great Awakening reshaped America's values, reenergized its churches, and redirected its mission.

Just as God moved mightily during America's early days, I believe He is doing it again. Watching the chaos of our modern world—the division, deception, and confusion—I believe we're approaching another Cane Ridge moment.

THE THIRD GREAT AWAKENING (1830s–1870s)

The Third Great Awakening marks a pivotal moment in American history. Some historians, including revival scholar J. Edwin Orr, view it as an extension of the Second Great Awakening, but the scale and global impact suggest otherwise. It was a fresh outpouring of the Holy Spirit.[20]

By the 1830s, America was grappling with the scourge of slavery and a widening gap between the rich and poor. Once again, God moved.

It began with Charles Finney, a young attorney. In 1821, Finney abandoned his legal ambitions after an encounter with God. He called it a "mighty baptism of the Holy Ghost." In *The Original Memoirs of Charles G. Finney,* he described the experience:

> Without any expectation of it, without ever having the thought in my mind that there was any such thing for me, without any recollection that I had ever heard the thing mentioned by any person in the world, the Holy Spirit descended upon me in as manner that seemed to go through me, body and soul. I could feel the impression, like a wave of electricity, going through and through me. Indeed it seemed to come in waves and waves of liquid love; for I could not express it in any other way. It seemed like the very breath of God. I can recollect distinctly that it seemed to fan me, like immense wings.[21]

From then on, Finney's mission was to win souls and awaken a slumbering nation.

His early revivals in upstate New York, including Evans Mills (1824–25), laid the groundwork. But his legendary Rochester, New York, crusade (1830–31) became one of the most spiritually impactful events in American history. Entire towns shut down. Businesses closed early. Taverns emptied. Courts fell silent. Even hardened skeptics were moved by the atmosphere of holiness.[22]

Finney partnered with Daniel Nash, known as "Father Nash," the revival's secret prayer warrior. Nash would quietly arrive in towns ahead of Finney, rent a room, and pray—sometimes groaning in the Spirit for hours—until a breakthrough came.[23]

Together, Finney and Nash created a revival model still used today: prayer prepares the ground, and preaching reaps the harvest.

"[Finney's] enormous success inspired a large number of 'professional evangelists' to come to the fore from the ranks of every major denomination," according to *Christianity Today*. "By 1840 the concept of large campaigns led by preachers who were not pastors of specific churches was generally accepted. From 1840 until the 1870s numerous preachers entered the ranks of traveling evangelists."[24]

To Finney, revival wasn't haphazard. It was the result of obedience, prayer, and God's miraculous intervention.

"Almost all the religion in the world has been produced by revivals," Finney wrote in "Lectures on Revivals of Religion." "God has found it necessary to take advantage of the excitability there is in mankind, to produce powerful excitements among them, before he can lead them to obey. Men are so sluggish, there are so many things to lead their minds off from religion, and to oppose the influence of the gospel, that it is necessary to raise an excitement among them, till the tide rises so high as to sweep away the opposing obstacles. They must be so excited that they will break over these counteracting influences, before they will obey God."[25]

Wave of national repentance

The revival soon spilled beyond Finney's meetings.

The Methodist Episcopal Church, fueled by camp meetings and circuit riders, doubled in membership between 1840 and 1842. Meanwhile, revivalists like Asahel Nettleton and Daniel Baker led powerful gospel campaigns throughout the South and Midwest, adding momentum to a rising wave of national repentance.[26]

Finney's influence also helped reshaped education and the abolitionist movement. As president of Oberlin College, he institutionalized revival values into academic life. He turned Oberlin into a hub of evangelical fervor, intellectual rigor, and social reform, especially concerning women's education and the abolition of slavery.[27]

Across towns and cities, the change was visible. Crime rates plummeted. Families were restored. Churches overflowed with seekers. A tangible fear of the Lord swept through communities, altering the atmosphere. It was as if a holy hush had settled over the land.

Revival wasn't accidental. It was mobilized. Finney taught believers to pray fervently and preach courageously. His theology framed revival not as a mystical experience but as a mission, one that required obedience, discipline, and action. Revival became a strategic battle plan for national reformation.

At the core of this plan was prayer. Intercession wasn't background noise; it was the foundation. Father Nash's strategy—arriving in towns early to wage war in the secret place—redefined revival preparation. His approach is still used by prayer ministries worldwide. Victory begins behind closed doors in spiritual warfare.

The fruit of this revival wasn't confined to church walls. It spilled into the streets, classrooms, and courts. Under Finney's leadership, Oberlin College became one of the first institutions in America to welcome both Black students and women.

THE FOURTH GREAT AWAKENING (1960s–1970s)

By the mid-twentieth century, America was unraveling. The assassination of President John F. Kennedy, the trauma of the Vietnam War, the rise of Marxist ideologies, the sexual revolution, and Watergate had turned the nation upside down. A generation that once sang in the pews now marched in protests, turned to psychedelics, and embraced existential despair.

THE EARLY FIRES OF THE JESUS MOVEMENT WERE LIT IN SOUTHERN CALIFORNIA THROUGH A SIMPLE BUT RADICAL DECISION: A PASTOR OPENED HIS CHURCH DOORS.

Trust in government collapsed. Confidence in the church eroded. The traditional family fractured. Many feared America was teetering on the brink of collapse.

Yet in the midst of this, the Holy Spirit moved again.

This time, revival erupted from the fringes—California beaches, communal homes, coffee shops, and open-air fields. It was raw and unapologetically supernatural. This wasn't a revival of the establishment. It was a revival of the outcasts, the addicts, the drifters, and searching souls.

This was the Jesus movement, as shown in Pastor Greg Laurie's 2023 movie *Jesus Revolution*, starring *The Chosen's* Jonathan Roumie as charismatic hippie preacher Lonnie Frisbee, Kelsey Grammer as Calvary Chapel's Pastor Chuck Smith, and Joel Courtney as Laurie himself.

A movement of hippies and miracles

The early fires of the Jesus movement were lit in Southern California through a simple but radical decision: a pastor opened his church doors. Chuck Smith embraced a group the church had largely ignored—barefoot, long-haired hippies searching for truth. He welcomed them without judgment, and the Holy Spirit did the rest.

Among them was Frisbee—perhaps the most unlikely revivalist of the era. A former drug user with a turbulent past, Frisbee carried a fierce anointing. His prophetic preaching, altar calls, and the accompanying signs and wonders resulted in supernatural encounters and mass conversions to Christ. Tens of thousands surrendered their lives to Jesus. Many were baptized in the Pacific Ocean at Pirate's Cove in Corona del Mar, California, where my wife, Irene, and I often enjoy scenic walks.

Music became the language of this revival. Artists like Larry Norman, Love Song, Keith Green, Andraé Crouch, and 2nd Chapter of Acts helped birth contemporary Christian music. Worship music was played at coffeehouses, in VW vans, and on street corners. House churches emerged, as well as street evangelists. Among them were figures like Duane Pederson, publisher of the *Hollywood Free Paper*, and Arthur Blessitt, a traveling preacher who carried a large wooden cross around the world.

What made the Jesus movement so powerful was its reach. It crossed denominational boundaries and transcended politics, and its impact still reverberates throughout the world today.

A hunger for the return of Christ

The Jesus movement shattered the stereotype of religion as cold or irrelevant. It made faith in Jesus intimate and relational.

Calvary Chapel exploded from a handful of people to thousands. Smith's preaching model became a template for churches around the world. He went through the Bible verse by verse and was open to anyone who showed up. Later, the Vineyard movement emerged under John Wimber, blending charismatic worship with healing and evangelism. Both became catalysts for global church planting.

Meanwhile, organizations like Youth With A Mission (YWAM), Campus Crusade for Christ, and Fuller Seminary expanded rapidly. Many converts became missionaries, pastors, church planters, and media pioneers. Christian radio, television, and publishing surged. The Word of God saturated the airwaves and the globe.

Most significantly, the movement ignited a renewed hunger for the return of Christ. Prophecy conferences boomed. People dug deep into Scripture, rediscovering the gifts of the Holy Spirit and the power of prayer. A biblical worldview returned to the forefront, as hundreds of thousands awakened to their calling in Christ.

"(The) Jesus movement...was significant on a number of levels," wrote Alex McFarland, a Christian apologist and former president of the Southern Evangelical Seminary. "Of primary significance was that in under a decade, millions of people throughout the US and internationally would find a personal, soul-saving relationship with Jesus Christ....Moreover, global Christianity to this very moment has been shaped by events reenacted in the *Jesus Revolution* movie. While much is made of the 'rise of the nones' in America, and that Gen Z is the 'least religious' demographic in US history, the fact is that Christianity around the world is growing rapidly. The Jesus movement is a large part of why this is the case....In the aftermath of the Jesus movement ministries formed that would take the message of Christianity throughout the world; also birthed were organizations that would take the Christian ethic of human relief and service throughout the world."[28]

FROM THE JESUS MOVEMENT TO THE "MOST SPIRITUALLY HUNGRY GENERATION"

The Jesus movement wasn't powered by political strategy or church programming. A generation cried out for the truth and heaven answered. But like past awakenings, the fire cooled. By the late 1980s, what had been free-flowing and Spirit-led became institutionalized, polished, and commodified.

Yet many prophetic voices believe the Jesus movement was only a foretaste.

They point to a final outpouring—a Fifth Great Awakening—that will eclipse every revival before it. A sweeping move of God where prodigals return and the remnant church arises in purity, fire, and authority. A generation without name or fame, marked by surrender, to carry the glory of God into the darkest parts of the world.

"God is about to send a tsunami of the Holy Spirit, a movement in the midst of gathering darkness," R. Loren Sandford, the late senior pastor at New Song Church in Denver, Colorado, wrote in *The Last Great Outpouring*.[29] "I have long prophesied that the end time outpouring of the Spirit will be greater than Pentecost, greater and more powerful than anything history has seen."

Evangelist Taylan Michael Seaman, founder of Revival Way Ministries, whose videos have reached hundreds of millions of people, said Generation Alpha and Generation Z are at the center of the revival now underway, and he called them "the most spiritually hungry generation that we've ever seen on the face of the earth."[30]

Seaman believes this generation's hunger for the supernatural will become a catalyst for revival.

"They're not going to be religious people who get stuck in a pew and they just become benchwarmers in the church," he said. "They're going to get baptized in the Holy Ghost and fire and carry it everywhere that they go. So I think what

God is doing in Generation Z and Gen Alpha right now is unlike anything we've ever seen, and I believe it's going to be the two generations that God uses to usher in the return of Jesus Christ."[31]

To watch my interview with Taylan Michael Seaman, scan the QR code or visit TroyAndersonBooks.com/seaman.

GOD IS GRACIOUSLY EXTENDING MERCY AND REVIVAL TO AMERICA

From Cane Ridge to Pirate's Cove, America's story is one of God's repeated mercy and grace, as unwarranted as it may be.

Once again, the hour is late. As we discussed at the beginning of this chapter, America is facing a civilizational collapse. But the United States is also experiencing an awakening. The question isn't whether God will move. The question is, Will we?

Encouragingly, Lifeway Research reports that Christianity continues to grow globally. Today, there are more than 2.64 billion Christians worldwide, with projections topping 3 billion before 2050. Meanwhile, the number of evangelical Christians is expected to rise from 420 million today to nearly 621 million by 2050. And from the humble beginnings of the Azusa Street Revival in 1906—when fewer than 1 million identified as Pentecostal—Pentecostal and Charismatic Christians are projected to top 1 billion by 2050.[32]

GOD IS NOT BOUND BY TRENDS.

In the United Kingdom, Bible sales have doubled and the number of young people attending church quadrupled from 2018 to 2024.[33]

"'It's incredibly heartening to see this renewed interest among young people in the life of the Church,' said Archbishop of York Stephen Cottrell."[34]

History reminds us: God is not bound by trends. He does not respond to polling data. He responds to prayer, fasting, and repentance. The evidence is hard to refute. In the 1740s, the First Great Awakening shattered religious apathy, birthing the American Evangelical movement. In the 1830s, Charles Finney's revivals in New York transformed cities, closing saloons and courts while opening hearts to Christ. The 1857 Fulton Street Revival, just before America's financial collapse, swept 10 percent of Manhattan into faith in Christ. In 1904, the Welsh Revival converted 7.5 percent of Wales in under a year. And in 1907, the Pyongyang Revival lit a fire that still burns in South Korea, now one of the most vibrant Christian nations on earth.[35]

These were not isolated miracles. They were the result of a partnership between God and humanity. In every great move of the Holy Spirit, you will find four elements:

1. A rediscovery of God

2. The gospel preached in power and clarity

3. A remnant devoted to prayer and repentance

4. Innovative evangelism that reaches young people[36]

And out of the fires of awakening new movements emerge. The American Bible Society (1816), The Salvation Army (1865), and Youth With A Mission (1960) are all revival-born institutions that helped shape the modern church.

Revival inspires, but movements endure. That's why every generation must steward its awakening carefully, lest the fire fade into memory.

A NATION ON THE LINE

America stands today in the early stages of collapse, unless the revival now unfolding keeps growing.

The prophetic blueprint has been written. In every generation, revival begins when a consecrated few take God at His Word, repenting, interceding, and believing He will rend the heavens again.

REVIVAL BEGINS WITH THE REMNANT. In Isaiah 57:15 the prophet Isaiah wrote, "For this is what the high and exalted One says—he who lives forever, whose name is holy: 'I live in a high and holy place, but also with the one who is contrite and lowly in spirit, to revive the spirit of the lowly and to revive the heart of the contrite.'"

If history teaches us anything, it's that revival begins with the remnant. It doesn't come from the top down, but from the ground up. From ordinary people with extraordinary faith in the miraculous power of the Holy Spirit.

The late Tim Keller, founder of Redeemer Presbyterian Church in Manhattan and co-founder of The Gospel Coalition, stated what revival is:

> I arrived at a definition of revival from reading history, from reading the Bible, and from my own experiences. Revival isn't something human beings do or the extraordinary apparition of the Holy Spirit. Real revival

is the intensification of the ordinary operations of the Holy Spirit. The ordinary operations of the Holy Spirit are conviction, conversion, assurance, and sanctification. When those operations are intensified across a church, denomination, city, or country, you've got revival.[37]

Revival awakens those asleep in the pews. It convicts the almost-Christian, the one close to faith in Jesus but never truly born again. It draws the lost, not through profound arguments, but through the presence of God.

THE HOLY SPIRIT'S INVITATION

A holy hunger is rising today. The world is weary of deception, distraction, and despair.

As in the past, God is looking for repentant hearts, for those who will cry out, "Lord, do it again in our time."

If you're reading this, consider this your invitation. You don't need credentials. You don't need a title.

You need a burden. A broken heart. A burning desire to see Jesus lifted high again in America and the nations.

The blueprint has already been written in blood, tears, and testimonies. Now the pen is in our hands. Will we live it?

Lord, revive us again, for Your glory.

CHAPTER 4

THE LIGHT AND THE GLORY

*I am well aware of the Toil and Blood and Treasure that it will
cost Us to maintain this Declaration, and support and defend these
States. Yet through all the Gloom I can see Rays of ravishing Light and
Glory. I can see that the End is worth more than all the Means.*
—JOHN ADAMS TO ABIGAIL ADAMS, ON THE PASSING
OF THE DECLARATION OF INDEPENDENCE[1]

A S A NEW follower of Jesus in the early 1980s, my youth pastor, Richard Wheeler, often invited me to travel with him when he spoke at churches, conferences, and Royal Rangers' Frontiersman Camping Fellowship "Pow Wows."

At these events, he retold American history by dressing in authentic period clothing—sometimes as a Pilgrim, mountain man, cowboy, or Revolutionary or Civil War soldier. His purpose was to highlight the often-neglected historical Christian perspective.

I learned a great deal about the true history of America—a much different version than the politically correct one taught in public schools, colleges, and universities today.

Then one day he told me about a book that chronicled God's hand in guiding the men and women who founded America—*The Light and the Glory: Did God Have a Plan for America?* by Peter Marshall, a Yale and Princeton Theological Seminary graduate, and David Manuel, a former editor at a major New York publishing house.[2]

Tim LaHaye, coauthor of the Left Behind series,[3] said this about *The Light and the Glory*: "*The Light and the Glory* reveals our true national heritage and inspires us to stay on God's course as a nation."[4]

As a youth, I read *The Light and the Glory*, captivated by stories of how Christopher Columbus believed the Holy Spirit directed him to discover America so God could use the nation to spread the gospel.

This chapter isn't just about the history of America that has been suppressed. It's about how the United States of America was founded on biblical principles by men and women, some deeply flawed, who believed, nonetheless, that they were part of a God-inspired mission.

Columbus, the Pilgrims, and the Puritans came to build the New World. "For we must consider that we shall be as a city upon a hill," Puritan leader John Winthrop said in his 1630 sermon "A Model of Christian Charity." "The eyes of all people are upon us. So that if we shall deal falsely with our God in this work we have undertaken, and so cause Him to withdraw His present help from us, we shall be made a story and a by-word through the world."[5]

CHRISTOPHER COLUMBUS AND THE BOOK OF PROPHECIES

An often-overlooked part of America's heritage is the role of Christopher Columbus, not just as an explorer, but as a follower of Christ.

In his obscure work *The Book of Prophecies*, Columbus recounted the inspiration he received from the Holy Spirit to undertake his perilous journey to the New World in 1492. According to Columbus, it was not just his navigational skills that led him to the Americas but the direction he received from the Spirit of God.

"Most exalted rulers: At a very early age I began sailing the sea and have continued until now," Columbus wrote in *The Book of Prophecies*. He continued:

> Our Lord has favored my occupation and has given me an intelligent mind....During this time I have studied all kinds of texts; cosmography, histories, chronicles, philosophy, and other disciplines. Through these writings, the hand of Our Lord opened my mind to the possibility of sailing to the Indies and gave me the will to attempt the voyage. With this burning ambition I came to your Highnesses....The Holy Spirit illuminated his holy and sacred Scripture, encouraging me in a very strong and clear voice from the forty-four books of the Old Testament, the four evangelists, and twenty-three epistles from the blessed apostles, urging me to proceed. Continually, without ceasing a moment, they insisted that I go on. Our Lord wished to make something clearly miraculous of this voyage to the Indies in order to encourage me and others about the holy temple....But finally, what Jesus Christ Our Redemptor said and had previously said through the mouths of his holy prophets came to be. And so one should believe that the other thing will also happen; and as witness to that, if what has been said is not enough, I offer the holy gospel in which Jesus Christ said that all things would pass away, but not his miraculous word. He also said that everything that had been said by him and written by the prophets must be fulfilled.[6]

This challenges the secular view of Columbus as merely a navigator who stumbled upon the Americas while seeking a trade route to the Indies.

"No mention had ever been made of his faith, let alone that he felt he had been given his life's mission directly by God," Marshall and Manuel wrote in *The Light and the Glory*. "Nor had we suspected that he felt called to bear the Light of Christ to undiscovered lands in fulfillment of biblical prophecy, or that he had been guided by the Holy Spirit every league of the way—and knew it."[7]

Columbus's voyage is symbolic prophetically of the larger mission the Pilgrims and Puritans would later embrace: that America was to be a nation set apart, guided by Providence.

In *God's Mighty Hand: Providential Occurrences in World History*, Richard Wheeler points out the dangers of Columbus's repeat voyages across the Atlantic. Columbus himself felt that he would have died if God had not preserved his life for a purpose.

Wheeler also speculates about what might have happened if Columbus had failed. The Muslims of that time were a dominant force, aggressively expanding into new lands in the name of Allah. Had Muslims settled the New World instead, countless millions would never have heard the gospel, and major historical events like the two World Wars would have turned out very differently.

AMERICA WAS TO BE A NATION SET APART, GUIDED BY PROVIDENCE.

"World War I and World War II would have had disastrous outcomes had America not been discovered by a Christian and founded on Christian principles set down by our godly forefathers," Wheeler wrote.[8]

PILGRIMS: THE MAYFLOWER COMPACT

More than a century after Columbus's discovery of the New World came a pivotal moment in American history with the Pilgrims' dangerous voyage to America and the signing of the Mayflower Compact in November 1620.

Fleeing persecution in England and seeking religious freedom, the Pilgrims made a covenant with God to build a society based on biblical principles. Their dedication of America to the "Glory of God, and Advancement of the Christian Faith" reflected their belief that their journey was part of God's larger plan to use America to spread the gospel.

"Lastly, (and which was not least,) a great hope and inward zeal they had of laying some good foundation, or at least to make some way thereunto, for the propagating and advancing the gospel of the kingdom of Christ in those remote parts of the world; yea, though they should be but even as stepping-stones unto others for the performing of so great a work," wrote Pilgrim leader William Bradford, a signatory to the Mayflower Compact and Governor of Plymouth Colony, in *Of Plymouth Plantation*.[9]

Daniel Webster, who served as Secretary of State and as a member of Congress in the nineteenth century, urged America to "not forget the religious character of our origin."[10]

"Our fathers were brought hither by their high veneration for the Christian religion," Webster wrote. "They journeyed by its light, and labored in its hope. They sought to incorporate its principles with the elements of their society, and to diffuse its influence through all their institutions, civil, political, or literary."[11]

The Puritans who followed the Pilgrims in the 1630s shared this divine sense of mission. As mentioned above, John Winthrop called the new colony a "city upon a hill," drawing from Jesus' Sermon on the Mount (Matt. 5:14), where Christ told His followers they are the "light of the world."

For Winthrop and the Puritans this metaphor represented a society meant to serve as a moral example to the world. Success would signal God's favor; failure, His judgment.

"Winthrop and his colleagues believed...that their errand was not a mere scouting expedition: it was an essential maneuver in the drama of Christendom," historian Perry Miller wrote in *Errand into the Wilderness*. "The Bay Company was not a battered remnant of suffering Separatists thrown up on a rocky shore; it was an organized task force of Christians, executing a flank attack on the corruptions of Christendom. These Puritans did not flee to America; they went in order to work out that complete reformation which was not yet accomplished in England and Europe."[12]

BIBLICAL PRINCIPLES AND AMERICA'S PROSPERITY

With God's help, the Pilgrims and Puritans built America by the sweat of their brows, with a focus on faith and a love for their families, communities, and country. They read the Bible, raised their children in the Word, and believed in the good news of Jesus Christ. That's why America worked.

Schools were built so children could study the Bible. They worked hard, as the Bible teaches, and reaped the fruit of their labors. They went to church and studied Scripture with their families.

The promise of 2 Chronicles 7:14 wasn't just a nice verse to them. It was the original American blueprint for survival. It shaped the belief that America's success was tied to its moral standing in God's eyes. Early Americans saw their nation as a work in progress, one that required constant self-examination and repentance to remain in God's favor.

Similar to the event in September 2020, The Return: National and Global Day of Prayer and Repentance on the National Mall, during the colonial era from 1607 to 1776, the Pilgrims and colonists often called for a Day of Humiliation, Fasting, and Prayer. These days were modeled after the sacred, solemn assemblies the ancient Israelites would hold at times of national crisis.

UNCONFESSED SIN IS ONE OF THE BIGGEST HINDRANCES TO REVIVAL TODAY.

Throughout the Revolutionary War period, the practice increased significantly. During the war, General George Washington ordered a day of national repentance to implore God to "pardon our manifold sins and wickedness, and that it would please Him to bless the Continental army with His divine favor and protection."

On March 30, 1863, at the height of the Civil War, President Abraham Lincoln proclaimed a National Day of Humiliation, Fasting, and Prayer:

> The awful calamity of civil war…may be but a punishment inflicted upon us for our presumptuous sins to the needful end of our national reformation as a whole people.…We have forgotten God.…We have vainly imagined, in the deceitfulness of our hearts, that all these blessings were produced by some superior wisdom and virtue of our own. Intoxicated with unbroken success, we have become…too proud to pray to the God that made us! It behooves us then to humble ourselves before the offended Power, to confess our national sins.[13]

Bruce Oliver, host of the top 100 Christian podcast *Talks for Christ,* said he believes unconfessed sin is one of the biggest hindrances to revival today.

"If it's pride, unforgiveness, immorality, or even division, God's Spirit is grieved and the flow of revival is blocked," Oliver said. "Revival is heaven sent, but without persistent, humble prayer, we'll miss the spark that ignites revival fires."[14]

To see my interview with Bruce Oliver, scan the QR code or visit TroyAndersonBooks.com/oliver.

"Revival doesn't start in the headlines. It starts in the heart. We need to encourage [people] to commit to daily prayer for our nation, beginning with their own repentance and walk with God. Scripture says, 'Draw near to God and He will draw near to you' (Jas. 4:8, NKJV). People need to become active in community events that point people to repentance and that point people's hearts back to Christ."[15]

PROVIDENCE AND THE AMERICAN REVOLUTION

As the American Revolution approached, God's Providence (His provision or assistance) played a central role in shaping the colonists' mindsets.

As Commander-in-Chief of the Continental Army, George Washington was known for his faith and conviction that God was guiding the colonies toward independence. He often credited Providence for their victories.

One famous example occurred during the Battle of Trenton in December 1776. Washington's troops were near collapse when a fierce winter storm suddenly cleared, allowing a surprise attack before dawn. Washington led his men across the icy Delaware River against Hessian mercenaries in Trenton, New Jersey. Peter Marshall and David Manuel wrote in *The Light and the Glory*:

> The Hessian garrison in winter quarters could be counted upon to be most heavily asleep, particularly if the schnapps had flowed as liberally as was customary on Christmas-tide. As Washington's troops loaded into the small boats on their side of the Delaware, a violent snowstorm and hailstorm suddenly came up, reducing visibility to near zero. The Hessians were totally surprised, that they could not believe what was happening. Henry Knox was there, and as he described in a letter to his wife, "The hurry, fright and confusion of the enemy was not unlike that which will be when the last trump will sound." In forty-five minutes of fighting, almost a thousand prisoners were taken. American casualties: two men frozen to death on the march; three men wounded. And the surprise to the young nation was also total. Washington had taken the offensive, in a stunning victory! "Never were men in higher spirits than our whole army is," wrote Thomas Rodney, and he spoke for much of the rest of America, as well. Was it a fluke, as Washington's detractors, now themselves in disfavor, muttered? Or was it, as Knox wrote, that "Providence seemed to have smiled upon every part of this enterprise"?[16]

The victory boosted morale and inspired re-enlistments. Washington interpreted the victory as a sign of divine favor, reinforcing his belief that their cause was just and God was guiding them.

The Declaration of Independence reflects the Founding Fathers' biblical worldview. When Thomas Jefferson wrote of "unalienable rights" endowed by the Creator, he was grounding the document in what the Bible teaches: all people are created equal by God and endowed with certain rights. The Founders believed our rights come from God, not kings, and governments exist to protect those rights.

The Christian influence of America's Founding Fathers

Biblical concepts—freedom, justice, and liberty—were woven into America's founding documents. The Founding Fathers were deeply influenced by Christian values, though their personal beliefs varied:

George Washington's prayers at Valley Forge and his calls for national unity under God are well-documented.

Thomas Jefferson, though a Deist, admired the moral teachings of Jesus and saw them as foundational to American ethics.

John Adams famously wrote that the Constitution was "made only for a moral and religious People. It is wholly inadequate to the government of any other."[17]

THE DECLARATION OF INDEPENDENCE: THE UNSHAKABLE FOUNDATION OF AMERICA

The Declaration of Independence isn't just a political document. It's a revolutionary statement that declared America's right to stand on its own.

Thomas Jefferson, one of its principal architects, made it clear: both the rights of nations and the rights of individuals are grounded in God's law. The colonies' right to exist "among the powers of the earth" was not arbitrary; it was granted by "the Laws of Nature and Nature's God." That's the law of God, as laid out in the Bible.[18]

Also, consider this famous line from the Declaration of Independence: "We hold these truths to be self-evident, that all men are created equal, that they are endowed by their Creator with certain unalienable Rights, that among these are Life, Liberty, and the pursuit of Happiness." Jefferson made it plain that our rights come from God, not government.[19]

This is what sets America apart. The Declaration was never intended to be a secular manifesto. It was a call to stand on the biblical principles of freedom, liberty, and God's guiding hand.

For decades the radical left and globalist elite have tried to erase God from our history. But the Constitution and the Declaration are faith-based documents, designed to protect freedom of worship and America's calling to be a light of liberty in the world.

AMONG SEVEN FORMS OF GOVERNMENT, THE BIBLE PREFERS ONE

Throughout history, governments have taken many forms. The Bible mentions several but gives a clear preference to one. These include the following:

Totalitarianism: A highly centralized government that does not tolerate differences of opinion or individualism. Communist and socialist regimes are totalitarian, as are dictatorships led by sultans, premiers, czars—or in Scripture, by pharaohs (Exod. 1–14), emperors (Luke 2:1), or Caesars (Mark 12:17).[20]

Monarchy: Rule by a king, queen, or emirate; often hereditary. Some monarchies are limited by higher law, like English kings under the Magna Carta. Israel's kings were supposed to be limited monarchs, required to write out God's laws (Deut. 17:18–20) and make a covenant with God (2 Sam. 5:3; 2 Kings 11:17). Most ignored these commands, becoming unlimited monarchs—a form of totalitarianism.[21]

Republic and Constitutional Republic: In this system, representatives elected by the people exercise power. A parliamentary democracy is a weaker form of a republic, where elected leaders hold sovereign power. A constitutional republic, as described in Exodus 18:21 and Deuteronomy 1:15–16; 16:18, places elected leaders under a higher law, a written constitution. John Adams called this "a government of laws and not of men." Jethro advised Moses to select capable men "who fear God, trustworthy men who hate dishonest gain" to serve as officials (Exod. 18:21).[22]

> THE CONSTITUTION AND THE DECLARATION ARE FAITH-BASED DOCUMENTS, DESIGNED TO PROTECT FREEDOM OF WORSHIP AND AMERICA'S CALLING TO BE A LIGHT OF LIBERTY IN THE WORLD.

Oligarchy: Power rests with a small elite group—such as an aristocracy or plutocracy. In Scripture, the Sanhedrin (Luke 22:66) functioned as a ruling oligarchy.[23]

Democracy: A government where the people hold sovereign power, making laws by direct majority vote. Ancient Athens pioneered this concept. Democracy is often unstable. John Adams called it "mob rule," and Benjamin Rush warned of "mobocracy," where passions override reason in democracies.[24]

Theocracy: Rule by religious leaders acting on God's behalf. In Scripture, Eli and Samuel led Israel before the monarchy. Today, many Islamic nations are ruled by ayatollahs or imams.

These seven forms of government encompass most systems seen throughout history. So where does America fit?

Many today believe the United States is a democracy, but that's not the case. John Adams warned, "Remember, democracy never lasts long. It soon wastes, exhausts, and murders itself. There never was a democracy yet that did not commit suicide."[25]

The Founding Fathers deliberately chose a constitutional republic, not a democracy. Article IV, Section IV of the US Constitution says, "The United States shall guarantee to every State in this Union a Republican Form of Government."[26]

Surprisingly, the Founders looked to Exodus 18:21 as a model for representative government:

> But select capable men from all the people—men who fear God, trustworthy men who hate dishonest gain—and appoint them as officials over thousands, hundreds, fifties and tens.
>
> —Exodus 18:21

"Significantly, this verse was directly cited by numerous Founding Fathers and had also been the subject of many influential sermons in the Founding Era," historians David Barton, Brad Cummings, and Lance Wubbels wrote in *The Founders' Bible: The Origin of the Dream of Freedom.*[27]

> Exodus 18:21 establishes a constitutional republic. With ancient Israel, God gave them this verse to choose their leaders after He first had given them a framework of laws to govern their nation. So, too, in America. Our Constitution, based on God's higher law—what the Founders titled "laws of nature and of nature's God," which they also described as the Moral Law—is the framework to govern our nation. It is a law higher than any elected officials and a law to which every citizen and government representative must conform.[28]

This higher law affirms inalienable rights given by God—life, liberty, property, self-defense, religious worship, and justice. America's government exists to secure these rights, not to grant or take them away.

"These rights are not subject to a majority vote—or to any other vote, ever," Barton, Cummings, and Wubbels wrote. "The officials we elect do not hold sovereign power but rule only beneath this higher sovereign law. Of the nearly 200 nations in the world, America is the most stable, operating well over two centuries under the same governing documents. But it is also the only nation uniquely and correctly identified by the *World Factbook* (a popular and heavily referenced annual publication of the Central Intelligence Agency) as a constitution-based federal republic—and this has been our form of government since given to us by our Founding Fathers in 1789."[29]

The Founders agreed. John Adams wrote to Benjamin Rush in 1807, "The Bible contains the most profound Philosophy, the most perfect Morality, and the most refined Policy, that ever was conceived upon Earth. It is the most Republican book in the world."[30]

Noah Webster, the "Father of American Scholarship and Education," echoed this in 1828:

> When you become entitled to exercise the right of voting for public officers, let it be impressed on your mind that God commands you to choose for rulers, *just men who will rule in the fear of God* [Exod. 18:21]. The preservation of a republican government depends on the faithful discharge of this duty; if the citizens neglect their duty, and place unprincipled men in office, the government will soon be corrupted. If a republican government fails to secure public prosperity and happiness, it must be because the citizens neglect the divine commands, and elect bad men to make and administer the laws.[31]

Webster's prophetic warning is exactly what we've seen take place in recent decades, with immoral presidents and other political leaders racking up our national debt astronomically, putting the republic in danger of collapse.

NO NATION HAS BEEN BUILT ON A FIRMER BIBLICAL FOUNDATION THAN AMERICA.

African American abolitionist Frederick Douglass summed it up: "I have one great political idea....That idea is an old one. It is widely and generally assented to; nevertheless, it is very generally trampled upon and disregarded. The best expression of it, I have found in the Bible. It is in substance, 'Righteousness exalteth a nation: but sin is a reproach to any people' [Prov. 14:34, kjv]. Sir, this constitutes my politics—the negative and positive of my politics, and the whole of my politics....I feel it my duty to do all in my power to infuse this idea into the public mind, that it may speedily be recognized and practiced upon by our people."[32]

No nation has been built on a firmer biblical foundation than America. We must defend that heritage. The rights Jefferson wrote about—life, liberty, and the pursuit of happiness—are more than just words on paper. They must guide every decision we make. America was made great by the faith of the Pilgrims, Puritans, and Founding Fathers, and only faith in God will keep us great.

AMERICA'S FOUNDING DOCUMENTS: PROTECTING FAITH AND FREEDOM

America's founding documents—the Declaration of Independence, Constitution, and Bill of Rights—were designed to protect faith and freedom.

One of the principal protections is in the First Amendment to the Bill of Rights, the 1789 document outlining the first ten amendments that guarantee Americans' civil rights and liberties.[33]

The First Amendment says, "Congress shall make no law respecting an establishment of religion, or prohibiting the free exercise thereof; or abridging the freedom of speech, or of the press; or the right of the people peaceably to assemble, and to petition the Government for a redress of grievances."[34]

The First Amendment is key. It guarantees freedom of religion—the right to practice your faith or not practice at all—while ensuring government stays out of your relationship with God. America was founded on the idea that you can worship freely or not at all, without state interference.

Here are key ways the founding documents protect faith:

The Establishment Clause: Keeping government out of religion

The Establishment Clause ensures the government cannot establish an official religion or favor one over another. It can't force religious practices or promote any particular faith. Whether you're Christian, Jewish, Muslim, or you believe something else, the government must not interfere in your beliefs.

The Free Exercise Clause: Protecting your right to worship

Equally important is the Free Exercise Clause. It guarantees your right to practice your faith, or not practice at all, without government interference. You're free to follow your beliefs, worship as you choose, or abstain altogether.

Religious Tests: No discrimination allowed

Article VI of the Constitution is clear—no religious tests for public office. The government can't bar you from running or serving because of your religious beliefs. That's discrimination and it's un-American. Whether you're Christian, Jewish, Muslim, or hold other beliefs, the Constitution says: "No religious Test shall ever be required as a Qualification to any Office or public Trust under the United States."[35]

Founding principles

When the Founding Fathers drafted the founding documents, they weren't just seeking to protect religious freedom; they sought to honor faith in God. They believed that faith and freedom go hand in hand.

They also recognized the need for what's now called the "separation of church and state"—a concept rooted in the First Amendment but a phrase that is often misused today. The Founders weren't trying to remove faith from public life; they wanted to prevent the government from controlling people's beliefs.

The phrase "separation of church and state" doesn't appear in America's founding documents. It's a myth perpetuated by secular activists attempting to erase the nation's Judeo-Christian heritage.[36] Robert Jeffress, D.D., senior pastor of the 14,000-member First Baptist Dallas, said:

> Listen long enough to the arguments of the American Civil Liberties Union, the Freedom from Religion Foundation or other left wing groups and you'll come to believe this version of America's history: You'll come to believe that America was founded by a wide diversity of people from many different faiths, some Deists, some atheists, and yes, a few Christians, but the Founders had one goal and that was to build a completely secular nation that was devoid of any religious, especially Christian, influence whatsoever. You'll be told that our Founders wanted to erect this unscalable wall around our country that would keep any spiritual influence from seeping into public life. That version of American history belongs in the same category as the story of George Washington and the Cherry Tree. It is an absolute myth....The truth is America was founded primarily, not exclusively, but primarily by orthodox Christians, and they founded this country upon the unchanging foundation of God's eternal truth. And furthermore, our Founders believed that our success as a nation depended upon our faithfulness to God's eternal Word, and though it is completely politically incorrect to say, the truth is this, America was founded as a Christian nation and our success as a nation depends upon our fidelity to God's Word.[37]

The phrase "separation of church and state" comes from Thomas Jefferson's January 1, 1802, letter to the Danbury Baptist Association of Connecticut. The Baptists, once persecuted in Europe, feared government interference in their religious practices. Jefferson reassured them, quoting the First Amendment and describing a "wall of separation"—not to remove God from government, but to protect the church from government overreach.[38]

"Jefferson's 'wall of separation' was obviously unidirectional, put in place to keep the government out of the church, not to keep God out of the government," wrote author, Bible teacher, and revivalist Eddie Hyatt. "His own actions affirm this, for as president, he took money from the federal treasury to pay for a missionary to the Kaskaskia Indian tribe and to build a church building for them in which to worship."[39]

The Founders never intended to strip God from public life. When George Washington took the first presidential oath of office with his hand on the Bible, he signaled his belief that biblical principles, including the Ten Commandments, were essential for a stable and prosperous nation. The day after ratifying the First Amendment, Congress proclaimed a National Day of Thanksgiving and Prayer. The Founders rejected an official state church like those in Europe, but they never intended to eliminate God from the public square.

DID THE FOUNDERS TALK ABOUT GOD?

While the Constitution doesn't directly mention God, the Founding Fathers were profoundly influenced by Judeo-Christian values and Enlightenment ideas.

The philosophers who shaped their views—including English thinker John Locke—believed God was the ultimate source of human rights and freedom. Locke, an "inspirer of both the European Enlightenment and the Constitution of the United States," helped embed the concept of natural rights, life, liberty, and property into America's DNA.[40]

THE FOUNDERS NEVER INTENDED TO STRIP GOD FROM PUBLIC LIFE.

These ideas are foundational to the Declaration of Independence, which affirms "unalienable Rights, that among these are Life, Liberty and the pursuit of Happiness." The Enlightenment taught that governments exist to protect these rights, not to infringe upon them.[41]

The Founders also embraced social contract theory: government works only with the consent of the governed. That's why America has elections and representative government. The government serves the people, not the other way around.

French philosopher Montesquieu's *The Spirit of Laws* introduced the idea of separating government powers into three branches—executive, legislative, and judicial—to prevent tyranny. The US Constitution put this brilliant idea into practice, protecting freedom.[42]

But the Founders knew freedom alone wasn't enough; virtue was essential. They believed that a moral society rooted in biblical values was the only way to sustain the republic. Without personal virtue, the system would collapse.

Of the fifty-five delegates at the Constitutional Convention, fifty-one were publicly affiliated with Christian churches of various established denominations. Two of them—Elias Boudinot and John Jay, the first Chief Justice of the Supreme Court—later founded and led the American Bible Society. Over two hundred years later, the American Bible Society continues the purpose set in motion by its founders, for the benefit of the whole nation: "We are on a mission to make the Bible available to every person in a language and format each can understand and afford, so that all may experience its life-changing message."[43]

Thomas Jefferson and Benjamin Franklin were Deists. Two other delegates were unorthodox or simply unknown in their affiliation. But even they recognized the need for a spiritual foundation for America. Jefferson and Franklin proposed a national seal depicting Moses leading the Israelites out of Egypt, following God in a pillar of fire.

Franklin himself famously urged the Continental Congress to begin its sessions in prayer, saying, "I have lived, sir, a long time, and the longer I live, the more convincing proofs I see of this truth that God governs the affairs of men, and if a sparrow cannot fall to the ground without His notice, is it probable that an empire can rise without His aid?"[44]

THREATS TO AMERICA'S HERITAGE

The threats facing America's Judeo-Christian heritage are immense and numerous: secularism, moral relativism, and globalism, to name a few.

These forces have gained alarming prominence in recent decades, eroding the country's biblical foundations. A new cultural climate is being perpetuated by the public educational system, media, entertainment industry, and Big Tech. These forces increasingly undermine the biblical values that America was built upon.

We face many challenges, but the need to protect and restore America's Judeo-Christian identity is too important for us to back down. America's future depends on the nation returning to its biblical roots.

Secularism has become a dominant force in modern American culture, pushing for a public square that is neutral toward or even dismissive of religion. In this climate, Christian beliefs are often marginalized under the guise of "inclusion" and "tolerance."

The First Amendment, designed to guarantee religious freedom, is frequently misinterpreted to promote a so-called "naked public square"—a term coined by Christian intellectual Richard John Neuhaus in *The Naked Public Square: Religion and Democracy in America*. This concept promotes the idea that religious speech is inappropriate in government, schools, and public life.[45]

Prayer in schools, once routine, is now banned or heavily restricted. Displays of religious symbols, such as the Ten Commandments, have been removed from courthouses and public buildings. However, in May 2025, Texas Gov. Greg Abbott signed Senate Bill 10—despite a federal court ruling against a similar Louisiana law—requiring public school classrooms in Texas to display the Ten Commandments.[46]

While I applaud Abbott and encourage other governors to follow suit, the removal of prayer and the Bible from schools has stripped America of basic moral guidance. The absence of faith in public life has led to spiritual emptiness, especially among younger generations who are less likely to attend church. Secularism's pursuit of neutrality has created a void where biblical truth and purpose once flourished.

"Did you know that for the first 150 years of our country, a school book called *The New England Primer* was used in schools across our country? The primer was filled with creeds, prayers, and even with Scripture verses that the students had to memorize," Jeffress said. "In fact, if you were going to graduate from the third grade, every student had to learn this acrostic from *The New England Primer*. Every letter of the alphabet represented a verse that the students had to memorize. For example, 'A wise son maketh a glad father, but a foolish son is the heaviness of his mother.'...'Except a man be born again, he cannot see the kingdom of God.'[47]

"Can you imagine what would happen with such a textbook today? We're not even allowed to acknowledge that there might be a Creator up there somewhere, that there's some Intelligent Designer up there who made us. Do you think that has any relationship with the increasing violence we're seeing in our schools when you teach children that they're nothing but animals? Don't be surprised when they act like animals."[48]

THE DECLINE OF THE FAMILY

Shifts in family structure and gender roles are also a threat to America's Judeo-Christian heritage.

The family, once the cornerstone of society and the primary institution for passing on moral values, has undergone dramatic changes in recent decades. Rising divorce rates, the increase of single-parent households, and the breakdown of marriage have reshaped the nation's social fabric.

At the same time, traditional gender roles rooted in biblical teaching have been redefined. The promotion of gender fluidity and the rejection of biological distinctions between men and women have contributed to a redefinition of the family.

These shifts have eroded the moral authority of the home, leaving a generation of young people without stable guidance from family or church. As a result, America faces growing social problems—rising poverty, substance abuse, youth violence, mental health crises, and moral confusion.

The loss of faith-based community has also fragmented social bonds. Churches once served as centers of moral support, civic engagement, and mutual care. Today, increasing secularization has left many Americans isolated, disconnected, and adrift in a culture where shared values are vanishing.

"Is our society better off today than when this assault on Christianity began 60 or 70 years ago?" asked Jeffress. "Today over 10 million teenagers in the U.S. drink alcohol regularly and 20 percent of those engage in binge drinking. Nearly 2,800 children die each year as a result of gun violence and another 14,300 are injured. Nearly 1 million babies were murdered in the womb last year, and one in four women in the U.S. will have aborted at least one of their children by the age of 45, and in 2011, over a half a million teenagers became pregnant with about 30 percent of those pregnancies ending in an abortion.

"Are those statistics just a coincidence? Not at all. Not when you consider God's warning to His own people, the nation of Israel, a warning that is just as applicable to us today as it was three thousand years ago. In Hosea 4:6, God says, 'My people are destroyed for lack of knowledge. Because you have rejected knowledge, I also will reject you from being priest for Me; Because you have forgotten the law of your God, I also will forget your children.'"[49]

America must remember this biblical truth: "Blessed is the nation whose God is the LORD" (Ps. 33:12).

THERE IS A RISING WAVE OF FAITH IN JESUS AMONG YOUNG PEOPLE, A TRUE SIGN OF HOPE.

THE NEED TO RESTORE AMERICA'S FOUNDATION OF FAITH

Despite these troubling trends, America's Judeo-Christian heritage is not beyond restoration. While secularism, moral relativism, and cultural shifts have eroded much of the nation's foundation of faith, there remains a deep hunger among many to return to the biblical principles that made America great. Encouragingly, there is a rising wave of faith in Jesus among young people, a true sign of hope.

We must pray this spiritual awakening continues to grow, reasserting the importance of faith in both public and private life. America must reclaim its Judeo-Christian identity by upholding values like personal responsibility, family integrity, and compassion. We need a renewed commitment to religious freedom, ensuring that the heritage that was integral to America's founding is preserved and protected for future generations.

Christian leaders and faith communities must take a more active role in addressing the challenges facing society. They must lead by example, teaching younger generations the importance of biblical values in everyday life and advocating for policies that reflect those values.

Political leaders must also recognize the central role faith has played in America's prosperity and work to protect its Judeo-Christian heritage.

America's founding principles still live in the hearts of millions. Through prayer, repentance, and a return to biblical values, our nation can restore its Judeo-Christian identity and once again shine as a light of hope in the world.

CHAPTER 5

REVIVAL: "IT'S LIFE AND DEATH"

*The pattern of judgment is that...after calling and calling and calling on
the nation turning away, He allows it to be shaken. He allows an enemy to
make a strike on the land. That happened in ancient times [to Israel] and
it happened in modern times with America. It happened with 9/11. God
allowed that. That was a shaking. The Lord gives the nation a window of
time to come back to Him, to either repent and go toward revival, or to go
away from God and head to judgment. We are now in a time where we have
increasing signs that the window is coming to a close and if we don't come
back to God, we head to judgment, so this is crucial. America needs revival.
It's not just a nice thing. It is the future of America. It's life and death.*
—*NEW YORK TIMES* BEST-SELLING AUTHOR RABBI
JONATHAN CAHN IN AN INTERVIEW FOR *GODSPEED*
MAGAZINE, "WILL THE WORLD TURN BACK TO GOD?"[1]

REVIVAL ISN'T OPTIONAL. As Rabbi Jonathan Cahn told me, "It is the future
of America. It's life and death."[2]

While we look back at past awakenings for inspiration, the need for a
fresh outpouring of the Holy Spirit has never been more urgent.

Sid Roth, host of *It's Supernatural!*, believes America's core issue hampering
revival is the divide between "religious Christianity" and "authentic Christianity."[3]

In John 17:3, Jesus said, "Now this is eternal life: that they know you, the
only true God, and Jesus Christ, whom you have sent."

"You can't get more specific than that," Roth said. "This is it, namely, that
they might be having an experiential knowledge of You. That's the key. The
operative word: *experiential* knowledge. Most people have head knowledge. I
had from the get-go experiential knowledge, and it took me a while to figure
out that most Christians had inherited knowledge from their parents. 'You go
to church because I tell you to go to church,' and that's the problem in America.
We are a nation that hasn't had experiential knowledge of God."[4]

Roth believes a "course correction" is coming—a move of God so profound
it will eclipse all previous revivals.[5]

The course correction is a glory that Haggai calls the "greater glory" [Hag. 2:9]. By definition the "greater glory" is something the world has never experienced. I like to put it this way: In my sanctified imagination, I know about all the revivals that the world has had since Jesus came and died and rose from the dead and is seated at the right hand of God the Father…All of the revivals we've had put together won't come close to touching what's coming.[6]

BONNIE BRAE HOUSE—BIRTHPLACE OF THE AZUSA STREET REVIVAL

On April 11, 2025, my wife, Irene, and I toured the birthplace of what Roth calls "experiential knowledge" of the Holy Spirit. We joined Wilma Berry, co-founder of the Azusa Street Mission & Historical Society, and Pastor Caleb Cooper at the Bonnie Brae House in Los Angeles to celebrate the 119th anniversary of the Azusa Street Revival.

This historic revival, which began on April 9, 1906, was led by William J. Seymour, the son of former slaves. It ignited one of the most powerful spiritual awakenings in modern history, becoming the catalyst for the Pentecostal and Charismatic movements—now totaling over 664 million adherents worldwide, with projections reaching 1 billion by 2050.[7]

Seymour, born in Louisiana in 1870, grew up Baptist and had early dreams and visions. After contracting smallpox in his twenties and losing sight in one eye, he moved to Houston in 1903, where he joined a Holiness church pastored by Lucy Farrow. She connected him with Charles Fox Parham, a teacher of the "Apostolic Faith" and speaking in tongues.[8]

Given that Texas law forbade blacks to be in classrooms with whites, Parham encouraged Seymour to listen to his lectures in the hallway. In 1906, Julia Hutchins invited Seymour to Los Angeles but rejected his teaching on tongues and padlocked the church door.[9]

Seymour then moved into the home of Richard Asberry at 214 Bonnie Brae Street. After a month of prayer and fasting, Seymour and several others were baptized in the Holy Spirit and spoke in tongues.[10] Jennifer A. Miskov, PhD, wrote in *Ignite Azusa*:

> In those early meetings at the Asberry house on Bonnie Brae Street, there were only about fifteen people….Then something happened that they had all been waiting and longing for. God crashed into that meeting like never before and someone started to speak in tongues….

> Ruth Asberry's cousin Jennie Evans Moore, who lived across the street, was resting on a stool, when she suddenly fell to the ground and began to speak in tongues....She recalled that it felt like a vessel broke inside of her and water "surged" through her entire being. When this rush came to her lips, she spoke in six different languages....Following this release, Jennie, who had never played the piano before, walked over to the piano and played it under the anointing while singing in tongues.[11]

As the crowds grew, Seymour preached from the front porch until it collapsed under the weight of the people. He then rented an abandoned African Methodist Episcopal church at 312 Azusa Street, fashioned a pulpit from shoebox crates, and founded the Apostolic Faith Mission.[12]

The *Los Angeles Times* soon reported on the revival, describing "colored people and a sprinkling of whites...breathing strange utterances and mouthing a creed which it would seem no sane mortal could understand."[13]

> History records that the supernatural fire of God was seen visibly resting on the Bonnie Brae home during the revival of 1906–1909. The fire department would show up...but the reality was that there was no physical fire as the Bonnie Brae House was engulfed in the Shekinah Glory of God....The glory of God was so strong that people's nubs would begin to transform into full arms and full hands as they began to grow back. Wheel chairs, canes and crutches lost their owners. Peg-legs were removed as the power of God restored brand new limbs."[14]

SAN FRANCISCO EARTHQUAKE FUELS AZUSA STREET REVIVAL

Just over a week after the Azusa Street Revival began, the 7.9 magnitude San Francisco earthquake struck on April 18, 1906. It killed over 3,000 people, destroyed 80 percent of the city, and was felt from Los Angeles to Southern Oregon. The disaster—described as "one of the most significant earthquakes of all time"—drove many, shaken by the calamity, to flock to Azusa Street seeking hope.[15]

Though the building was only 40 by 60 feet, as many as six hundred people packed inside while hundreds crowded the windows. The *Los Angeles Daily Times* reported the "weird babble of tongues" at the meetings. However, attempts to scoff at the revival only attracted more people to the meetings. "Anyone could be seen shouting, dancing, jerking, shaking, weeping, laughing, falling into trances, or speaking or singing in tongues,"[16] Jeff Oliver writes in *Pentecost to the Present.* Rick Joyner adds, "Some of the local Holiness churches had lost so many members they had to close their doors and join the revival by default."[17]

Frank Bartleman, an itinerant Holiness preacher, reported for the *Way of Faith in South Carolina* that "Pentecost has come to Los Angeles, the American Jerusalem."[18]

> The first issue of *The Apostolic Faith* [Seymour's own newspaper] went out to 5,000 and soon to over 50,000 subscribers around the world. The train station a half mile away continually unloaded passengers arriving from all over the continent as news of the revival spread through both the religious and secular press.[19]

As thousands experienced the revival, many returned home, sparking similar moves of the Spirit. Missionaries carried the message to Africa, South America, and beyond, helping launch the global Pentecostal and Charismatic movement.

PROPHECY OF A GREAT END-TIMES REVIVAL

During the Azusa Street Revival, Seymour prophesied that an even greater revival would erupt more than a century later.[20] In my interview with Pastor Caleb Cooper, he told me:

> One of the markings of the great Azusa Street Revival is that William J. Seymour said, "The color line is washed away by the blood of Jesus." So when we look back at that revival, it paints a picture of what God wants to do obviously on a more massive scale. We were in the Bonnie Brae house together, Troy, and one of the words that's been declared for quite some time actually came up in the meeting. Many revivalists that are watching this, they know that it was prophesied in about a hundred or 110 years...there would be a revival greater than Azusa that would come in these last days...the latter and the former rain converging, and that will be a new thing when we see a culmination of every move of God all happen at one time in our generation.[21]

To watch my interview with Caleb Cooper, scan the QR code or visit TroyAndersonBooks.com/cooper.

During my visit to the Bonnie Brae House, about a dozen ministers and believers prayed in tongues, prophesied, and cried out for revival in California, America, and the world. It was a sacred moment—I was honored to be a part of it. One minister prophesied I would "document" this unfolding revival, inspiring people today and future generations to join in this new move of the Holy Spirit.

AIMEE SEMPLE MCPHERSON, THE MEDIA, AND HOLLYWOOD

After visiting the Bonnie Brae House, Irene and I toured the Foursquare Heritage Center in Echo Park—the Parsonage of Aimee Semple McPherson. We also visited Azusa Street, where a simple plaque commemorates the great revival that sparked a global movement.

As Wilma Berry, co-founder of the Azusa Street Mission & Historical Society, showed me the plaque, I remembered September 26, 2020, during The Return: National and Global Day of Prayer and Repentance—the historic gathering on the National Mall in Washington, D.C.

That day on Azusa Street, we were part of a small event involving about a hundred people broadcast on GOD TV. Irene and I were accompanied by Jerry Moses, a former megachurch pastor and Assistant to the President at CBN, Movieguide, and Benny Hinn Ministries. I led our group in a prayer for revival in the media, Hollywood, America, and the world.

> **GOD HAS USED THE MEDIA TO SPREAD THE FLAMES OF REVIVAL IN THE PAST.**

As a former *Los Angeles Daily News* reporter who worked in downtown Los Angeles for many years covering Los Angeles County government, the courts, and Hollywood, I was aware of how God has used the media to spread the flames of revival in the past. The Azusa Street Revival spread, in part, because the press told the story. The same thing happened with Billy Graham's crusades, Aimee Semple McPherson's services, the Jesus movement, and Campus Crusade for Christ.

Over the last century, Hollywood has made movies and TV series that have inspired countless millions of people to become followers of Jesus—*The Ten Commandments, The Greatest Story Ever Told*, the *Jesus* film, *Jesus of Nazareth, The Passion of the Christ, The Chosen, Jesus Revolution*, and many others.

"Southern California is the primary portal on earth for biblical Christian movements, Christian leaders, Christian churches, and numerous global movements of God," said Paul McGuire, a former counterculture radical who has lived in Southern California since the 1970s and has spent decades "studying and experiencing revival." He even had a vision of an end-times awakening, which we included in our 2015 book *The Babylon Code*.[22]

> Southern California and Los Angeles [the City of Angels] birthed Bill Bright and Campus Crusade for Christ, Chuck Smith and Calvary Chapel, Jack Hayford and The Church on the Way, Mel Gibson and *The Passion of the Christ*, and Aimee Semple McPherson, founder of the Foursquare Church. McPherson reached millions....Hollywood and the biggest stars of the time like Charlie Chaplin would flock to her services. And she was a woman—perhaps controversial to some. But many massive global revivals came out of Southern California, like the Azusa Street Revival, which has resulted in [hundreds of millions] of people around the world being filled with the Spirit and saved.
>
> Billy Graham's breakthrough crusade held in Los Angeles was green-lighted by the billionaire William Randolph Hearst, who ran his media empire from Northern California and told his editors to "Puff Graham." Demos Shakarian and his Full Gospel Businessmen's Fellowship International, which started in Clifton's Cafeteria in Los Angeles, carried revival to presidents like Ronald Reagan and countless millions of businessmen around the world. Splitting off from Calvary Chapel was the Vineyard Movement spreading signs and wonders globally. Hal Lindsey with his book *The Late Great Planet Earth*, which resulted in millions of salvations, started at the University of California, Los Angeles....You and I have been placed in the center of this invisible spiritual network by God. In the spiritual realm, Southern California is a global birthing portal from God.[23]

IS A MAJOR MOVE OF THE HOLY SPIRIT BEGINNING?

I first met McGuire sixteen years ago in 2009 while covering a prophecy conference at Calvary Chapel Chino Hills for the *Los Angeles Daily News* (which also served as inspiration for my first cover story in *Charisma* magazine, titled "Last Days Fever"). When I look back over the past sixteen years, I can't help but see the supernatural hand of God guiding our steps.

From 1991 to 2011, I worked as a newspaper reporter. But after that encounter with McGuire, God opened countless doors. He's graciously allowed me to spread His message on platforms I never imagined.

Since then, I've written hundreds of stories for *Charisma*, Reuters, *Christianity Today, Newsmax*, CBN News, The Christian Post, Townhall, WND, *Outreach, Prophecy Watchers, SkyWatch Magazine*, and more. I've also had the honor to serve as executive editor of *Charisma*, senior editor of Godspeed Magazine, and executive editor of The Return International.

Since 2015, I've written nine books—*The Babylon Code, Trumpocalypse, The Military Guide to Armageddon, The Military Guide to Disarming Deception, Revelation 911, Your Mission in God's Army, The Trump Code, I've Been to Heaven*, and now *Designated Disrupter*—six of them number one Amazon bestsellers so far. *Revelation 911* made Newsmax's "Rising Bestsellers" list, and *I've Been to Heaven* just hit number one "Hot New Release" in the "Near-Death Experiences" category.[24]

I've also been interviewed by hundreds of media outlets—Newsmax TV, CBN News, Daystar, TBN, *Jewish Voice with Jonathan Bernis*, SkyWatch TV, *The Washington Times, New York Post*, Coast to Coast AM, *The Strang Report*, Real America's Voice, and many more. Through our newsletters like Revelation Watchers, Battle Ready News, Prophecy Investigators, and Inspire Literary Group, the gospel message has reached countless people around the world.

But this is not about media appearances or bestsellers. It's about the mission God gave us—to proclaim the good news of Jesus Christ, alert the world to the lateness of the prophetic hour, awaken the church to this pivotal moment in history, and help inspire hope in an end-times awakening before Christ's return.

It's proof that when you say yes to God's call, He can indeed do "immeasurably more than all we ask or imagine, according to his power that is at work within us" (Eph. 3:20). As retired US Army Chaplain and Colonel David Giammona and I wrote in *Your Mission in God's Army*, anyone willing to enlist in "God's Army" can make an impact.

The Bible confirms this:

- Ephesians 2:10: "For we are God's handiwork, created in Christ Jesus to do good works, which God prepared in advance for us to do."

- Acts 1:8: "But you will receive power when the Holy Spirit comes on you; and you will be my witnesses in Jerusalem, and in all Judea and Samaria, and to the ends of the earth."

- Romans 8:28: "And we know that in all things God works for the good of those who love him, who have been called according to his purpose."

- Exodus 9:16: "But I have raised you up for this very purpose, that I might show you my power and that my name might be proclaimed in all the earth."

As I've shared before, Billy Graham told me in 2013 what America needs to do: Repent and turn back to God (2 Chron. 7:14; Acts 3:19; Joel 2:13). This is our "Nineveh moment."

One of the greatest miracles I've witnessed was The Return 2020 on the National Mall in Washington, D.C. It was truly supernatural to watch Rev. Kevin Jessip, Rabbi Cahn, and thousands of believers there who understood what was at stake.

Since then, along with our "40 Days to Save America" and "77 Days to Take Back America" campaigns of prayer, fasting, and repentance, we've seen the miraculous reelection of President Trump, a spiritual turnaround in America and the world, and the first waves of revival taking place, especially among young people. Paul McGuire said to me in an interview:

> As you know, I have spent a lifetime studying and experiencing revival, especially, over the last number of years beginning with the vision I had [on July 4, 2012, about the possibility of a "biblical, last days revival," as detailed in *The Babylon Code*]. Miraculously, the Lord opened up many doors for me to develop personal relationships and meet with many of the world's greatest champions of revival like Bill Bright, Jack Hayford, Chuck Smith, Pat Robertson, and many others who prayed for me personally. Then together with you, we seeded the possibility of a present-day revival into large numbers of Christians through our books and interviews.
>
> We are in a last-days spiritual war in the church and outside of the church. It is all about controlling the narrative as servants of Christ. The reality we live in is often based on falsehoods, personal human agendas, and delusions. When you write from the place of truth, legitimate spiritual power from "On High" is conferred upon you. You become God's agent of revival and a powerful transmitter of revival.[25]

A LUKEWARM, "COUNTERFEIT" CHRISTIANITY IN A DANGEROUS WORLD

Let us return to Rabbi Cahn's warning—"America needs revival. It's not just a nice thing. It is the future of America. It's life and death"—and Sid Roth's call for a "course correction." The question is whether the church realizes just how close America is to a "civilizational collapse" and how urgent the need for revival is.[26]

The revival now underway faces extraordinary headwinds. America is grappling with the erosion of biblical values, the collapse of the nuclear family, and the rise of anti-Christian and anti-Semitic ideologies. Political polarization is at an all-time high. Meanwhile, existential threats loom—from Russia's nuclear saber-rattling, China's rising global dominance, and Iran's pursuit of nuclear weapons, to globalist agendas like the World Economic Forum's "Great Reset" and the United Nations' "Agenda 2030" plans, threatening national sovereignty and religious freedom.

Before President Trump's historic reelection in 2024, America caught a glimpse of what totalitarianism looks like: pandemic lockdowns, church closures, pastor arrests, and the government pushing medical mandates that harmed many people. Polls showed widespread distrust in the 2020 presidential election, with a Monmouth University survey finding that 30 percent of Americans—and 68 percent of Republicans—believe Joe Biden only won due to voter fraud.[27]

THE REVIVAL NOW UNDERWAY FACES EXTRAORDINARY HEADWINDS.

During the Biden years, Americans witnessed soaring inflation, a border crisis, wokeism, censorship, and foreign criminals flooding the nation. Trump's border czar, Tom Homan, estimates there are about "600,000 illegal aliens in the U.S. with a criminal conviction."[28]

Amid these dangers, Sid Roth says, "most Christianity in America is at the lukewarm stage, which is counterfeit."[29]

Roth cited Jesus' rebuke to the Laodicean church in Revelation 3:14–17:

> These are the words of the Amen, the faithful and true witness, the ruler of God's creation. I know your deeds, that you are neither cold nor hot. I wish you were either one or the other! So, because you are lukewarm— neither hot nor cold—I am about to spit you out of my mouth. You say, "I am rich; I have acquired wealth and do not need a thing." But you do not realize that you are wretched, pitiful, poor, blind and naked.

"[Jesus] said, 'I'd rather you be hot or cold,'" Roth explained. "You're either in or out....Mario Murillo is one of the top evangelists I believe in the world. He's a friend of mine, and I went to one of his tent meetings for the first time. I watched everyone worshipping God. And if you had asked me, I'd say everyone was a believer. But when it came time for the altar call and hundreds stood up to receive the Lord, I'm thinking, 'Didn't I just see hundreds of people worshipping God?' There's something missing in American Christianity."[30]

Despite the "lukewarm" state of the church, Roth believes America's greatest days could still be ahead, but it "could go either way."[31]

"And that's based on prayer and it's based on obedience," Roth said. "You see, you can have a thought to do something. You can dismiss it with your peanut brain that doesn't have all the facts. Make a fool of yourself as long as it's not unbiblical—take a step. You know what that's called in the Bible? Faith. You know what the Bible says, 'Without faith it is impossible to please God' [Heb. 11:6]. And believe it or not, if you have had experiential knowledge of God, you're one of His best, and your greatest days are ahead of you."

Roth is especially stirred by the coming "greater glory."

"It's a game changer," Roth said. "I can't get beyond what it'll look like. We've never seen it, but I believe this is God's last mercy on planet earth. Now, how long will it last? I don't want to be like [apostle] Paul who wrote the Book of Hebrews and starts out by saying, 'In these last days...' [Heb. 1:2]. He thought any minute now Jesus was going to return. But I think that way too, and that's a good way to live because you don't know when your end will come.[32]

"I'm just very grateful to God that He's kept me in good health [until age 85] and I can do anything He puts in front of me because of His goodness. I'm reminded of Moses. He said, 'God, show me your glory.' [See Exodus 33:18.] And God used a synonym for the word 'glory.' And God said, 'I'll display My goodness before you.' [See Exodus 33:19.] A synonym of 'glory' is 'God's goodness' and the 'greater glory' is coming. What more could we ask for?"[33]

FROM COLUMBUS TO THE GREAT AWAKENINGS TO THE "GREATER GLORY"

What began with Columbus's Holy Spirit–inspired journey to the New World, was followed by the Pilgrims' dedication of America to the "advancement of the Christian faith" in the Mayflower Compact, and continued with the Great Awakenings of the eighteenth and nineteenth centuries, the Azusa Street Revival, and the Jesus movement of the twentieth century must now serve as a rallying cry for a new generation. We must fulfill Jesus' final instruction to His disciples in Matthew 28:16–20 and make disciples of all nations.

Our world finds itself adrift today, filled with doubt, riven with political division, yet searching for meaning and purpose.

The Great Awakenings and revivals of the past were more than emotional outbursts of excitement; they were turning points in history. They inspired people to lift up the poor, widows, and orphans; confront injustice; and establish institutions of charity and education.

From the abolition of slavery after the Civil War to waves of social reforms, these revivals were not merely revivals.

Today, as we face the challenges of our modern world, we need the Holy Spirit's awakenings that reshaped America before to restore our hope again.

"I think we forget that the Holy Spirit is always at work," said Bishop Daniel Timotheos Yohannan, president of the global mission agency GFA World:

> It's not dependent on us or dependent on our programs or our systems or even data. God cares more about His people than we do. God cares more about the hurting than we do, and God will show up in people's lives when they desire Him. And I think in every generation when things get dark, things get difficult, whether it's persecution or politics or challenges or secularism, God seems to show up faithfully in each generation to inspire and encourage and to push people forward. And this is why I have so much hope for the younger generations. They're going to surpass me. They're going to go further than me. They're going to do better than me. They're going to take the gospel further around the world. I'm so excited that they can go faster and better and they can bring the gospel and be a light to the whole world better than I can. And I think that's the hope that we need to have. I think the darker things get, the brighter things also are when it comes to God. God has His people everywhere. It may be a mighty minority, like Gideon with his three hundred, but that mighty minority can do great things.[34]

To watch this interview with Bishop Yohannan, scan the QR code or visit TroyAndersonBooks.com/yohannan.

PART II

PROPHECY, POLITICS, AND AWAKENING

CHAPTER 6

HOW TRUMP'S PRESIDENCY INTERSECTS WITH BIBLE PROPHECY

For no prophecy was ever produced by the will of man, but men
spoke from God as they were carried along by the Holy Spirit.
—2 PETER 1:21, ESV

A T A TIME of massive global disruption, threats of nuclear war, and catastrophic natural disasters of biblical proportions—when 63 percent of
evangelical Christians believe we are "living in the end times" and nine
in ten pastors say current events align with what Jesus warned would happen
before His return—many are looking at how President Donald Trump fits into
unfolding biblical prophecies.[1]

For many followers of Christ, Trump's return to the White House is seen as
part of God's plan for America and the world.

As we discussed in chapter 2, there are prophetic voices who have compared
Trump to Cyrus the Great, the Persian king who helped the Israelites return
from exile. Others view him as a modern-day Jehu, the disrupter who exposed
and addressed the corruption of his time.

Voices like Rabbi Jonathan Cahn, Lance Wallnau, and Joseph Z believe
Trump has been chosen to challenge the Deep State and pave the way for
national repentance and revival.

RABBI JONATHAN CAHN: TRUMP AND JEHU

Over the years, I've interviewed many faith leaders on how America may fit
into God's prophetic timeline, including Cahn. His 2012 book *The Harbinger*
ignited a national conversation about judgment and the need for repentance.
More recently, he's drawn parallels between Trump and Jehu.

Remember, Jehu was a warrior king, raised up by God to disrupt the entrenched
powers, tear down the idolatrous altars of Baal, and rid Israel of corruption.

Jehu wasn't part of the establishment. Nonetheless, he was anointed by God to challenge the wicked rulers of his time, including Jezebel and Ahab, who had led Israel into apostasy. Likewise Trump, also an outsider, came onto the political stage rough and unpredictable. He won reelection vowing to "drain the swamp" and push back against globalist policies that many view as a threat to American sovereignty and religious freedom.

At the National Faith Advisory Board's Inaugural Faith Summit in 2024, Cahn said Trump was "born to be a trumpet of God, a vessel of the Lord, with a destiny to overturn America's 'cult of Baal' and end the sacrifice of millions of unborn babies" through the overturning of Roe v. Wade, the 1973 Supreme Court decision legalizing abortion.[2]

LANCE WALLNAU: A DIVINE DISRUPTION

Political commentator Lance Wallnau sees Trump as a modern-day Cyrus, the outsider king chosen by God to free the Jews from Babylonian captivity and rebuild Jerusalem.

FOR MANY FOLLOWERS OF CHRIST, TRUMP'S RETURN TO THE WHITE HOUSE IS SEEN AS PART OF GOD'S PLAN FOR AMERICA AND THE WORLD.

Like Cyrus, Trump is a figure who came from beyond the halls of power, yet God is using him for a higher purpose.

Wallnau has cited Trump's decision to move the US embassy from Tel Aviv to Jerusalem as pivotal, mirroring Cyrus's decree allowing the Jews to return to the Promised Land.

"I believe Trump is the chaos candidate who has been set apart by God to navigate us through the chaos coming to America," Wallnau wrote in *God's Chaos Candidate*. "With him in office, we will have authority in the Spirit to build the house of the Lord and restore the crumbling walls that separate us from cultural collapse."[3]

JOSEPH Z: A POPULIST REVIVAL

Prophetic voice Joseph Z also views Trump as a figure God chose to restore America to its Judeo-Christian roots. He sees Trump's leadership as part of God's bigger plan to ignite revival.

"I believe that he is fulfilling prophecy that is similar to what you write about and many of us talk about, and that is the Cyrus prophetic word," Joseph Z said. "I believe he is fulfilling a prophetic purpose for the body of Christ at this time. And I believe that God is raising him up to not only rescue America, but help the church get through and fulfill the Great Commission for our generation."[4]

To watch this interview with
Joseph Z, scan the QR code or visit
TroyAndersonBooks.com/josephz.

In 2015, before Trump took office, Joseph Z stood in Trump Tower asking God who would win the election. The answer stunned him.

"I said, 'God, is America going to go down? Is it going to burn? Is it over with?' And the Spirit of the Lord roared to me in Trump Tower and said, 'No, America has one more round, because the young lions are coming.'...I believe if we stand as the righteous, we will push aside this onslaught of what I call the wicked lizard overlord mafia that answer to their goblin masters trying to run this place into the dirt," Joseph Z said.[5]

Before the 2024 election, Joseph Z told me Trump's reelection would ignite a "populist revival."[6]

"I believe the revival we've all been praying for and believing God for is going to come," he said. "It'll be a populist revival. I believe the followers of Donald Trump, or those that are having rallies and gatherings...[are] a catalyst for revival. I believe God is using politics to wake up the nation, but I believe the church will come in and induce revival through some of these gatherings, because when they realize politics doesn't have the answers they're looking for, the church will rise up."[7]

Trump's policies, especially his support for Israel and religious freedom, are in Joseph Z's view good signs, but he has a warning:

"The Lord spoke to me [following Trump's reelection] and said, 'The church is the nuclear deterrent,'" Joseph Z said. "I got a witness in my spirit that said... If we get to July [2025] without a nuclear incident...we're going to see the turn of the tide."[8]

"I believe we're in sixteen years of redemptive instability where we'll see a turnaround and victory come. I believe we could see twenty years of life that begins the rebuild to the year 2040; I believe God has a marker on that year....The word of the Lord for 2025 is that we as the body of Christ, the ecclesia, are to storm Babylon. We are to continue rising in prayer, pushing back [against] this nefarious agenda of witchcraft, darkness, social evils, this woke ideology, this control over our economics, this wickedness that's happening with an invasion of our nation."[9]

TRUMP THE DISRUPTER

These faith leaders see Trump's role as a disrupter, helping break the grip of entrenched powers on the United States—the Deep State, globalists, and the political elite.

Whether it's through his defense of Judeo-Christian values, foreign policies, or resisting the establishment, they believe God is using Trump to accomplish a bigger plan.

In my last book on Trump, *The Trump Code,* I explored the curious parallels between Trump and the nineteenth century novels *The Baron Trump Collection* by American lawyer Ingersoll Lockwood. They seemed to have predicted his rise to power in uncanny ways.

> **WE'RE AT A TIPPING POINT. EITHER WE RETURN TO GOD OR WE FACE COLLAPSE.**

As the book approached its release date in September 2024, I asked questions on social media that ignited debate, including a post on my Prophecy Investigators' account on X (formerly Twitter) featuring an image of the book and the headline: "Judgment or Revival—Great Awakening or Great Reset?"[10]

It garnered over 2.6 million views and generated hundreds of comments.

Could these novels written in the 1890s have foreshadowed Trump's rise? Could the mysteries of time, the work of Nikola Tesla and Albert Einstein, and prophetic destiny play a role in the events we're witnessing now? Is Providence guiding events in ways we barely comprehend?

Now, in *Designated Disrupter,* I'm asking a deeper question: Could God be using controversial figures—Trump, Tucker Carlson, Jordan Peterson, Russell Brand, and many others—not just to disrupt politics and culture but to inspire a global spiritual awakening?

I believe America is in the "Nineveh moment" foreseen by famed evangelist Billy Graham. We're at a tipping point. Either we return to God or we face collapse.

My friend Joseph Z understands the importance of the prophetic moment we're living in:

"Troy, your data on the story of Baron Trump and his Uncle Don, and all these things that are happening in this narrative, are so profound they're actually breathtaking," Joseph Z said. "There's a Latin term called *sensus plenior*…a deeper, fuller meaning that happened before, is happening again, and repeating itself. What I see is a repeating anointing with a *sensus plenior* where Donald Trump is…fulfilling the purposes of God."[11]

INFLUENCERS: SHAPING THE GLOBAL CONVERSATION

We're living in a chaotic era, a period of time marked by political polarization as well as a spiritual void that has left millions of people searching for meaning and purpose.

Yet, a surprising trend is emerging. Influential voices from outside the church are now openly talking about their faith in Christ, capturing the attention of millions.

People like Jordan Peterson, Russell Brand, Tucker Carlson, Joe Rogan, Trump, and many others are inspiring a broader conversation about the role of faith in the public sphere.

These influencers are unlikely catalysts for revival. Yet their message is that faith in Christ isn't just relevant; it's the antidote to the crises America and the world are facing.

Jordan Peterson: The psychological significance of the biblical stories

Few people have ignited interest in the Bible like Jordan Peterson. As a psychologist, best-selling author, and cultural thinker, he's reaching millions hungry for meaning in a world drowning in nihilism. He's become one of the most influential thought leaders of our time—especially among young men.

Peterson's exploration of Christian thought has inspired a wave of interest in the Bible. In his books—*12 Rules for Life* and *We Who Wrestle with God*—he draws heavily from biblical stories, offering interpretations in light of modern psychological principles. By reframing the Bible for a secular generation, he's prompted many to take the Bible more seriously.

In his 2017 lecture series "Psychological Significance of the Biblical Stories," Peterson argued the Bible is deeply embedded in our cultural framework and can provide a sense of purpose and direction.[12]

At the Isabel Bader Theatre in Toronto, Canada, Peterson addressed this mystery:

> You might think, well, why bother with this strange old book at all? And that's a good question. It's a contradictory document that's been cobbled together over thousands of years. It's outlasted kingdoms—many, many kingdoms. It's really interesting that it turns out that a book is more durable than stone. It's more durable than a castle. It's more durable than an empire....[It's] so evanescent—how can it be so long living? So there's that. That's kind of a mystery....We don't understand how [these Bible stories] came about. We don't really understand how they were put together. We don't understand why they had such an unbelievable impact on civilization. We don't understand how people could have believed them. We don't understand what it means that we don't believe

them now, or even what it would mean if we did believe them. And then on top of all that...no matter how educated you are, you're not educated enough to discuss the psychological significance of the biblical stories....

When I look at the stories in the Bible...how it happened to motivate an entire culture for 2,000 years and to transform the world—like, what's going on? How did that happen? It's by no means obvious. One of the things that bothers me about casual critics of religion is that they don't take the phenomenon seriously. And it's a serious phenomenon, not the least because people have the capacity for religious experience and no one knows why that is.[13]

Russell Brand: From chaos to Christ

Russell Brand's metamorphosis is a striking example of the social shift we're seeing. Formerly the poster child for Hollywood excess—a wild, rebellious, and hedonistic comedian—Brand has become a humble voice for spiritual awakening.

His journey of faith has been remarkable. Through his podcast and massive following on YouTube, he has wrestled openly about addiction, cultural collapse, and the desire for transcendence. Now his search has led him into the arms of Christ.

Speaking of his baptism, Brand said:

Something occurred in the process of baptism that was incredible, overwhelming. I felt changed, transitioned....This is new for me. I'm learning, and I will make mistakes. But this is my path now. And I already feel incredibly blessed, relieved, nourished, held. It's been an incredible experience....I'm so grateful to be surrendered in Christ.[14]

During a time of deep cynicism, Brand's vulnerability is disarming. He's reaching the disillusioned, the addicted, and those searching for hope.

When a celebrity with his platform gives his life to Jesus, the ripple effects can be powerful.

Tucker Carlson: Revival is coming

The former host of *Tucker Carlson Tonight* on Fox News, Tucker Carlson is known for his sharp political commentary, but few know how his faith in Christ shapes his worldview.

Surprisingly, like many of those I interviewed for *Designated Disrupter*, he believes America's survival depends on a reset of American morality.

In an interview with former Navy Seal Shawn Ryan, Carlson said:

I don't have too many great insights into things or prophetic feelings. I'm very conventional, but the one thing that I really felt strongly a couple of years ago—really strongly, I felt it overwhelmingly like from outside me—was that there's some form of religious revival coming. I felt that really strongly.[15]

Joe Rogan: Ease the confusion of the unknown

Joe Rogan may not be the first name that comes to mind when you think of Christianity. But in today's media world his influence is colossal.

Who could forget his popular, freewheeling, three-hour interview with President Trump shortly before the 2024 presidential election? The interview has garnered over 59 million views on YouTube alone.[16]

After Trump won the election, many pundits agreed going on Rogan's show (which he did on the advice of his son Barron Trump) helped him win not only the youth vote, but the election itself.

"To describe 2024 as the first podcast election would be an exaggeration. But not, I think, much of one," wrote *The Times* columnist James Marriot in his article "How Joe Rogan helped Donald Trump to win America." "Podcasts have exploded in popularity ever since the last American election and are now perhaps the most formidable and underrated force in the new online media. Anybody who doubts this should take note of Trump's victory rally, which featured a shout out to the 'mighty and powerful Joe Rogan.' Allies of the 45th (and soon to be 47th) president evidently believe that he owes at least part of his victory to Rogan. They are very plausibly correct in that analysis."[17]

As host of *The Joe Rogan Experience,* the most downloaded podcast in the world, Rogan has become an unlikely conduit for spiritual conversations.

Despite identifying himself as spiritual, not religious, Rogan often has deep conversations about God with his guests. Jordan Peterson and other Christian thinkers frequently talk about the Bible on his show.

One moment stood out to me during his interview with British evolutionary biologist Richard Dawkins. Rogan said:

> People find great comfort in these belief systems. I've often said it gives them a scaffolding for their structure of the world, their ethics, and their morals. They can use religion as some sort of mechanism to help them get by, something that they can climb on to ease the confusion of the unknown.[18]

Donald Trump: Faith as a national rallying cry

Since his reelection, Trump has significantly elevated the importance of faith in America's national conversation. Throughout his first and second terms, Trump made no secret of his support for Christianity and the important role it plays in the United States.

At the National Prayer Breakfast in 2017 he said:

> We will be a safe country, we will be a free country and we will be a country where all citizens can practice their beliefs without fear of hostility or a fear of violence. America will flourish, as long as our liberty, and in particular, our religious liberty is allowed to flourish. America will succeed, as long as our most vulnerable citizens—and we have some that are so vulnerable—have a path to success. And America will thrive, as long as we continue to have faith in each other and faith in God.[19]

A NEW ERA OF INFLUENCE IN PROPHETIC TIMES

People like Jordan Peterson, Russell Brand, Tucker Carlson, Joe Rogan, Trump, and others are igniting a global conversation about faith.

They are using their platforms to inspire millions to reconsider the power of God to transform their lives. In an often-hostile world, they are offering hope, wisdom, and the biblical truth that faith in God is critical to navigating life's many challenges.

The rise of these "designated disrupters" comes as many prophecy experts believe the world is in a prophetic acceleration toward the end-times events described in Scripture.

Throughout history, few periods have been marked by the sheer magnitude of crises we are experiencing today—record levels of debt, new technologies like artificial intelligence and digital currencies that make the "mark of the beast" (Rev. 13) system possible for the first time in history, and the growing specter of global thermonuclear war.

THE WORLD IS IN A PROPHETIC ACCELERATION TOWARD THE END-TIMES EVENTS DESCRIBED IN SCRIPTURE.

The Bible warns that as we approach "the end of all things" (1 Pet. 4:7, MEV) the fulfillment of prophecies will accelerate. Astrophysicist Hugh Ross, founder of Reasons to Believe, notes that of the Bible's 2,500 prophecies, about 2,000 have already been "fulfilled to the letter—no errors."[20]

Now revival is spreading. But as prophecy expert Paul McGuire warns, this awakening is coming with fierce resistance.

McGuire says that "God's people need to step up their game." Since the advent of AI technology, we're entering a world previously only imagined in movies like *The Matrix*. The revival that is building in America and the world is being counterattacked viciously by the Deep State and the occult elite. In ourselves, we don't have enough power. We desperately need the *dunamis* power of the Holy Spirit to overcome the darkness. McGuire says he is optimistic but calls this moment in history "the greatest spiritual battle in the history of the world."[21]

This is where we are at—a global spiritual awakening colliding with occult and demonic powers trying to stop it. What happens next depends on how we as the church respond.

PANDEMICS, NATURAL DISASTERS, AND PROPHECY

If you study Bible prophecy and follow global events, it's hard to miss the parallels between Scripture and today's headlines.

Jesus warned in Matthew 24, Mark 13, and Luke 21 that the last days would be marked by wars, famines, pestilences, and earthquakes.

> For nation will rise against nation, and kingdom against kingdom. And there will be famines, pestilences, and earthquakes in various places. All these are the beginning of sorrows.
> —MATTHEW 24:7–8, NKJV

Now, with super-hurricanes, mega-earthquakes, exploding volcanoes, devastating tsunamis, and other catastrophic disasters pummeling the planet on a regular basis, these warnings are today's headlines. The COVID-19 pandemic alone killed over 7 million people, shut down nations worldwide, crashed the global economy, and spread global fear. For many, it was a prophetic wake-up call—a glimpse of the global shaking Scripture says will precede the end.[22]

During the pandemic, we saw widespread despair, chaos, and a loss of trust in nearly every institution. A Pew study found that 72 percent of Americans said COVID-19 widened political and social divisions. Over a million Americans died, many of us know someone who was hospitalized or died, and many are still battling long COVID.[23]

My precious wife, Irene, nearly died in November 2022 when she was hospitalized for seventeen days with severe COVID pneumonia, severe sepsis, acute pancreatitis, and several other life-threatening conditions. A doctor told me she only had a 50-50 chance to live, so I asked all our friends and family to pray for her, and we believe God saved her life. Afterward, the hospital sent us a gargantuan bill. Again, everyone prayed, we submitted all our financial information to the hospital, and by what we believe was another miracle of God, the hospital forgave the entire bill. What are the chances?

For prophecy watchers, the pandemic was a precursor, a warning sign of the tribulation. COVID-19 was a glimpse of the chaos the Book of Revelation describes—a wake-up call for the world.

WARS AND RUMORS OF WARS

Jesus warned us clearly: "You will hear of wars and rumors of wars, but see to it that you are not alarmed. Such things must happen, but the end is still to come" (Matt. 24:6).

We're living in that prophecy now. As someone who's reported on the intersection of geopolitics and biblical prophecies for many years, I've seen the progression of the headlines, moving the world toward the apocalyptic events described in the Bible.

As Rabbi Jonathan Cahn pointed out in *The Harbinger*, the September 11, 2001, terrorist attacks were a key prophetic event, perhaps setting in motion the "beginning of sorrows" described in Matthew 24–25. *The Harbinger* detailed how the same nine signs of judgment that ancient Israel experienced before its destruction 2,600 years ago are reappearing in America today.

THE WORLD IS A POWDER KEG READY TO EXPLODE, AND ONLY THE HAND OF GOD AND PRAYERS OF THE SAINTS ARE HOLDING BACK THE UNTHINKABLE.

"We are living in prophetic times, critical times," Cahn said following Trump's reelection. "The answer is not even the window. The answer is that which the window was given for; the answer is revival. For if we change the government but do not change the people, the unchanged people will change the government back. If we turn the laws but we don't turn the hearts, then the unturned hearts will turn the laws back again. The only way America can be great again is for America to turn back to the God who made America great in the first place....I'm charging you. Don't let it stop. Continue. Let's pray every day for revival until it comes."[24]

Following the September 11, 2001, terrorist attacks came the Global War on Terror involving major military interventions in Iraq and Afghanistan. Since then, we've witnessed Russia's invasion of Ukraine, Russian leader Vladimir Putin's regular threats of nuclear war, North Korea's threats of nuclear war, and growing concerns that China will attack Taiwan, potentially triggering World War III.

These aren't random conflicts. They're part of unfolding biblical prophecies that track with the Book of Revelation. Wars have always existed, but our generation faces something entirely different—global conflicts with the threat of nuclear war, artificial intelligence, autonomous weapons, coordinated swarms of robots, deadly drones that dramatically change the nature of warfare, and now the move of warfare into space.

The world is a powder keg ready to explode, and only the hand of God and prayers of the saints are holding back the unthinkable.

THE GREAT RESET AND MARK OF THE BEAST

Record levels of global debt and economic instability are other signs of the end times.

The Book of Revelation tells us that in the last days, a global financial system will emerge where "[no one can] buy or sell unless they had the mark, which is the name of the beast or the number of its name" (Rev. 13:17).

For many centuries it was hard to imagine how this prophecy might come true. But today with electronic banking, digital currencies, artificial intelligence, and the growing surveillance state, it's possible for the first time in history.

For end-times watchers, an especially troubling development that raised people's prophetic radars occurred when the World Economic Forum called for the "Great Reset of capitalism" in 2020.[25]

Former World Economic Forum Chairman Klaus Schwab gained notoriety after he released his book *COVID-19: The Great Reset* shortly after the pandemic started, prompting many prophecy experts to question whether the "Great Reset" was merely a new name for the "new world order."

Meanwhile, the precarious state of America's economy cannot be overstated. Our national debt has exploded to nearly $37 trillion, close to $110,000 for each person in the United States. The dominance of the dollar is under increasing threat. The shift toward a cashless society is accelerating. A "Great Reset" of the economic system is not beyond the realm of possibility.[26]

While I was writing this chapter, Trump signed the GENIUS Act. This new law regulates stablecoins, demands monthly reserve disclosures, and expands government oversight of digital assets. Trump said it will secure America's leadership in cryptocurrencies and digital finance. Critics warned it could open the door to unprecedented financial surveillance and control by both government and corporations.[27]

I believe Trump's motives are patriotic. He's trying to save America from disaster, restore prosperity, and protect our future. But prophetically, perhaps God is allowing these events to unfold so that the events of the Book of Revelation can be fulfilled on His prophetic timeline. Daniel 2:21 reminds us that God raises up leaders and sets times and seasons. Even well-intentioned actions can move us closer to biblical prophecy being fulfilled.

The financial system the apostle John foresaw two millennia ago on the island of Patmos is beginning to take shape. We are moving toward a world where global commerce can be monitored, restricted, and controlled by centralized authorities.

IS AMERICA IN BIBLE PROPHECY?

One of the biggest questions I hear is whether America is in Bible prophecy.

For centuries America has called herself the shining city on a hill—what President Ronald Reagan called the "last best hope" of the world.[28]

But what happens when a country founded on godly principles falls into apostasy? As discussed in chapter 3, many prophecy experts believe America's growing decadence is following the pattern of ancient empires that collapsed. While the Pilgrims and Puritans saw America as the new "Jerusalem," some prophecy experts today have cast the United States as a modern-day Babylon.[29]

In our book *The Babylon Code*, McGuire and I asked whether the "great whore...seated on many waters" that is destroyed by "fire" in Revelation 17 and 18 could represent America. The apostle John described a nation that enriched the merchants of the earth, boasting, "I rule as a queen; I am no widow, and I will never see grief" (Rev. 18:7, NRSVUE), and then is destroyed in a single hour: "In one hour all this wealth has been laid waste!" (Rev. 18:17, NRSVUE).[30]

Could this be a prediction of a sudden nuclear strike on New York City or America?

Revelation 18:9–10 says:

> When the kings of the earth who committed adultery with her and shared her luxury see the smoke of her burning, they will weep and mourn over her. Terrified at her torment, they will stand far off and cry: "Woe! Woe to you, great city, you mighty city of Babylon! In one hour your doom has come!"

The chapter goes on to say that the "merchants of the earth will weep and mourn over her because no one buys their cargoes anymore" (Rev. 18:11)—with "every sea captain, and all who travel by ship, the sailors, and all who earn their living from the sea" (Rev. 18:17) remaining "far off," watching "the smoke of her burning" (Rev. 18:18).

Could it be that the ship captains will keep their distance because they are afraid of nuclear radiation?

The Bible mentions nations like Israel, Iran (Persia), Russia (Magog), China (the Kings of the East), and a revived Roman Empire but is silent about America. Why?

Some believe it's because the United States will be weakened—crushed by its soaring debts, divided by civil strife, or devastated by the rapture, the belief that Christians will be supernaturally taken to heaven before the tribulation period begins, removing many members of its government, military, police and fire services, and private sector workforce, creating a chaotic situation.

> *GOD IS GIVING US A WINDOW OF TIME TO RETURN TO HIM AND HELP BRING IN THE END-TIMES HARVEST.*

Others believe that America may ultimately align with the Antichrist system, becoming part of the global government, economic, and universal religious system that Revelation describes.

Will America continue to shine the light of the gospel to the world in these last of the last days? Or will we follow the path of many other civilizations that collapsed when they forgot their Creator?

That's the dilemma we face, and time is running out. Whether we are witnessing the beginning of events that will lead to those described in Revelation or a hopeful reboot of our nation—Trump's vision of a "true golden age for America"—I believe God is giving us a window of time to return to Him and help bring in the end-times harvest.[31]

TRUMP, ISRAEL, AND PROPHECY

When it comes to Bible prophecy, few topics are more important than Israel. For most evangelical Christians, supporting Israel is about standing with God's chosen people.

That's one of the reasons why Trump's two presidencies—both his first and second terms—have prompted so much discussion. Many believe his rise to power is part of God's plan to defend Israel in a world that is often hostile to the Jewish people.

Genesis 12:3 (ESV) says, "I will bless those who bless you, and him who dishonors you I will curse, and in you all the families of the earth shall be blessed."

One of the most prophetic moments of Trump's first term happened in

December 2017 when he recognized Jerusalem as Israel's eternal capital. Then in May 2018 he moved the US embassy from Tel Aviv to Jerusalem.[32]

The Bible, especially in the Old Testament, places a major emphasis on the importance of Jerusalem in God's covenant with His people. In Zechariah 8:3 (NKJV) the prophet refers to Jerusalem as the "City of Truth" and "Mountain of the LORD of hosts, The Holy Mountain."

For centuries Jerusalem has been at the center of God's redemptive plan for humanity. Trump's actions are seen as a modern fulfillment of that covenant.

"I think that America needs Israel," said Rabbi Jonathan Bernis, founder of Jewish Voice Ministries International. "Genesis 12:3 says [God] will bless those that bless the children of Abraham. I'm not saying that this means America and Christians that are pro-Israel should be defending every action of the Israeli government....In fact, we should be critical of decisions that are made by a largely secular leadership that has not embraced the gospel and does not treat believers in Jesus in Israel well. That's a reality."[33]

Bernis said Genesis 12:3 is about God's faithfulness to Israel, even in their state of unbelief, and His commitment to preserve them as a people.[34] Jeremiah 31:35–36 says, "This is what the LORD says, he who appoints the sun to shine by day, who decrees the moon and stars to shine by night, who stirs up the sea so that its waves roar—the LORD Almighty is his name: 'Only if these decrees vanish from my sight,' declares the LORD, 'will Israel ever cease being a nation before me.'" Bernis said:

> [Today,] Israel is not only surviving but prospering even in their state of unbelief because God is faithful and God is committed to their redemption in His time and His plan. The US fundamentally needs to stand with Israel and Israel's preservation and survival, which again doesn't mean that [Americans] agree with everything that Israel does. We have to call out Israel on bad decisions. They have to operate with proper ethics.
>
> But fundamentally it's imperative for the blessing on America to continue to stand with Israel. And sadly, there is a growing movement among believers, evangelicals, and conservative leaders that are beginning to turn against Israel....We're dealing not with flesh and blood, but principalities and powers, and the spirit of the Antichrist is manifested very strongly in anti-Israel, anti-Jewish, anti-Semitic views that creep in—beginning with anti-Zionism.[35]

To watch my conversation
with Rabbi Bernis, scan
the QR code or visit
TroyAndersonBooks.com/bernis.

STANDING AGAINST THE GLOBALISTS

Unlike many presidents, Trump has frequently aligned himself against the globalist agendas of the United Nations, World Health Organization, and World Economic Forum. Seen through the lens of Bible prophecy, his opposition to globalist agendas is a critical line of defense against powerful forces that want to undermine American sovereignty.[36]

The globalists' push for a world government has long concerned Bible prophecy scholars. The Bible warns in Daniel and Revelation of a global dictator who will dominate the world during the tribulation period.

In Revelation 13, the apostle John described two beasts: the Antichrist and the False Prophet. The first beast rises from the sea, empowered by Satan. The second beast deceives humanity into worshipping the first beast and oversees a global economic system linked to the "mark of the beast."

Revelation 13:16–18 (MEV) says:

> He causes all, both small and great, both rich and poor, both free and slave, to receive a mark on their right hand or on their forehead, so that no one may buy or sell, except he who has the mark or the name of the beast or the number of his name. Here is a call for wisdom: Let him who has understanding calculate the number of the beast. It is the number of a man. His number is six hundred and sixty-six.

By rejecting globalist policies and defending America's borders, Trump has become—whether intentionally or by God's supernatural design—a stopgap measure against this coming world order.

As McGuire explains, Trump is helping fulfill the original mission of the Pilgrims and Puritans who had a "very clear vision" for America.[37]

> People need to really understand because they've been indoctrinated with all this Marxist socialism undermining America, [which says], "America's evil, America's bad." All of those are lies. America is not

perfect, but it's not evil and it's not bad. God...has a special plan for America, a special destiny for America...shining the light of the gospel throughout the world....We're different, not that we're better, but we're different and unique from all the other nations because of our DNA code, if you will, which comes right out of the Word of God.[38]

America exists to show the world the contrast between God's plan for humanity and the counterfeit utopias promised by humanism, socialism, and communism.

Think about it—the reality of the Garden of Eden, a paradise so beautiful and awesome, that the God of love planned for every man and woman to live eternally inside the Garden of Eden. That's a snapshot of God's loving vision for every person to live in...the Garden of Eden. Then contrast that to humanism and man-centered philosophies and beliefs....The communists [say], "We're going to give you heaven on earth. We're going to give you paradise." The socialists and Marxists use those words, but when you look at what they produce, it's the hellish opposite of the Garden of Eden.[39]

It's a nightmare—totalitarianism, mass deaths, gulags where people freeze to death, the slaughtering of hundreds of millions....All of these nations are brutal, totalitarian—[George Orwell's] 1984 Big Brother hell on earth societies....The purpose of America is to show the entire world the difference...how [God] fills human institutions with light, love, justice, righteousness, creativity, imagination, and yes, prosperity.[40]

With this in mind, Trump's opposition to globalist policies—whether related to trade, climate accords, or international health mandates—is a prophetic stand against the totalitarian system the apostle John warned would ultimately gain control of the world. Trump's rejection of the World Economic Forum's "Great Reset" and United Nations' "Agenda 2030" plans aligns with biblical prophecy and resisting forces that seek centralized global control.[41]

One of Christ's last instructions to His disciples was, "Occupy till I come" (Luke 19:13, KJV), meaning to diligently carry out the responsibilities entrusted to us until His return.

A CALL TO NATIONAL REPENTANCE

The world's mounting crises are not just signs of the end times but a call to action. For America, the prophetic alarm is sounding. Faith leaders like Billy

Graham, Reinhard Bonnke, Sid Roth, Paul McGuire, Pastor Paul Begley, and many others have warned for years: America must repent, turn from sin, and return to the covenant the Pilgrims made with God in the Mayflower Compact.

While I was writing *Designated Disrupter*, Mike Kerr, founder of Hear the Watchmen, asked for an interview with McGuire and me. On Kerr's show, McGuire delivered an important message: America is facing one final chance to repent, turn back to God, or face collapse.[42]

McGuire shared two prophetic visions he received— one on July 4, 2012, and another on July 4, 2025. In the first vision, detailed in our book *The Babylon Code*, McGuire recounted how while in deep repentance for his own sins and the sins of America, he was overwhelmed by an intense burning sensation, followed by a satellite-like view of America from above. He saw glowing dots throughout California, which morphed into people standing in worship. God revealed to him that this was His highest desire for America—a nationwide revival, spreading from the West Coast to the East, North to South, and ultimately around the world.[43]

> AMERICA'S ORIGINAL PURPOSE IS TO BE A "CITY ON A HILL," SHINING THE LIGHT OF THE GOSPEL TO THE WORLD.

However, the vision came with a warning: This move of the Holy Spirit is conditional upon national repentance, the intercession of prayer warriors, and America's acceptance of the truth of the Word of God. "The revival is not guaranteed," McGuire said. "God's people must awaken from their slumber, stop playing church and take ownership for what's happening."[44]

PAUL MCGUIRE: AMERICA'S LAST CHANCE

Then on July 4, 2025, McGuire received a second vision. Awakened from a deep sleep—a metaphor for the spiritual condition of much of the church today—he described an encounter where God showed him the current state of America and what's at stake.

> The Lord said, "I want My people to stand against the darkness and quit making excuses." And then the hard thing that the Lord told me was that, "I'm giving you one last chance. This is it." What we do now is going to set in motion the immediate and long-term future. The stakes are so high now because of AI and genetic engineering and the replacement of human jobs with robots and the coming nanochip implant

that's already here (the microchip implant, the cashless society)—They're erecting a totalitarian state.[45]

McGuire warned of the World Economic Forum's "Great Reset" plan. He said:

We all know the "Great Reset" is nothing more than a rebranding of the term "new world order." New world order meant a Luciferian, godless, one-world government, one-world religion, and one-world economic system. The World Economic Forum changed their title to the "Great Reset" to sucker punch people, and that's what they're trying to implement. So we have one last chance, and we can defeat the enemy to whatever degree God gives us the ability, but we must be…empowered by the Holy Spirit. If we go into a spiritual battle, or try to take a stand without the direct anointing of power from on high and the Holy Spirit, we will go down so hard we won't even be a faint memory in history.[46]

McGuire said God is calling His people to restore the American Dream—not materialism, but the covenant vision of the Pilgrims and Puritans. America's original purpose is to be a "city on a hill," shining the light of the gospel to the world.

I believe Trump's role in this battle is prophetic. Like a modern-day Jehu, Trump is a flawed but strong leader, raised up to disrupt the corrupt globalist system.

When Trump announced in 2016 that "Americanism, not globalism, will be our credo" as his platform for president, it was a direct challenge to the new world order.[47]

STEPPING INTO YOUR GOD-GIVEN ASSIGNMENT

The world is at a prophetic crossroads. The "Great Reset," "Agenda 2030," digital currencies, AI, and centralized global control are real threats. But this is a time for courage. How do we respond?

1. Partner with the Holy Spirit: Jesus promised us a helper—the Holy Spirit—to guide us through difficult times. Seek His wisdom daily. Pray for discernment to act in faith, not fear.

2. Stay Informed: Watch global trends—digital currencies, AI, and globalist agendas. These are not random events. They align with biblical prophecies. Watch, pray, and prepare.

3. Defend Sovereignty and Liberty: Support leaders and policies that protect national sovereignty, religious freedom, and the sanctity of life. The rise of global control is part of the end-times battle between the forces of God and Satan.

4. Promote National Repentance and Revival: Revival starts with us. Pray for America's return to its Judeo-Christian roots. Stand for truth, defend biblical values, and help rebuild America's foundation of faith in Jesus.

This is not just about surviving what's ahead. It's about discovering and stepping into the mission God has for your life during one of the most exciting times in history to be a believer—the period of time before Christ's return.

Don't miss out on what He's planned for your life from the "foundation of the world."

"Just as He chose us in Him before the foundation of the world, that we should be holy and without blame before Him in love" (Eph. 1:4, NKJV).

CHAPTER 7

THE HOLLYWOOD REVIVAL

*I think it comes down to this. If you want to see a revival, do revival-like
things, stop waiting for some emotional experience, just go out and do
what God's called you to do. Only God can send a revival, but only I can
preach the gospel. Now,s God has chosen to reach people through people,
but there's a rejuvenating, refreshing thing about sharing your faith.*
—PASTOR GREG LAURIE IN AN INTERVIEW ABOUT
HIS MOVIE *JESUS REVOLUTION*.[1]

JUST AS JESUS was a radical counterculture celebrity of His time, movie stars,
rock stars, and other influencers are helping ignite a new Jesus Revolution
today, inspiring a new generation to follow Christ into unlikely places as old
as the traditions of Christianity itself.

Today, revival is unfolding on movie sets, in recording studios, at stadium
press conferences, during viral live streams, and on social media feeds.

From Hollywood to Spotify, from Netflix to TikTok, the world's most recog-
nizable names are talking about Jesus, and millions are listening.

At a time when Christianity is often marginalized or mocked in mainstream
culture, an unexpected trend is emerging: Celebrities, musicians, tech moguls,
and sports icons are changing the game. They're disrupting cultural expectations, reaching people churches might never reach and inspiring conversations
about Jesus.

From podcast interviews to postgame speeches, from red carpets to concert
stages, the seeds of revival are being spread by the most unlikely messengers.
Worship leader Sean Feucht said:

> I think of the verse that says, "The Lord gave the word; Great was the
> company of those who proclaimed it" [Ps. 68:11, NKJV]. So, I think
> that you are going to start seeing these words of revival and awakening
> [being] reiterated...and blasted [out] in arts, media, entertainment—all
> these places. I think a big part of our heart is that we want to see the
> fame of Jesus cover the earth "as the waters cover the sea" [Hab. 2:14],
> and that looks like movies and TV shows and [YouTube] channels...
> promoting God's Word, shining His light. So yeah, I'm all for it. The

kingdoms of the world will become the kingdoms of our Lord [Rev. 11:15], and it's exciting to see.[2]

Today, cultural influencers—including actors, producers, rock stars, tech titans, athletes, and media personalities—are sharing their faith in Jesus, pointing millions toward God. They are becoming His "designated disrupters" in a pop culture revival unlike anything we've seen.

What's happening reminds me of an experience I had when I was writing a 2015 cover story for *Charisma* magazine titled "Jesus Goes to Hollywood." In my three-decade career as a journalist, writing thousands of stories, it's one of my favorites. As part of my research for the article, my wife, Irene, and I got to meet and take pictures with Hollywood movers and shakers Mark Burnett and Roma Downey (*Touched by an Angel, The Apprentice, The Bible*) at their Malibu home overlooking the Pacific Ocean. Charisma Media Founder Stephen Strang sent us on assignment to interview them. Roma—whose home was filled with Joan of Arc statues—was amazed to discover that my ancestor poet and playwright Friedrich von Schiller wrote *The Maid of Orleans* play that helped popularize the Joan of Arc story. She and Irene hit it off instantly, with Roma walking arm-in-arm with Irene around the backyard, chatting like they were old friends.

The *Charisma* magazine cover showed a picture of Jesus' sandal-clad foot about to step on a Hollywood Walk of Fame star. The story delved into the resurgence of faith-based movies and television shows, exploring whether Hollywood could contribute to an awakening. The story's subtitle captured its essence: "With the flood of faith films hitting theaters, many say believers have an unprecedented opportunity to spread the Good News. Will Hollywood help Christianity make a comeback, regain its influence in culture and inspire another spiritual awakening?"[3]

> CULTURAL INFLUENCERS— INCLUDING ACTORS, PRODUCERS, ROCK STARS, TECH TITANS, ATHLETES, AND MEDIA PERSONALITIES— ARE SHARING THEIR FAITH IN JESUS, POINTING MILLIONS TOWARD GOD.

Then in 2023, to my surprise, *Newsweek* released what seemed to be the follow-up story: "Jesus Takes Hollywood."

The cover showed an image of Jesus holding a movie set clapperboard, signaling "action" on set. When I saw it, it struck me as God's sense of humor. I told my friend Jerry Moses about it. Jerry is the former assistant to the president at Movieguide, Ted Baehr. He agreed it seemed more than coincidental, and he sent a copy of the magazine to Baehr, believing he would be inspired by it. The *Newsweek* article explored how "Hollywood and the entertainment industry are in the midst of a 'revival moment' of faith-based projects that are unifying the body of Christ and amplifying light across a dark world," according to a *Crosswalk* report on the article and trend.[4]

Actor Jonathan Roumie, who plays Jesus in *The Chosen* TV series, wrote an Instagram post featuring the *Newsweek* cover:

> Our collective projects, @thechosentvseries and @jesusrevolutionmovie are at the heart of this revival moment in culture and entertainment. It's a pivotal moment in time on so many levels; for culture, politics, faith, ideology, and entertainment, among others. I can see the pendulum swinging upwards; the praise—skyward bound, the naysayers losing ground, and the willingness to build bridges and unify the fractured body of Christ in simply celebrating together. The thrust of my mission continues to be to amplify and shape how and where the light falls on earth through the gifts I've been blessed with, the realms of influence in which I've been given authority, and the specific capacity to shoulder what I can (though I struggle quite often). That said, submission on the most spiritually fundamental level reigns supreme…and I cannot wait to see how the Divine continues to permeate the earthly, armed with His regiment of rugged, culture-catalysts.[5]

Roumie's remarks and the *Newsweek* cover story come as Hollywood is planning to release several major motion pictures in the coming years that will further help amplify this "revival moment," including the following:

- Mel Gibson's sequel to *The Passion of the Christ*—*The Resurrection of the Christ,* a two-part series of films slated for release in March and May of 2027.[6]

- *The Way of the Wind*, a film about the life of Jesus from director Terrence Malick.

- *Among the Outlaws*, the remake of the *Jesus* film, the 1979 movie viewed over 11 billion times, with 679 million decisions to follow Christ.[7]

- *JESUS*, the animated remake of the *Jesus* film, scheduled for release in 2026.

Meanwhile, shortly before his inauguration, President Trump named legendary actors Mel Gibson, Sylvester Stallone, and Jon Voight as his "Special Ambassadors" to Hollywood to help rejuvenate the struggling entertainment industry. Trump posted this to Truth Social:

> It is my honor to announce Jon Voight, Mel Gibson, and Sylvester Stallone, to be Special Ambassadors to a great but very troubled place, Hollywood, California. They will serve as Special Envoys to me for the purpose of bringing Hollywood, which has lost much business over the last four years to Foreign Countries, BACK—BIGGER, BETTER, AND STRONGER THAN EVER BEFORE! These three very talented people will be my eyes and ears, and I will get done what they suggest. It will again be, like The United States of America itself, The Golden Age of Hollywood![8]

Shortly afterward, prophetic voice Brandon Biggs, known for predicting the July 13, 2024, assassination attempt on President Trump (he saw the president get shot in the ear before it happened), made a surprising declaration: "A mighty move of God is coming to Hollywood, like the Shekinah Glory on Azusa Street."[9]

HOLLYWOOD'S UNLIKELY TURN TOWARD CHRIST

My wife and I love movies. Like millions of other people, we find something powerful about sitting down together to watch a masterfully told story unfold on the big screen at our local movie theater or on our television.

Films have a way of reaching into our hearts that few other mediums can match. They transport us, challenge us, and often leave us reflecting long after the credits roll. That's why it's no surprise that God is using Hollywood as a catalyst for revival today.

Movies aren't just entertainment; they're modern-day parables. Through cinematic storytelling, biblical truths are breaking into living rooms, smartphones, and theaters worldwide—whether it's on the big screen or livestreaming through Netflix, Amazon Prime, Apple TV+, or YouTube.

As a journalist who has spent decades covering politics, faith, and entertainment, I've discovered that the Holy Spirit often moves in unexpected ways. Today, God is using movies and TV series to draw people to His Son Jesus.

Many films and TV series are contributing to this unfolding revival, but a few stand out.

MEL GIBSON'S RETURN: THE RESURRECTION
AND BATTLE FOR SOULS

I'll never forget watching *The Passion of the Christ* when it was released in theaters in 2004. Watching the sheer brutality of what Jesus endured during His trial and crucifixion brought tears to my eyes.

The film had a major impact on my life, playing a role in my shift from mainstream journalism to becoming a writer for Christian and conservative media outlets and an author of Christian books.

The film stunned the world, grossing over $609 million globally, with more than 60 million tickets sold in the United States alone. It remains one of the most successful and controversial faith-based films ever made.[10]

In a January 2025 interview with Joe Rogan, Gibson addressed the fierce opposition he faced at the time.

"There was a lot of opposition to it," Gibson said. "I think if you ever hit on that subject matter, you're going to get [pushback]....His sacrifice was for all mankind—for all our ills and all the things in our fallen nature....I was born into a Catholic family. I'm very Christian in my beliefs...so I...believe this stuff to the full."[11]

Now Gibson is stepping back into the arena with *The Resurrection of the Christ*, an otherworldly exploration of good versus evil.

"The next film I'm going to do [will]...tackle this question—that there are big realms, spiritual realms," Gibson said. "There's good, there's evil, and they are slugging it out for the souls of mankind. And my question is: Why are we even important—little old flawed humanity? Why are we important in that...the big realms are slugging it out over us?"[12]

GOD'S TIMING IS NEVER ACCIDENTAL.

The project took Gibson and his team, including *Braveheart* screenwriter Randall Wallace, more than six years to write.

"It's really ambitious," Gibson said. "It goes from...the fall of the angels to the death of the last apostle."[13]

The focus of the film is the resurrection of Christ.

"Who gets back up three days later after he gets murdered in public? Who gets back up under his own power?" Gibson asked. "Buddha didn't do that."[14]

God's timing is never accidental. As revival is breaking out across America and the world, *The Resurrection of the Christ* is arriving at a prophetic moment.

After more than two decades of silence, the cinematic continuation of the gospel story will come to life on big screens in theaters worldwide, showing a new generation that Christ's resurrection isn't a story from the distant past, but the defining event of history.

Gibson, who lost his Malibu home in the Los Angeles wildfires while he was in Austin, Texas, to record the interview with Rogan, is sixty-nine years old this year (2025). Completing a project of this magnitude is no small task. That's why my wife and I, along with many others, are praying for his health and for inspiration to finish the assignment God has given him.[15]

This may well become the most powerful sermon Hollywood ever delivers.

THE *JESUS* FILM REMAKE: THE GOSPEL FOR A NEW GENERATION

The original 1979 movie *Jesus* has reached more people than any other film in history—more than 11 billion viewings and over 679 million recorded decisions for Christ.[16]

I watched the *Jesus* film at the theater a few months after I became a follower of Jesus. The film chronicled the life of Jesus and His disciples as told in the Book of Luke.

To my surprise, I learned decades later from Paul McGuire, my coauthor of *The Babylon Code* and *Trumpocalypse,* that he had written the marketing plan for the *Jesus* film at the request of Campus Crusade for Christ International founder Bill Bright. Bright's organization financed the film produced by John Heyman, a famous British film and TV producer.

Now, a good friend of mine—a prominent Hollywood filmmaker—is spearheading a modern remake of the movie. He and his team are going to retell the gospel story with cutting-edge cinematic technologies to help capture the hearts of new generations.

"The story of Jesus has never been more relevant, or accessible than it is right now, and it's about to reach every last corner on earth," said Josh Newell, executive director of the Jesus Film Project. "There are some estimates that there are billions of people today who have never heard of Jesus. And I'm here to tell you that there is a plan to reach everyone, everywhere in the next decade."[17]

This new movie has the potential to reach additional billions of people with the good news of Jesus Christ, helping fulfill the Great Commission—Jesus' final instruction to His disciples to take the gospel to all the world.

In Matthew 28:19–20, Jesus said:

> Therefore go and make disciples of all nations, baptizing them in the name of the Father and of the Son and of the Holy Spirit, and teaching

them to obey everything I have commanded you. And surely I am with you always, to the very end of the age.

Looking back and connecting the dots, God truly works in mysterious and amazing ways.

JESUS REVOLUTION: REVIVAL ON THE BIG SCREEN

Pastor Greg Laurie's 2023 blockbuster movie *Jesus Revolution* captured the most significant spiritual awakening in modern times—the Jesus movement of the late 1960s and '70s.

The film stars Jonathan Roumie (*The Chosen*) and Kelsey Grammer, bringing to the screen the story of hippie preacher Lonnie Frisbee, Pastor Chuck Smith, and Pastor Laurie.

Roumie, who plays Jesus in *The Chosen* TV series, said he read the "phenomenal" script and instantly decided to play Frisbee, whose "story was amazing and heartbreaking and beautiful, and a testament to God's grace."[18]

> I mean, Christ appeared to Lonnie in a vision that told him, before he ever met Chuck Smith, that he was going to bring thousands of hippies to Himself, to Christ. And he looked out in this vision at the Pacific Ocean, and instead of being filled with water, it was filled with people, with hippies just yearning for God. And that's exactly what he did. He also professed to Greg Laurie that he saw that God was going to use Greg to minister to thousands of people as well....So he was prophetic, he was apostolic, he was charismatic, and he worked with the Spirit intimately, and he was in love with Jesus Christ.[19]

Jesus Revolution isn't just about an awakening that occurred decades ago. Revival is happening again, and Jesus is calling His followers to share "the hope that is in you" (1 Pet. 3:15, NKJV).

THE HOLY SPIRIT CAN AT ANY TIME AWAKEN A GENERATION, AND OFTEN WITH UNEXPECTED PEOPLE.

Pastor Laurie, whom I've interviewed many times over the years, is a great example of this. Not only does he lead a megachurch with Harvest Church, but he's also reaching millions through Harvest Crusades—and now he's expanded into movies with *Jesus Revolution*.

At the Harvest Crusades event at Angel Stadium in Anaheim, California, on July 19, 2025, a capacity crowd of over 45,000 people attended, with an additional 200,000 online viewers. This marked the second consecutive year the stadium has been packed out. The one-night event saw over 6,500 people make professions of faith, marking one of the most powerful responses in its 35-year history.[20]

"The heart of the Harvest Crusade, for the past 35 years, has been the proclamation of the Gospel," Laurie said. "When the invitation to follow Christ was given, so many people came forward that the Fire Marshals had to stop them, with others backed up in the aisles—a first for Angel Stadium."[21]

This is what happens when God calls and we answer.

Today, *Jesus Revolution* is resonating with Gen Alpha, Generation Z, and Millennials. Many are hungry for the same kind of love-based revival that swept through America in the late 1960s and '70s. *Jesus Revolution* reminds us that the Holy Spirit can at any time awaken a generation, and often with unexpected people.

THE CHOSEN: A CINEMATIC REVIVAL EVENT

We've watched *The Chosen* grow from a crowdfunded experiment into a global movement. With more than 770 million views and theatrical screenings of recent episodes, *The Chosen* has become one of the most watched TV series worldwide.[22]

In homes, theaters, and churches, people are watching the story of Jesus and His disciples come to life in a way they've never seen before. The series is giving believers a renewed passion for sharing their faith. Skeptics are being drawn into the gospel account. *The Chosen* has become one of the most powerful evangelistic tools of our time.

One of the most compelling aspects of *The Chosen* is the backstory. Few stories are as inspirational as the personal journey of Dallas Jenkins, creator of *The Chosen* and son of Jerry Jenkins, coauthor of the Left Behind series of fictional end-times thrillers that sold over 65 million copies.

After his last film, *The Resurrection of Gavin Stone*, bombed at the box office, Jenkins was devastated. Facing the potential end of his career, he and his wife decided to pray.[23]

That night, his wife told her husband that she felt God was telling her: "I do impossible math."[24]

They knew it was a reference to the story of Jesus feeding the five thousand (Matt. 14:13–21). They realized that their job wasn't to figure out how to multiply the loaves and fish. That's the miracle Jesus performed. Their job was to simply bring what they had to the table.

Later that night, Jenkins sat at his computer, mulling over what he thought he had done wrong. Then a Facebook message popped up. It was from a man named Alex, a casual acquaintance from years earlier.

"Remember, it's not your job to feed the 5,000," Alex wrote. "It's only to provide the loaves and fish."[25]

Dallas was stunned. This biblical story, the feeding of the five thousand, had been the focus of his and his wife's prayers.

Jenkins messaged Alex back: "Can I ask you why you said that to me?"[26]

Alex replied that he had resisted telling him, but God put it on his heart to tell him.

That was the turning point that helped launch *The Chosen*.

At the time, producing a crowdfunded, multi-season series about the life of Jesus seemed nearly impossible. But the message from Alex seemed like confirmation from heaven. It wasn't about success or failure. It was about obedience. Jenkins would provide the loaves and fish, and God would handle the math.

Today, people in every corner of the globe are watching *The Chosen*. The impact of Jenkins's obedience to God is staggering.

My wife and I recently watched Roumie's documentary on Amazon Prime, telling the story of how he was picked to play Jesus. Like Jenkins, we saw how raw and broken he was before *The Chosen*. He had only a small amount of money left in his bank account when Jenkins called him, asking if he'd like to play Jesus. Now it's become the role of a lifetime.

Many of the actors and actresses involved in the project have since shared testimonies of the impact of the series on their lives.

This is what happens when God calls ordinary people to extraordinary tasks. He's not asking us to feed five thousand. He's just asking us to bring what we have.

WHEN HOLLYWOOD BECOMES A PULPIT

For decades I, along with many others and the incredible team at the Hollywood Prayer Network, have been praying for revival in Hollywood. Today, I believe we are beginning to witness a faith-inspired media revolution starting to unfold.

What the entertainment industry is creating are catalysts for revival—from *The Chosen* to *House of David* to a TV series under development that will chronicle the first few centuries of Christianity. God is raising up often forgotten and "canceled" people in the entertainment industry who are now reaching tens of millions of people.

From streaming series to Hollywood blockbusters, this new wave of storytelling is helping fulfill the Great Commission in ways few could have imagined a decade ago.

For decades, many Christians considered Hollywood a taboo place for people of faith. For too long followers of Jesus shunned Hollywood, giving the devil free reign to influence the kinds of movies and TV shows the entertainment industry creates. The results were predictable—with most movies and TV shows filled with sex, violence, and occult-inspired content.

Over the years, I've spoken to and interviewed Christian producers, directors, screenwriters, actors, and actresses in Hollywood who told me that they believe the industry is a major demonic stronghold. One man said he had a terrifying dream in which he saw gigantic walls of darkness surrounding Hollywood.

> THE HOLY SPIRIT IS RAISING UP VOICES TO REACH THE WORLD, MAKING THESE CULTURAL DISRUPTERS POWERFUL AGENTS OF REVIVAL.

But something has shifted spiritually in a miraculous way that only the Holy Spirit could bring about. God is disrupting the status quo and raising up courageous witnesses of Christ in the entertainment industry.

Actors, actresses, producers, directors, rock stars, and influencers—some of the most iconic names in the world—are stepping into the spotlight, talking about their faith in Jesus, drawing the attention of millions of people.

The Holy Spirit is raising up voices to reach the world, making these cultural disrupters powerful agents of revival.

TRAILBLAZERS IN FAITH-BASED MOVIES

Jim Caviezel

"Jesus is as controversial now as he has ever been. Not much has changed in 2,000 years."[27]

Actor Jim Caviezel risked his career to portray Jesus in *The Passion of the Christ*. Since then, he's remained one of Hollywood's most courageous Christian voices, calling America to repentance and revival.

Mel Gibson

"I'm not a preacher, and I'm not a pastor. But I really feel my career was leading me to make *The Passion of the Christ*. The Holy Ghost was working through me on this film, and I was just directing traffic. I hope the film has the power to evangelize."[28]

Gibson has faced decades of backlash for making *The Passion of the Christ*. Yet he presses on. His upcoming film, *The Resurrection of the Christ*, may become one of the most daring gospel statements in cinematic history.

Jonathan Roumie

> I'm saying these words and hearing myself say them—I don't feel
> worthy to be saying them....And [Dallas Jenkins] puts his hand on my
> shoulder and he says, "Brother, none of us are truly worthy but here we
> are. I mean it's you and me. We're doing this that the world may know
> His story, those who haven't heard His story, we know the impact that
> He's had on the world and on our lives personally."...And I thought,
> "He's right. He's right. For whatever reason God saw fit to put me in
> that role and not somebody else."[29]

Before *The Chosen*, Roumie was nearly broke. His surrendering to God led to
the role of a lifetime, transforming not just his career but his walk with Christ,
helping inspire a global media revival.

Roma Downey and Mark Burnett

Roma Downey: "My faith is central to who I am so it plays a big role in
everything in my life. I am fortunate that much of my working life has been
about sharing inspiration and hope. I believe in God and am eager to share His
message of love with everyone."[30]

Mark Burnett: "Doing this 'on the screen' would allow millions of people to
discover the Bible. We knew we couldn't teach it, but we could create an emotionally connecting dramatization that might make them open [or reopen] the
Book....For that is what the Bible is. A story, the story of God's love for his
people, the greatest love story ever told."[31]

The creations of this Hollywood power couple—from *The Bible* miniseries to
the *Son of God* movie—have reached millions, proving that biblical stories can
captivate mainstream audiences.

ICONS COURAGEOUS ABOUT THEIR FAITH

Sylvester Stallone

"The character of *Rocky* was built on the idea that he was chosen to do something. That's why the first image in *Rocky* is the picture of Christ. This is a story of
faith, integrity and victory. Jesus is the inspiration for anyone to go the distance."[32]

Stallone's gratitude to Christ has surprised many. Known for *Rocky* and
Rambo, he now encourages his fellow stars to lean into faith in God, even under
the Hollywood spotlight.

Mark Wahlberg

"Obviously, you know, God didn't come to save the saints. He came to save the sinners. We've all had things and issues in our lives, and we want to be better versions of ourselves, and through focusing on my faith, it's allowed me to do that."[33]

Wahlberg's faith drives his life. He promotes fasting, morning prayer, and Catholic discipline as the antidote to Hollywood's culture of self-promotion.

Denzel Washington

> Number one: Put God first….Everything that I have is by the grace of God….Forty years ago…I was flunking out of college. I had a 1.7 grade point average….I was sitting in my mother's beauty shop….And I'm looking in the mirror and I see behind me this woman under the dryer and…she said, "Boy you are going to travel the world and speak to millions of people."…Well I have traveled the world and I have spoken to millions of people, but that's not the most important thing….I've kept God in my life and it's kept me humble. I didn't always stick with Him but He always stuck with me.[34]

Washington has long been open about his Christian faith, but in 2024 he took it a step further, obtaining his minister's license. Known for films like *The Book of Eli* and *The Equalizer*, Washington frequently speaks about the importance of prayer and listening to God's call on our lives.[35]

Matthew McConaughey

"First off, I want to thank God because that's who I look up to. He's graced my life with opportunities that I know are not of my hand or of any other human hand. He's shown me that it's a scientific fact that gratitude reciprocates."[36]

After a period of agnosticism early in his life, McConaughey has since gone public with his faith. In a 2025 interview with *Relevant* magazine he said, "I'm a believer. I believe in God."[37]

Jon Voight

"God is real, He knows us and is on our side….If I'm going to be a vessel for God, I better be cleaner than I was….I am afraid of offending God. Because God is everything. God is love. God is all these beautiful things, beauty, everything. And how can I live up to that? I need a lot of help. I think that is the fear of the Lord. It keeps you on track."[38]

Voight's interviews cut through political and generational lines, calling Americans to return to biblical values.

FAITH IN POP CULTURE

Chris Tucker

"I'm back to, you know, back to the stand-up comedy, man. And you're absolutely right. I'm from the Church of God in Christ. I was raised up [in the] Church of God in Christ....My mom used to make us go to church man, and I'm so glad she did. You know that made me who I am today, you know? I talk about it in my stand up, you know, being raised in church and all that good stuff man. But I've been having a great time."[39]

At the height of his career, the comedian and actor walked away from blockbuster roles to honor his Christian faith. Today, his comedy is clean and Christ-centered.

Alice Cooper

"Drinking beer is easy. Trashing your hotel room is easy. But being a Christian, that's a tough call. That's real rebellion."[40]

The original shock rocker now mentors young artists and speaks about his faith, showing that true rebellion is following Jesus Christ.

Hailey Bieber

"We're constantly evolving, especially in Jesus. Our relationship with Christ is going deeper and deeper....Where I was before I was a wife and who I was before I was a wife is not who I am now."[41]

Together with her husband, Justin Bieber, Hailey is part of a new wave of young celebrities working to make faith and family a priority.

Candace Cameron Bure

"My faith is the foundation of who I am. It is the compass by which I make all of my decisions in my life and career. My faith in Christ is not something I leave at the door when I go to work and only put on at home. It goes with me everywhere."[42]

From *Full House* to faith-based movies, Bure courageously shares her faith in an industry where that's often discouraged.

Dennis Quaid

"The most important thing is to be authentic. I'm a Christian. That's who I am....I have a personal relationship with [Jesus]."[43]

Quaid has overcome addiction and brokenness through faith in Christ. Today, he shares his testimony to help others.

SPORTS ICONS

Deion Sanders

"I'm not going to be ashamed of the Gospel. That's what my Bible tells me. And I'm going to proclaim my Lord and Savior Jesus Christ wherever I want to. Ain't nobody gonna tell me not to give love and respect to my Lord and Savior that has blessed me, has pulled me up from suicidal thoughts, and a multiplicity of things that you don't know."[44]

"Coach Prime" doesn't just want to build winning teams; he's helping raise up disciples of Christ. Sanders, a former NFL athlete nicknamed "Prime Time," is now a college football coach known as "Coach Prime" who openly leads his players in prayer.

Tim Tebow

"I don't know what my future holds, but I know who holds my future."[45] From Heisman Trophy winner to NFL quarterback to missionary, Tebow's courage to share his faith in Christ on and off the field continues to inspire millions.

Nick Foles

"To me, relationship in Christ is a relationship, not a religion, and I'm just grateful for it. God always has a plan; you just got to trust it."[46] After leading the Philadelphia Eagles to a Super Bowl victory, Foles gave credit to God. His humility under pressure set a standard for what winning looks like.

THE CELEBRITY REVIVAL

These celebrities aren't claiming to be perfect; they're thanking God for His amazing grace. Their courage is disrupting Hollywood norms, inspiring curiosity in Jesus among millions of their fans. What's happening is bigger than the testimonies of Hollywood stars. It signals a tectonic shift in the culture of influence. From rock legends to A-list actors, filmmakers to comedians, athletes to tech moguls, these cultural icons are bringing Christ into the public square. In my interview with him, international prophetic voice Joseph Z commented:

> I believe we are in the...next Great Awakening. In other words, it's not about to happen. It is happening. And that happens every so often. Revival is history. As you know, people begin to experience revival and many times they don't even know they're in the middle of it. In other words, there's so many things going on that are distractions with the culture, the narrative of society, and yet there is an awakening....

Should Jesus tarry, I believe we will look back at this season and realize what a Great Awakening we were in.

We recently saw the passing of [Black Sabbath frontman and reality TV star] Ozzy Osborne, and there's reports coming out that he received a Bible and began to hear the gospel right before the end. Now, only the Lord knows what happened, but that is quite a testament to the fact that we are in a different time than we once were. So yes, I believe we're in a Great Awakening. I believe that we are seeing revival nationwide. We just have to have eyes to see, ears to hear, and hearts that discern what's actually happening. It is taking place right now.[47]

This isn't the revival the church expected, but it's the awakening the Holy Spirit is inspiring. The testimonies of these celebrities are helping to create a ripple effect of spiritual hunger around the world.

The question is: Will the church recognize this moment, rise to the occasion, and help disciple the millions of mostly young people now coming to faith in Jesus? Evangelist Taylan Michael Seaman, founder of Revival Way Ministries, said:

Oh my goodness, if the church won't respond, God will pick anybody. God chose a donkey [to speak] when He couldn't get a prophet [to obey Him; see Numbers 22:21–39]....I love the church of the Lord Jesus Christ, and there's a lot of phenomenal churches out there, but...the reality is there's a lot of pastors, ministers, evangelists, and people in church who think God needs them more than they need God.

God does not need you. God will use you if you lay down your life, but [He] does not need you. He always has a remnant. And if there's no remnant available, He will go find people like Trump...Joe Rogan...all these celebrities that are being radically saved....God used a man like [Elon Musk] to [bring] freedom of speech back into social media, back into America, which really, no matter how you slice and dice it, shifted the entire election and saved the United States of America from what could have been, honestly, some form of destruction.[48]

In the words of the apostle Paul: "I tell you, now is the time of God's favor, now is the day of salvation" (2 Cor. 6:2).

CHAPTER 8

THE ALPHA AND GEN Z AWAKENING

I think the enemy overplayed his hand and tried to isolate and rage and divide and confuse a generation. And I think God is moving. People are realizing secular progressivism is empty and hollow, and people are looking for meaning and truth and faith. So you're seeing a great returning, and I think that's just going to continue.
—WORSHIP LEADER SEAN FEUCHT IN AN INTERVIEW FOR *THE INSPIRE SHOW* WITH TROY ANDERSON.[1]

The tyrant dies and his rule is over, the martyr dies and his rule begins.
—SOREN KIERKEGAARD, *THE JOURNALS OF KIERKEGAARD*[2]

FEW PEOPLE HAVE influenced Generations Z and Alpha like the late Charlie Kirk. As the founder of Turning Point USA, he was not only a popular conservative activist but a mobilizer of young people who long for truth in a time of confusion. His voice carried weight because it spoke to the heart of their anxieties and hopes, challenging them to embrace Jesus Christ and the cause of freedom and liberty.

Barna Group research shows Generation Z is both the most digitally connected and one of the most spiritually searching generations in modern history.[3] They are skeptical of institutions, yet increasingly open to authentic encounters with God. Faith leaders such as Greg Laurie have observed that "Something is happening with this young generation. They are really hungry for spiritual truth."[4]

Kirk understood this. He didn't soften his message to appeal to the culture. Instead, he spoke with courage, embodying the kind of fearless faith that is inspiring a new generation of designated disrupters.

In announcing "The American Comeback Tour" on February 11, 2025, Kirk said, "The American comeback is powerful and real, and it's sweeping the nation. However, one of the last strongholds of far-left, increasingly insane and out-of-touch ideologues is found inside the formerly hallowed halls of higher education. We have many of these purveyors of anti-American indoctrination on the run, but when they regroup, they will do so from inside the academy. So we will take the fight to them. America's students are still only given one side of the story, the leftwing side, so we intend to continue balancing the scales and equipping local students to fight for their values. If you're a progressive, you get to come to the front of the line and make your best argument, and I'll make mine, as TPUSA celebrates the free exchange of ideas."[5]

Kirk saw that winning the next generation was essential to the future of America and the church. His ability to bring together thousands of students at campuses across the nation demonstrated that the next generation is not lost to apathy or secularism but is rather on the brink of revival.

He also reminded young leaders of the personal cost of conviction: "I want to be remembered for courage for my faith…the most important thing is my faith in my life," Kirk said.[6]

His tragic death has become a galvanizing moment for a generation.

As Generations Z and Alpha navigate a world defined by political division and cultural upheaval, Kirk's legacy challenges them to rise with courage. His life and death are a heroic example to a new wave of leaders courageously declaring the gospel in schools, universities, and the online world. The future of America may very well rest in the hands of these young disrupters, empowered by the Holy Spirit, and guided by those who went before them.

A PROPHETIC TURNING POINT FOR GENERATIONS Z AND ALPHA

The spiritual hunger among Generations Z and Alpha is unmistakable. Into this pivotal moment stepped Kirk, who mobilized millions of young people through Turning Point USA.

From stadium gatherings to campus chapters, his message awakened a generation to the reality that faith and courage must be lived publicly.

Then, on September 10, 2025, at Utah Valley University, Kirk was in mid-debate when an assassin's bullet struck him down. Law enforcement officials declared it an act of political assassination. For millions of students and families, a prophetic voice had been silenced, yet Kirk's message could not be stopped.

Only a few days after his death, Charlie's wife, Erika Kirk, emerged as a leader of her generation. "You have no idea the fire that you have ignited within this wife. The cries of this widow will echo around the world like a battle cry," she declared.[7] Her words spread as quickly as the news of his death, inspiring millions of people.

A special memorial event in Kirk's honor took place September 21, 2025, at the State Farm Stadium in Glendale, Arizona, with 90,000 to 100,000 people in attendance and millions watching on television or online.[8]

"I challenge the ministers out there to talk about what the Bible says and not what the leftists say," Ben Carson, former Secretary of Housing and Urban Development, told attendees at the "Charlie Kirk Remembrance: A Life Well Lived" memorial. "And get on board, get on board of the revival that is coming. We are not going to be able to stop it."[9]

Kirk's legacy is what the Holy Spirit is using to inspire a new generation to pick up his mantle and join the revival movement.

"I believe that Charlie is a modern-day prophet," said Andrew Kolvet, executive producer of *The Charlie Kirk Show* and one of Kirk's longtime friends. "Prophets go into a culture, into a town, into a city, and they call it to repent. And if you don't want to repent, then you're not going to like that message.... [Kirk] was a guy that confronted evil head-on. He didn't pull punches. He said exactly what the truth was. And if you don't want to hear the truth, you will despise the truth, and that's why they despised Charlie."[10]

Charlie's martyrdom and Erika's rising leadership illustrate how God is raising up young disrupters to change history.

"The world needs Turning Point USA," Erika said at the event. "It needs a group that will point young people away from the path of misery and sin. It needs something that will lead people away from hell in this world and in the next. It needs young people pointed in the direction of truth and beauty, and so I promise you today every part of our work will become greater....Charlie and I were united in purpose. His passion was my passion, and now his mission is my mission. Everything that Turning Point USA built through Charlie's vision and hard work, we will make ten times greater through the power of his memory."[11]

At the end of her speech, in a heartfelt moment that seemed to fulfill Kim Clement's prophecy that a modern-day Esther would bring the "oil of gladness" and healing to America, she forgave her husband's alleged assassin, Tyler Robinson, helping to diffuse the division, hatred, and violence permeating society.

"I forgive him because it was what Christ did and is what Charlie would do," she said. "The answer to hate is not hate. The answer we know from the gospel is love and always love. Love for our enemies, and love for those who persecute us."[12]

THE JESUS EFFECT: THE MISSION CONTINUES

Amid Erika's grief over her husband's death, the movement Charlie helped build is growing exponentially. *The Charlie Kirk Show* continues to broadcast, reaching millions with the unapologetic truth of the gospel.

At the memorial, President Trump described Kirk as a "giant of his generation and above all, a devoted husband, father, son, Christian, and patriot."[13]

"He was violently killed because he spoke for freedom and justice, for God, country, for reason, and for common sense," Trump said. "He was assassinated because he lived bravely, he led boldly, and he argued brilliantly without apology. He did what was right for our nation. And so on that terrible day, September 10, 2025, our greatest evangelist for American liberty became immortal. He's a martyr now for American freedom. I know I speak for everyone here today when I say that none of us will ever forget Charlie Kirk, and neither now will history. Because while Charlie has been reunited with his Creator in heaven, his voice on earth will echo through the generations and his name will live forever in the eternal chronicle of America's greatest patriots. He will live forever.

"To Charlie's incredible and beautiful widow, Erika, we know the weight of this monumental loss is almost unbearable. But even in the midst of heartache and pain, too great to even fathom, you have somehow found the strength and deep faith to be a comfort to millions and millions of people. And thank you very much, Erika. Thank you very much. Today, an entire nation wraps its loving arms around you and your beautiful children. We share in your immense and overwhelming sorrow, and we vow that we will do everything we can to ensure that your children grow up in a land where their father is honored and revered as a great American hero. That's what he is."

Trump said he would posthumously award Kirk the Presidential Medal of Freedom at the White House.[14]

"Charlie Kirk started with only an idea to change minds on college campuses, and instead he ended up with a far greater achievement: changing history," Trump said. "The lesson of Charlie's life is that you should never underestimate what one person can do with a good heart, a righteous cause, a cheerful spirit, and the will to fight, fight, fight....

"Today Charlie Kirk rests in glory in heaven for all eternity....We grieve for the friend and leader that we have lost, but we go forward, strengthened by his faith...and inspired by his example to defend the country he lived for, for the freedoms he died for, and the values in which he so deeply believed."[15]

A MOVEMENT OF YOUNG PEOPLE CRYING OUT TO GOD

Today, revival isn't just breaking out at memorial events, stadiums, beaches, rooftops, and on the streets. It's also unfolding on TikTok feeds, viral YouTube videos, livestreamed prayer sessions, and even the gaming universe.

The generations many assumed would drift away from Jesus Christ—Generation Z and Generation Alpha—are leading today's faith revolution, many of them inspired by Kirk's courageous example.

Corné J. Bekker, dean of the School of Divinity at Regent University, said:

> We are seeing in the United States...[and] really all around the world a movement of young people crying out to God and coming to the Lord in the thousands if not hundreds of thousands. We are seeing a sea of young people surrendering their lives to the Lord. You see this in movements like The Send and other places where young people are crying out to God and saying, "Here I am, send me" [Isa. 6:8]....We are seeing this movement on university campuses, we're seeing it in churches, and we're seeing it in the formation of new churches....What's amazing to me is that [most of] the people that are coming are under the age of 25...so where for decades we saw young people leaving the faith, we are seeing the beginning of a reversal of this.[16]

In many cases, young people are not discovering Jesus in traditional ways. They're finding Him through videos and podcasts on their smartphones. From TikTok evangelists to YouTube preachers, from Discord discipleship groups to repentance podcasts, this new wave of awakening is changing the rules of evangelism.

And with the loss of trust in the mainstream media—what President Trump calls "fake news" or the "enemy of the people"—the road has been paved for something unforeseen: a youth-led, technology-powered revival.[17]

"If we look at the trends, right now we're seeing some of the major platforms that have been filled with disinformation...get defunded," international prophetic voice Joseph Z said. "We're seeing different celebrity voices lose their platforms. Even network television is shaking....We're seeing that shaking because people have access to [unfiltered and unbiased] information [on YouTube, podcasts, etc.]."[18]

Amid this sea change in how people consume media, God is raising up young podcasters, influencers, and revivalists who are harnessing the digital revolution to help fulfill the Great Commission.

"I like to say it this way: 'God's going to raise up the outcast, turn 'em into a broadcast with a podcast,' and we're going to see so much of that come forward and…bring truth to the culture," Joseph Z said. "This is the age of information and God wants the truth out. So I believe that's why He's doing it. He's using those who have a heart and a conviction to follow His truth in government, the church, the marketplace, and entertainment….The Word of the Lord will not be chained. It will come forward. So it's part of this [new] Great Awakening. It really is."[19]

While standing inside Trump Tower in 2015, Joseph Z asked God what the future held.

"The Lord spoke to me and said that the young lions would come," he said. "I believe this is that generation—Gen Alpha. They will live up to their name; they really will."[20]

"YOUNG LIONS" ON THE DIGITAL MISSION FIELD

> Therefore go and make disciples of all nations, baptizing them in the name of the Father and of the Son and of the Holy Spirit, and teaching them to obey everything I have commanded you. And surely I am with you always, to the very end of the age.
>
> —MATTHEW 28:19–20

The Great Commission has never been confined to a particular place or region. From a hillside in Galilee to Europe's gothic cathedrals to America's frontier meeting houses to Asia's underground churches, the Good News of Jesus Christ has overcome many barriers. Today, the mission field is expanding into the digital world.

YOUNG PEOPLE ARE NOT DISCOVERING JESUS IN TRADITIONAL WAYS.

YouTube, Instagram, and TikTok are the new frontiers of evangelism and have become digital gateways for people to encounter God. Just as Johannes Gutenberg's printing press placed the Bible in the hands of the masses, algorithms are now carrying the gospel into the lives of a generation seeking purpose, meaning, and a connection to the divine.

We are witnessing a new reformation. The pulpit is no longer fixed; it's mobile, embedded in reels, comment threads, and live streams.[21]

"While screen time, apps and global connectivity are advances that older generations had to learn and adapt to, young adults have been raised knowing little else," Barna CEO David Kinnaman said. "It's to be expected that as technology transforms society, impacting even the simplest of daily activities, younger generations will find new ways to harness these tools—including for spiritual growth, faith sharing and church engagement."[22]

Why is digital evangelism so effective? One word: Authenticity. Generations Alpha and Z aren't looking for polished sermons. They are looking for what is real. In a world of curated personas, a testimony filmed on a shaky smartphone has more power than a carefully staged production.

During a time of shrinking attention spans, short videos have become highly popular. A 45-second reel can lead to a midnight salvation. A YouTube comment thread can turn into an online prayer room. Sean Dunn, founder of Groundwire Ministry, said:

> It's because the people…are desperate because they're discovering what they have been relying on is empty, void, and doesn't work. Young people are waking up and they're not saying, "I'm going to hell." They're waking up and saying, "I'm going through hell." And when they go through struggles and challenges, they run usually to entertainment and bad decisions. But what they're really looking for is the peace…that passes all understanding [Phil. 4:7]. They're looking for joy. We know the joy that is indescribable and full of glory, and they're searching for these things—these meaningful relationships—and we know the One who never leaves. Everything that they crave Jesus offers.[23]

To watch my interview with Sean Dunn, scan the QR code or visit TroyAndersonBooks.com/dunn.

By uploading poignant videos to social media platforms that address the challenges young people are experiencing, Dunn said they are seeing hundreds of thousands of people reaching out to their online volunteers and asking questions like, "How can I have a meaningful relationship, because everybody takes advantage of me?"[24]

> We use disruptive media to connect with their pain, connect with their crisis, suggest Jesus is the answer, and then invite them into a conversation. And that's really kind of the secret sauce that is helping them understand that God is relevant. This is crazy, but the majority of the alternative media would want us to think that the majority of people in our nation are atheists. They're not. They believe in God; they just

ignore Him. And because they believe in God, we don't need to convince them that God is real. We need to remind them that He's relevant. He becomes relevant the moment that He intersects with whatever crisis they're going through. I wish that young people were waking up and saying, "How do I get to heaven?" Most of them are saying, "How do I get through the day?" And so if you meet them [where they are], then you can also introduce Jesus as the eternal solution that they need to consider.[25]

TIKTOK EVANGELISTS AND VIRAL REVIVAL MOMENTS

"And those who are wise shall shine like the brightness of the sky above; and those who turn many to righteousness, like the stars forever and ever" (Dan. 12:3, ESV).

In a time when the truth is drowned out amid the digital noise, a wave of young evangelists is rising—the "young lions" Joseph Z foresaw, shining from bedrooms, dorm rooms, and dashboards lit by LED lights. As the prophet Daniel foretold, the wise are leading many to Christ, one video at a time.

We are seeing the rise of digital evangelists, not seminary-trained but smartphone-equipped and empowered by the Holy Spirit. Their message is powerful: Jesus saves, heals, and transforms lives.

"I didn't grow up in the Christian church by any means," evangelist Taylan Michael Seaman said. "I grew up about as far away from God as you really could get. My family didn't serve the Lord. I never heard the gospel properly preached to me other than one time when I was 12 years old. But other than that, I did not hear it again until I was 21....I was an absolute heathen [who] ended up going to a Christian college somehow....I went on a football scholarship."[26]

While playing football in college, Seaman got injured, became hooked on painkillers, and began drinking alcohol on a regular basis.

> I found myself in a position where at 20 years old, I could not have a conversation normally with somebody unless I had alcohol in my system. And I found myself not able to sleep at night or do my homework unless I had Adderall in my system or Percocet or Hydrocodone. So, basically, I was a 20-year-old drug addict and alcoholic without really even knowing it, and I was stuck in a very, very dark place. It was in that time...when I hit rock bottom, I called out to God.
>
> I had a faithful man who had been mentoring me in business a bit.... And he would every once in a while slip in the gospel if I had a problem. He would say, "Oh, well the Bible says this." And at first it didn't really click with me, I would just notice, "Oh, he must be a Christian. It's

their job. They kind of have to mention the Bible." But he was a great guy and...I actually felt good when I was around him. And so because I felt good, I wanted to be around him more. Little did I know that was the presence of God, but I came to find out about a year later....

One day he finally brought me to a breaking point more or less and said, "Hey, today is your day and the gospel requires us to make a decision. I've been mentoring you for a little over a year now, and the Bible says you're either all in or you're all out. And I think right now you need to make the decision of whether or not you want to fully give your life to Jesus." And in that moment, I believed—and him, me, and God as my witness—he baptized me in the black hills of South Dakota in a pool. I went under a dead man, and I came back up alive under Christ.[27]

Since then, Seaman said his "life shifted" and "everything changed." About a year later, he was baptized in the Holy Spirit and knew he was called to go into full-time evangelism.[28]

Ever since then, the early months of 2019, I have been preaching the gospel primarily full time. And although I was kicked out of college twice before I got saved—we call that a double portion as Christians—I ended up going back to school when I was saved and filled with the Holy Spirit and realized that the theological degree that I was going after didn't necessarily carry what I thought it carried. See, before I got saved, I thought all Christians were the same. But then once I got filled with the Spirit, I realized that that's not exactly how it is. I realized there was some...family drama in the body of Christ. And so I actually ended up dropping out of college and went into full-time evangelism. And I've been doing that now for the last five years as a full-time evangelist.[29]

Testimonies like Seaman's of freedom from addiction, anxiety, gender confusion, and suicidal despair are widespread today. Hashtags like #JesusTok, #FaithStory, and #ChristianTikTok have garnered millions of views. Why? Because in a world saturated with fake personas, the power of real encounters with the Holy Spirit is what young people are searching for.

A 45-SECOND REEL CAN LEAD TO A MIDNIGHT SALVATION.

The impact isn't just online. Teenagers are watching gospel clips, walking into churches, and giving their lives to Jesus. Atheists are binge-watching testimonies and accepting Christ. Baptisms are taking place in bathtubs. Bible studies are forming in DMs. Group chats are turning into fasting chains.

Drawn by the Holy Spirit in their digital universe, Generations Alpha and Z are so hungry for Jesus that many are now showing up at crusades, churches, and other events, looking for a touch from God. One man who couldn't get into the July 2025 Harvest Crusade even climbed over Angel Stadium's fence in Anaheim, California, to get saved. Pastor Greg Laurie said the man is a "symbol of Gen Z right now," remarking:

> Something is happening with this young generation....They have access to more tools and information than ever before, yet they are called The Hopeless Generation....But what we just saw at the Harvest Crusade is so encouraging. This generation of young people showed up in droves! Gen Z is reaching out to God.[30]

The mainstream media has largely ignored this phenomenon, but a global move of God is taking place. The Holy Spirit is flooding the platforms once blamed for spiritual apathy and using them to call the prodigals home. This is the revival we never saw coming. And it's already here, one clip and once fence jumper at a time.

DIGITAL EVANGELISM

> How, then, can they call on the one they have not believed in? And how can they believe in the one of whom they have not heard? And how can they hear without someone preaching to them?
>
> —ROMANS 10:14

While long videos are good for discipleship, it's often short videos that open the door to the gospel. Platforms like Instagram Reels, YouTube Shorts, and TikTok have become places where young people hear testimonies and become fascinated with Jesus. In sixty seconds or less, the Holy Spirit is reaching young people, inspiring repentance, and awakening a generation that scrolls more than it sits in churches.

For Generations Z and Alpha, these platforms have become mission fields. With many young people not attending church, the digital world has become a powerful tool for spreading the Word of God.

Brock Eastman, branding director for "The Action Bible," told *The 700 Club*: "We like to think about...bringing the Bible to life in a different way for this generation…with graphic novels. This Bible appeals to them because they like that kind of, 'Oh, I can see the images of the story moving and there's a narrative.'"[31]

Today, many of the voices reaching young people aren't pastors or theologians. They're young believers, storytellers, and Spirit-filled digital creators—speaking the language of their generation.

Here are a couple of them:

- **Isaiah Saldivar**, a courageous leader in deliverance and spiritual warfare, reaches millions across YouTube, TikTok, and Instagram. He hosts a weekly podcast called "Revival Lifestyle" that is in the top 1 percent of podcasts in the world. He is calling his generation to awaken to the reality of the supernatural and the authority of the believer.[32]

- **Jenny Weaver**, once a "homeless drug addict, self-cutting Wiccan," encountered Jesus and never looked back. Her powerful testimony has inspired viral live streams of worship, prayer, and revival. Now leading a global online community, Weaver embodies the redemptive power of the gospel.[33]

PODCAST PROPHETS AND YOUTUBE REVIVALISTS

While short reels inspire curiosity, longer videos help cultivate deeper growth in the Lord. YouTube channels and podcasts offer a place for conversations about faith, discipleship, and purpose.

According to Edison Research, 63 percent of Americans ages 13–24 listened to a podcast in the month prior to the survey. They're not just listening for entertainment. Many are seeking meaning and guidance in life.[34]

"As a Gen Z'er and a researcher at Edison, I can say this with confidence: audio isn't just what we listen to—it's how we make sense of who we are and escape the chaos of daily life," Edison Research's Manager of Research Salma Aly said. "Things are getting real—sometimes too real—and audio is helping us cope. In fact, 63 percent of Gen Z agree that audio helps them get through difficult times."[35]

Here are a few young podcasters:

- **Ruslan KD**, a Christian hip-hop artist turned cultural commentator, addresses faith, politics, and worldview through his popular YouTube channel. Of Armenian descent, he was a refugee from Azerbaijan when he moved to the United States as a child. His commentary challenges young adults to live a life grounded in the Bible.[36]

- **Tim Ross**, through his show *The Basement*, hosts Spirit-led interviews that explore the human soul. Honest and emotionally raw, the podcaster and social media influencer covers taboo topics with wisdom and humility.[37]

- **Allie Beth Stuckey's** *Relatable* podcast helps young women rise above cultural confusion. A wife and mother of three, she's a courageous voice for biblical womanhood. Author of the *New York Times* bestseller *Toxic Empathy: How Progressives Exploit Christian Compassion,* she speaks regularly at churches about the importance of political engagement and combating the lies of progressivism.[38]

HOW THE COLLAPSE OF LEGACY MEDIA IS CHANGING EVERYTHING

"See, the former things have taken place, and new things I declare; before they spring into being I announce them to you" (Isa. 42:9).

We are living in a seismic prophetic shift, a time when the influence of legacy media is receding and new platforms are rising to tell the truth. For generations, the mainstream media set the agenda and molded society.

But today, God is raising up unexpected voices to speak not through corporate media but digital streams. What was once a stronghold of control—media gatekeepers—is being replaced by a decentralized move of God.

Traditional media is in decline. The credibility once held by media outlets like CNN, MSNBC, ABC, and even Fox News has eroded to historic lows, especially among younger people. According to Gallup and Pew Research, Millennials and Generation Z are not turning to cable news for information. Today, just 16 percent of Generation Z have a "great deal" or "quite a lot" of trust in the news media.[39]

Instead, young people are flocking to YouTube, Spotify, Substack, Rumble, and TikTok. They are hungry for truth that's uncensored and free from corporate and globalist control.

As a journalist for several decades, I've seen firsthand how stories about faith and religion were often dismissed by editors as unnewsworthy. In other cases, reporters and editors would put their own spin on religious news, often with a subtle tone of mockery.

But that era is over. The mainstream media's power and control is in decline. In their place stands a wide-open digital world. Now, anyone with a smartphone and a message can reach millions.

Today, a new generation of believers is rising with the fire of the Holy Spirit. They're preaching Christ and reaching hearts where it matters most—on the platforms young people pay attention to.

The decline of the mainstream media hasn't just created a vacuum. It has opened a door for the gospel, and God is filling it with revolutionary voices of truth.

NEW VOICES FILLING THE VOID

Today, many influencers are using their platforms to awaken a generation to the love of Christ. Some of these figures include:

Sean Feucht

Founder of the *Let Us Worship* movement, Feucht emerged as a courageous voice during the lockdowns, leading outdoor worship gatherings that went viral. This included an iconic march over the Golden Gate Bridge in San Francisco at the beginning of the COVID-19 pandemic. While playing the guitar and singing to the crowd, "God birthed a movement…with a 'Gideon-sized' army that refused to back down from fear and governmental tyranny. A new era of church BOLDNESS was born and a revival that would sweep across America!" Often shunned by the media, Feucht turned to alternative platforms and social media to broadcast his outdoor gatherings, helping inspire a spiritual resistance against tyranny in cities across the country.[40]

Mike Signorelli

A pastor and revivalist, Mike Signorelli reaches millions through YouTube, Facebook, and Rumble. Known for his teaching on deliverance and spiritual warfare, he is equipping a new generation to walk in freedom and biblical authority. The founding pastor of V1 Church, V1 College, and V1 Community Impact, he and his wife regularly host marriage conferences.[41]

A GENERATION CRAVING TRUTH AND BOLDNESS

Today, traditional broadcasters are being replaced by Holy Spirit–led believers using the latest technologies to help fulfill the Great Commission.

Revival today is digitally driven, global in scale, and unstoppable. Podcasts, livestreams, and Substack newsletters are bypassing gatekeepers to deliver the raw gospel truth to a generation hungry for what's real. Joseph Z said:

> One of the favorite things of this generation is to watch debates that bring intellectual stimulation where there's outcomes. That's why Charlie Kirk is so successful in what he does….So for the pastors, for the leaders, what you need to do is not be afraid to talk about politics in the pulpit. You need to be not afraid to talk about moral issues directly in the pulpit. You need to not hold back on this generation. They're craving truth and they're craving boldness. And if pastors and leaders will simply, for lack of a better word, stop preaching pretty-pretty-pony gospel messages, and start standing up and preaching the truth of the gospel—be not afraid to confront the culture and deal with things head on—you're going to see young men and women that are looking for that mentorship, that leadership, line up behind you and follow you. And that is God's way. I believe that's something we need to really encourage our pastors to do.[42]

If the church doesn't recognize this, we risk missing a revival that's already breaking out—not in the pews, but in pixels. Generations Z and Alpha aren't waiting for platforms; they're building them. YouTube, TikTok, and Discord have become modern sanctuaries where lives are changed and the gospel moves at the speed of bytes.

CONTENT CREATORS BECOME CHAPTERS OF CULTURE

"Their voice has gone out into all the earth, their words to the ends of the world" (Rom. 10:18).

We are witnessing what the apostle Paul foretold two millennia ago—the gospel spreading around the globe via smartphones and other new technologies. In this prophetic hour, God is raising up a new breed of messengers, not defined by titles but by their anointing.

These content creators aren't just feeding the algorithm; they're feeding souls in the ever-scrolling landscape of social media. They've become trusted guides and relationship mentors.

A couple of influencers in this digital reformation include:

Tovares and Safa Grey (Godly Dating 101)

Through reels, memes, and honesty, the husband-and-wife team of Tovares and Safa Grey offer biblical relationship advice to a generation navigating love and purity in a hookup culture. Authors of *Godly Dating 101: Discover the Truth About Relationships in a World That Constantly Lies,* their content is helping draw singles into Christ-centered conversations about dating and marriage.[43]

Emily Wilson Hussem

With compassion and conviction, Emily Wilson Hussem, a YouTuber, author, wife, and mother, encourages young women to embrace purity and Christ-centered living. Her reels are filled with biblical wisdom on faith, dating, and motherhood.[44]

GAMING: THE REVIVAL YOU DIDN'T SEE COMING

"I have become all things to all people so that by all possible means I might save some" (1 Cor. 9:22).

In this new era, revival isn't just preached—it's played. For Generations Z and Alpha, gaming is a retreat where friendships are formed and revival is taking place.

From Twitch streams to metaverse churches, Fortnite to Minecraft, the gospel is spreading in these virtual realms, meeting a generation where they live and play.

Christian gamers are turning voice chats into prayer meetings. Salvation stories are unfolding between Roblox rounds. Discord servers are filling with testimonies. Faith is showing up in pixels, prayer emojis, and livestream intercession. The church has left the building and entered the game.

Nick Yeh grew up playing video games. Like many people born in the 1990s, he remembers his first Gameboy Color, loading up Pokémon Blue, playing Smash and Double Dash on GameCube, and playing Halo with his youth pastor.[45] Yeh, now a volunteer for InterVarsity Christian Fellowship, says:

> Playing video games helped me develop a relationship with [Jesus]....I've found ways that gaming can be a part of joining God in mission. I queue up in public lobbies in Call of Duty and I talk to other players online. I share a bit about my story and try to find ways to share who Jesus is in my life....I believe that gaming can be a form of ministry. It can teach us to embrace places of discomfort and to love one another in that.[46]

An innovative type of missionary is arising—armed with today's hi-tech armor of God (Eph. 6:10–18)—the gaming controller. They're ministering through Minecraft, discipling in Discord, and preaching through PlayStation. On platforms like YouTube Gaming, Twitch, and VR spaces, they're leading worship, hosting Bible studies, praying for their fellow gamers, and bringing the gospel into the digital world where millions are gathering.

What once looked like escapism has become a mission field. For countless Generation Z and Alpha youth, this may be their first and only encounter with the transformative message of Christ.

The Barna Group found 41 percent of teenagers have never opened the Bible and just 20 percent read Scripture weekly.[47] Today, only 4 percent of Generation Z have a biblical worldview, yet 88 percent play video games.[48] However, independent game developers are looking to turn the tide.

In the Bible-themed video game Gate Zero, players—living in 2072 when a global authoritarian regime controls all information, suppressing the Bible—travel through time to explore ancient Israel circa AD 30, completing missions, evading capture, and unraveling "riddles that reveal profound truths."[49]

"We really want to dive into creating a video game for the younger generation to be able to experience Jesus and to be able to get familiar with the stories and the events from the Bible," said Arve Solli, head of Bible X, the developer of Gate Zero. "This game might be the only Bible some people read, so that's basically what we want to do. We want to take players back—back to origin, back to zero and make them able to dive into this huge world of the biblical stories and events."[50]

From Roblox to VRChat, worship services, baptisms, and prayer gatherings are taking place in these immersive virtual worlds. What was once considered digital fantasy is now fertile ground for sharing faith.

In the heart of gaming platforms and metaverse spaces, young people are discovering the Bible. These aren't just games. They've become the new town squares for a searching generation.

If the church ignores this digital frontier, we risk losing a generation. It may not look like what we expected to happen, but it's exactly where God promised He would be: wherever the people are.

DISCIPLING A DIGITAL AWAKENING

The Alpha and Generation Z revival is flourishing now. The gospel is going viral but momentum and excitement over something new isn't enough. Like the seed in shallow soil (Matt. 13:5–6), faith without depth withers. If we stop at views and shares, we'll miss the great harvest God intends.

The opportunity is unprecedented. One Spirit-filled clip can reach millions.

As Scripture declares, "Their voice has gone out into all the earth" (Rom. 10:18). Generation Z craves powerful worship, honest testimonies, and the truth.

But viral faith can be shallow. Spiritual soundbites stir emotions but rarely transform lives. The apostle Paul's words contain great wisdom: "Preach the word; be prepared in season and out of season; correct, rebuke and encourage—with great patience and careful instruction" (2 Tim. 4:2). Discipleship requires Bible reading, community, and accountability.

This is a wake-up call for the church. Don't just count clicks and views. Shepherd these young souls, find mentors for them, ground this generation in the Word of God, and encourage real-life fellowship.

Generations Z and Alpha aren't waiting; many of them are leading this revival. "In the last days, God says, 'I will pour out my Spirit on all people. Your sons and daughters will prophesy, your young men will see visions...'" (Acts 2:17).

Revival is happening. The only question is whether we will disciple them or miss what God is doing.

Joseph Z offered this wisdom on how followers of Christ can get in alignment with what the Holy Spirit is doing and help evangelize and disciple new believers:

> I like to say it this way: Every believer on a micro level, in their individual walk, needs to read the Bible until it starts talking back to 'em. That's number one. Number two, they need to be filled with the Holy Spirit. They need to be filled with the Spirit of God and spend long amounts of time in prayer. You do your part and then collectively the body of Christ does its part....The body of Christ is called to be the number one superpower in the world. We can impact nations, we can impact society...and we will see the goodness of the Lord.[51]

CHAPTER 9

PROPHETS, PRESIDENTS, AND AMERICA'S DEFINING HOUR

I looked through the tunnel and then I could hear them singing even louder, "From glory to glory." And I asked the Father, "What is this?" And He said, "This is the Great Cloud of Witnesses."
—BRANDON BIGGS IN A VISION OF THE GREAT CLOUD OF WITNESSES[1]

I N A POWERFUL live stream that opened with him singing and worshipping the Lord in his home, prophetic watchman Brandon Biggs described a heavenly vision in which he heard the Lord speak audibly: "I'm here, Brandon."

The presence of God filled the room with a tangible presence so thick that his wife, Diana, collapsed to the floor, weeping, overcome by the fragrance of the Lord—the scent of honeysuckle.

As he continued to worship, Biggs heard the voices of heaven join in—a heavenly choir of saints singing, "From glory to glory, He's changing us, changing us."

Brandon then saw a tunnel open in front of him, glowing with colors like cotton candy—pastel purples, pinks, and blues. Drawn through it, he entered what he described as a heavenly realm where the "great cloud of witnesses" (Heb. 12:1) was gathered in prayer.

"I said to Him, 'What are they doing?' And He said to me, 'Brandon, this is a prayer group.' I said, 'A prayer group in heaven? Why are they praying?' He said, 'Brandon, they're praying on assignment for the revival that's about to take place on the Earth.' He said, 'They're assisting you.'"[2]

God told Biggs a "great move of My presence" was coming, pouring out His Spirit in a "mighty revival." He saw tens of thousands born again in Minnesota, with revival "hotspots" spreading nationwide. "The bluer the state, the greater the harvest," the Lord told him, showing hotspots in California, Oregon, Washington, and Nevada. The revival, God said, would be like popcorn: "That's the way this next revival is going to be....They're going to be popping up all over the place."

God warned it would not be controlled like Asbury, Brownsville, or other revivals: "They try to limit God and how He's doing things," Biggs said. "The

Lord said, 'You're not going to corral what's about to happen with your Pharisee thinking....Heaven and earth are about to collide with the greatest harvest of souls and the greatest demonstrations and manifestations of My glory that this world has ever seen before....People have seen glimpses with [the Azusa Street Revival], with the Brownsville [Revival], with the Welsh Revival...but what I'm about to do—there is no comparison to what is about to happen in these last days.'"[3]

THE DEFINING HOUR HAS ARRIVED

History is marked by pivotal moments—times when nations must choose between revival or judgment.

The Bible records many such moments:

- **Sodom and Gomorrah**—destroyed for their extreme wickedness.

- **Egypt**—judged through the ten plagues (Exod. 7–12), leading to Israel's deliverance.

- **Canaanites**—conquered because of their abominations.

- **Israel and Judah**—exiled for idolatry, disobedience, and rejecting God's commands.

- **Nineveh**—spared when its people repented after Jonah's warning.

We are living in such a time now. In my eight previous books investigating whether we are approaching the end-times described in Scripture, I've shown how God has given countless warnings—through biblical prophecy and modern-day prophetic voices.

The Bible speaks of this exact time: "Multitudes, multitudes in the valley of decision! For the day of the LORD is near in the valley of decision" (Joel 3:14).

For years, prophetic voices have warned that a great reckoning is coming. Today, the world shakes under the weight of decadence, corruption, and satanic evil. Presidents, prophets, and patriots are asking what lies ahead for America and the world.

We are witnessing what the Book of Hebrews calls a "shaking"—a divine disruption of biblical proportions: "Once more I will shake not only the earth but also the heavens" (Heb. 12:26).

This is not just the political upheaval of Donald Trump's return to the White House. It is a divine reordering, preparing the way for what my *Revelation 911* coauthor, Pastor Paul Begley, calls the "Great Harvest Revival."[4]

We believe it has already begun and will accelerate during the tribulation, for as Isaiah said: "When your judgments come upon the earth, the people of the world learn righteousness" (Isa. 26:9).

Revelation 7:9–17 describes a great multitude saved during the tribulation: "After this I looked, and there before me was a great multitude that no one could count, from every nation, tribe, people and language, standing before the throne and before the Lamb" (Rev. 7:9).

Today, political and faith leaders are confronting globalists who seek to dismantle the freedoms the Western world has long enjoyed. This is our Nineveh moment—a brief window for repentance and a return to God, or a descent into collapse under the Antichrist system. Joseph Z said:

> I believe that [America is] ours to lose right now. I believe the Spirit of the Lord wants the church to intercede. Intercession is one of the biggest things we can do at this moment to push these things back....All these people that are trying to bring about a globalist environment even in America. But America is the firewall. We are indeed the last frontier to hold the line. And I believe we have a great opportunity that can push this out for another generation if we do our job well at this time. So I believe that the globalist structure has already been shaken.
>
> I believe America has one more round it's got to stand. It will push this globalist agenda backwards as long as the church keeps rising because the gates of hell cannot overcome the *Ecclesia*. And when we continue to rise, we will stop their agenda. But the moment the church shrinks back, the globalist agenda will take a step forward. So that is ours to lose right now.[5]

A PROPHETIC PATTERN IS REPEATING

Throughout history, God has raised up unlikely leaders to deliver nations in crisis.

Gideon was hiding in fear when the angel of the Lord called him to lead Israel—not with thousands, but with three hundred handpicked warriors. God reduced his army to ensure victory came by His power, not human strength: "With the three hundred men that lapped I will save you and give the Midianites into your hands" (Judg. 7:7).

David, a young shepherd, was not man's choice to be king but God's. He slew Goliath, defended Israel, and turned the nation back to God: "For man looks on the outward appearance, but the LORD looks on the heart" (1 Sam. 16:7, MEV).

Moses, at the age of eighty, resisted God's call, citing his stutter. Yet God chose him to confront Pharaoh, break Egypt's political and economic power, and lead Israel through the miraculous parting of the Red Sea to the Promised Land.

Moses, Gideon, and David weren't flawless, but they were obedient. At times of national peril, God used them to change history.

Now America stands at a similar crossroads—between spiritual compromise and a call to return to God. Once again He is raising up leaders—not perfect, but chosen—to confront the globalists (modern-day Pharaohs) and prepare the way for revival: "So I sought for a man among them who would make a wall, and stand in the gap...but I found no one" (Ezek. 22:30, NKJV). This time, designated disrupters are standing in the gap. The question is, Will we respond or fall?

TRUMP AND THE GIDEON, DAVID, AND MOSES TRIFECTA

My biblical studies, research, and interviews over the years have uncovered a prophetic pattern linking ancient Israel with modern America—a connection the Pilgrims and Puritans often noted in their literature.

Trump fits within this paradigm. His role is prophetic and multifaceted, defying the expectations of both faith leaders and political pundits. Respected prophetic voices—Rabbi Jonathan Cahn, Lance Wallnau, Dutch Sheets, and Kim Clement—have described him as a disrupter, raised by God for a specific assignment in America's defining hour upon the world stage.

LIKE GIDEON, LIKE DAVID, LIKE MOSES

In this prophetic moment, Trump's assignment mirrors that of three unexpected figures God raised up to bring deliverance in times past—Gideon, David, and Moses.

Like Gideon

In his second term, Trump has gathered a small, handpicked team of disrupters and reformers. Despite relentless attacks from activist judges and the mainstream media, his movement—like Gideon's three hundred—has seen miraculous victories against overwhelming odds.

Like David

Trump is a flawed yet chosen leader who faces today's giants while carrying the weight of a nation's destiny on his shoulders. On July 25, 2015, Kim Clement prophesied a change in the White House that the Holy Spirit would use to bring revival:

"For there shall arise leaders that shall speak the truth in this nation, and I will give them one more chance," says the Lord...."And there shall arise men and women that shall pray in the White House, and they shall bring the latter rain into this nation and onto the earth," says the Lord.[6]

Like many of Clement's prophecies, this has proven accurate—Trump's second term has been marked by prayer gatherings at the White House. On the National Day of Prayer, May 1, 2025, he reflected on America's spiritual heritage:

TRUMP HAS WORKED TO DEFEND AMERICA'S LEGACY OF FAITH.

Across every chapter of our grand American story—from General George Washington's humble prayer at Valley Forge to Reverend Billy Graham's legendary rallies in the heart of Manhattan to the somber National Prayer Service in the wake of the September 11, 2001 attacks, our greatest leaders have always recognized the necessity of faith, prayer, and devotion to God. As President Washington famously stated..."Of all the dispositions and habits which lead to political prosperity, religion and morality are indispensable supports."[7]

Trump has worked to defend America's legacy of faith, creating task forces to combat anti-Semitic, anti-Christian, and other forms of religious bias. On the National Day of Prayer he also spoke of his personal commitment to religious freedom:

I will never waver in safeguarding the right to religious liberty and protecting God in our public square....On July 13, 2024, my faith took on new meaning. An assassin's bullet came within a quarter of an inch of ending my life. In that instant, as Secret Service crowded around and knocked me to the ground, I felt what seemed to be the supernatural hand of God. I believe that God spared my life for a reason—to save our country and restore America to greatness. It serves as a sacred reminder of our Creator's infinite goodness, guidance, and grace.[8]

Like Moses

The globalist system has become a modern-day Pharaoh, enslaving nations through technocratic control and digital surveillance.

Like Moses confronting Pharaoh, Trump is leading America toward an exodus from this tyranny: "So now, go. I am sending you to Pharaoh to bring my people the Israelites out of Egypt" (Exod. 3:10).

AMERICA'S REVIVAL

While I was writing this chapter, the White House's YouTube channel released a video titled "6 Months of Power: President Trump's Comeback. America's Revival."[9]

In just six months, Trump signed a wave of executive orders, jump-starting the economy and securing America's borders. Key achievements included the following:

- **Border security**—Over 600 known or suspected terrorists deported; Immigrations and Customs Enforcement (ICE) arrested over 100,000 illegal alien criminals, including 2,700 from the Tren de Aragua gang.[10]

- **Economic revival**—Retail sales surged, gas prices dropped, and markets hit record highs; inflation held at 2.1 percent, a level not seen since the first Trump administration.[11]

- **Global financial wins**—Over $2 trillion expected by 2034 in signed international agreements, with record tariff revenues already coming in.[12]

- **Historic tax relief**—On July 4, 2025, Trump signed the "One Big Beautiful Bill" that cut waste and delivered one of the largest tax cuts in US history, raising take-home pay by up to $13,300.[13]

Like Moses leading the exodus, these actions are breaking the grip of the globalists and paving the way for revival.

THE GIDEON 300

Just like the biblical account of Gideon, Trump leads what can be called the Gideon 300—a team of political leaders, reformers, and cultural disrupters tasked with shaping national and global policies for America's comeback.

Political reformers

- **JD Vance,** Vice President—Advocate for faith, family, and national revival, representing a new generation defending biblical values and constitutional principles.[14]

- **Mike Johnson,** Speaker of the House—Quotes Scripture from the House floor, saying, "My faith informs everything I do." A champion of religious liberty and defender of America's Judeo-Christian heritage.[15]

- **Scott Bessent,** Secretary of the Treasury—Architect of the "3-3-3" plan: cut the federal deficit to 3 percent of GDP, hold GDP growth to 3 percent, and add 3 million barrels of oil per day by 2028—breaking globalist control and restoring middle-class prosperity.[16]

- **Howard Lutnick,** Secretary of Trade—Driving the "America First" agenda to restore sovereignty and bring jobs and factories back to US soil.[17]

- **Stephen Miller,** White House Deputy Chief of Staff for Policy—Plays a key role in shaping "America First" policies on national security and immigration.[18]

- **Pete Hegseth,** Secretary of Defense—Oversaw the strike that destroyed Iran's nuclear capabilities, averting global catastrophe.[19]

- **Kash Patel,** Director of the Federal Bureau of Investigation—National security expert, author of *Government Gangsters,* and leading figure in dismantling the Deep State.[20]

- **Susie Wiles,** White House Chief of Staff—First woman in the role, credited as the architect of Trump's 2024 reelection.[21]

Legal and cultural reformers

- **Pam Bondi,** Attorney General—Former Florida attorney general confronting Deep State corruption; in August 2025 she launched a grand jury probe into alleged Obama-era intelligence fabrication.[22]

- **Mike Huckabee,** Ambassador to Israel—Pastor, broadcaster, and pro-Israel advocate mentoring new Christian leaders.[23]

Prophetic cultural disrupters

- **Tulsi Gabbard,** Director of National Intelligence—The first American Samoan elected to Congress, Gabbard oversees eighteen US intelligence agencies. She's a fierce defender of constitutional freedoms and free speech.[24]

- **Robert F. Kennedy Jr.,** Secretary of Health—Medical freedom champion and Trump's ally in the "Make America Healthy Again" campaign.[25]

- **Karoline Leavitt,** White House Press Secretary—Youngest ever in the role, expanding access to new media voices.[26]

THE WHITE HOUSE FAITH OFFICE

Like Gideon's army, Trump has chosen his team for their courage to confront powerful forces seeking to destroy America. The Gideon 300 is standing in the gap, tackling some of the nation's most intractable problems.

Beyond this core team, a growing number of members of Congress, governors, state legislators, local officials, and grassroots leaders are joining the movement. They are openly professing faith in Christ, defending religious liberty, and rejecting globalist agendas.

They are part of a faithful remnant committed to preserving America's founding values and advancing repentance and revival. While these leaders fight on the political and cultural front lines, prayer warriors and intercessors are working behind the scenes to shift the spiritual atmosphere.

One of Trump's most significant actions has been creating the White House Faith Office, led by Pastor Paula White-Cain. Announced on February 7, 2025, the office will "empower faith-based entities, community organizations, and houses of worship to better serve families and communities." Housed under the Domestic Policy Council, it consults faith leaders on policies to "better align with American values" and elevate grant opportunities for faith-based and community organizations.[27]

The announcement followed Trump's order establishing the Task Force to End the War on Christians, comprised of Cabinet members and key agencies working to "end the anti-Christian weaponization of government." Trump pledged the task force would "move heaven and earth to defend the rights of Christians and religious believers nationwide."[28]

While I'm in the White House, we will protect Christians in our schools, in our military, in our government, in our workplaces, hospitals and in our public squares, and we will bring our country back together as one nation under God, with liberty and justice for all....Without God, we are isolated and alone, but with God, the Scripture tells us, all things are possible.[29]

Faith leaders and advisers

These faith leaders have participated in White House prayer gatherings, policy discussions, or voiced strong support for Trump:

- **Pastor Paula White-Cain,** Chair of the White House Faith Office and senior spiritual adviser to Trump—Founder of Paula White Ministries and a *New York Times* best-selling author, she is married to Jonathan Cain of the iconic band Journey.[30]

- **Franklin Graham,** President of Samaritan's Purse and the Billy Graham Evangelistic Association—Led prayers at the 2025 inauguration and White House Easter services. "I don't know if in our modern history we have had a president publicly communicate the gospel as clearly as this—and I thank God for it," Graham said. "On the National Day of Prayer, the president...protect[ed] people of faith by signing an executive order to establish a Religious Liberty Commission....I have never forgotten the legacy of my Scottish ancestors who immigrated to America for the freedom to worship Jesus Christ....I look forward to...boldly proclaiming the truth of God's Word and the life-changing gospel."[31]

- **Robert Jeffress,** Senior Pastor of First Baptist Dallas—Frequently advises the White House on religious liberty issues. "Thank God for this president," Jeffress said. "One of the great ironies in history is going to be [when] people look back and see that it took a secular, New York real-estate tycoon from New York City to put faith back into its proper place in American life."[32]

- **Greg Laurie,** Pastor of Harvest Christian Fellowship— Regularly invited to White House events and supports national revival. He, too, has noticed the amazing trends among Generation Z that we discussed in chapter 8. "The data told us

Gen Z was walking away from Christianity," Laurie wrote. "Instead, they're walking toward it....As Charlie Kirk says, 'They don't want fluff. They want the unfiltered Gospel of Christ....' This isn't just church talk. It's showing up in pop culture: Two Christian songs (Brandon Lake & Forrest Frank) are on the Billboard Hot 100. 'The Chosen' and 'House of David' are topping streaming platforms."[33]

- **Rev. Samuel Rodriguez,** President of the National Hispanic Christian Leadership Conference and faith adviser to the White House—In March 2025 he joined other leaders in the Oval Office to pray for Trump. "With gratitude and humility, we pray for President Trump," Rodriguez said. "You assigned him. You appointed him. You anointed him for such a time as this. We ask You to cover him with the blood of Jesus, empowering him to advance an agenda of righteousness and justice, truth and love. Protect him from all evil as he undergirds our nation with the firewall of our Judeo-Christian value system. Fulfill Your purpose in his life."[34]

> WHILE THESE LEADERS FIGHT ON THE POLITICAL AND CULTURAL FRONT LINES, PRAYER WARRIORS AND INTERCESSORS ARE WORKING BEHIND THE SCENES TO SHIFT THE SPIRITUAL ATMOSPHERE.

- **Alveda King,** Evangelist, civil rights leader, pro-life advocate, and niece of Martin Luther King Jr.—She called for unity as Martin Luther King Jr. Day and the Presidential Inauguration fell on the same day, January 20, 2025. "When peripherals collide, convergence is imminent," King said. "The convergence of these events cannot be just a coincidence, and January's March for Life, in particular, gives us a chance to reflect on the progress we have made in the movement. Through our prayers, our hope, and our continued hard work, we can finally rejoice that there is a light at the end of the tunnel."[35]

- **Lance Wallnau,** Prophetic commentator and one of three evangelical leaders who accurately predicted Trump's 2016 victory—On the "Encounter Today" podcast, he said Trump has been

raised up by God to dispatch "statesman evangelists" worldwide for a global revival. "Jesus told me that Trump was going
to be put back in office for the sake of the nations," Wallnau
said. "I thought...he was coming back just for making America
great, but the Lord said, 'Oh no, his agenda is America, but
for America's interest to be secured, there has to be a reordering of the global community.'...Trump will create a *Pax
Romana*; a period of peace realigning nations....He is raised
up as God's instrument for the sake of the nations....Trump
himself, I believe, is going to not only establish America's
trade relationships with these nations, but there will come a
point where the statesman evangelists are going to come along.
Meaning, nations are going to start to open up to the movement of reformation happening here....It's a movement toward
Judeo-Christian values....Trump is the catalyst of the global
reformation happening."[36]

- **Ché Ahn,** Co-founder of The Call with Lou Engle and senior
  pastor of Harvest Rock Church in Pasadena, California—
  Recently announced his 2026 campaign for governor, aiming
  to inspire more Evangelicals (one in five Californians are
  Evangelicals but few go to the polls) to vote and potentially
  shift California red after many years as a blue stronghold. With
  fifty-four electoral votes, the state could dramatically impact
  America's political future. Ahn writes: "California has long
  been a bellwether. What happens here doesn't stay here—it
  spreads. Our policies, innovations, and cultural shifts often
  lead the nation. That's why this race for governor matters far
  beyond our state lines. It's not just about changing who holds
  office. It's about changing what we expect from leadership....
  It's often said that as California goes, so goes the nation. If
  that's true, then what we do here in 2026 matters more than we
  realize. Because if we can turn things around here—if we can
  build a state where families can afford to stay, small businesses
  can grow, and every life is treated with dignity—then we're not
  just changing a state. We're giving the nation a new example of
  what's possible."[37]

- **Mario Murillo,** Evangelist, revivalist, and author of *It's Our Turn Now: God's Plan to Restore America Is Within Our Reach*— Speaking at a Texas tent revival in May 2025, he issued a prophetic warning in his sermon "What Is Next for America?" as opposition to Christians, conservatives, and patriots intensifies ahead of the 2026 midterm and 2028 presidential elections. "God revealed that the church has three and a half years to wake up, unify, get on fire, and begin speaking out....Donald Trump and the Republican Party are not going to save this nation, it's already too late. So there's one thing left...God's got an army!... Unity, particularly unity in the church and between churches. Unity throughout the body of Christ. The answer is the destruction of division."[38]

GOD'S GOT AN ARMY!

These faith leaders are members of Adonai's army. They form a diverse yet unified front: evangelical, Charismatic, Pentecostal, intercessory, and prophetic voices providing counsel and covering the White House in prayer.

This is not a ceremonial alliance but a partnership between faith and governmental leaders. Prominent ministers such as Franklin Graham, Robert Jeffress, Pastor Greg Laurie, Alveda King, Rev. Samuel Rodriguez, Ché Ahn, Mario Murillo, Dutch Sheets, Rabbi Jonathan Cahn, and others are speaking at national events, calling the nation to repentance.

Patriots in Congress, along with conservative and Christian media, are aligning with these leaders, recognizing that the stakes extend beyond politics to the possibility of national and global revival. Rabbi Jonathan Bernis said:

> I think that there's a resurgence of church involvement both in the Protestant and Catholic world, and God is being reintroduced in our government. I think it's a genuine move of God. It's not the culmination; it's the beginning. It's kind of the dew before the great rain. And I'm confident...that we are going to see a revival in America...that's greater than the Jesus movement of the early 1970s. It's going to be profound....And for those that have eyes to see, it's really visible. Look at the numbers. Churches are growing and that's a shift from the last two decades.[39]

Barna Group data reflects this shift: While only 20 percent of Americans attend church weekly today (down from 32 percent in 2000), 39 percent of Millennials now attend weekly—up from 21 percent in 2019—surpassing both Generation X and Baby Boomers. Although most churches remain below pre-COVID-19 attendance levels, many report returning members and an influx of guests.[40]

PROPHETS, KINGS, AND REVIVAL

The creation of the White House Faith Office and Trump's partnership with faith leaders reflects an encouraging biblical model:

- **King Jehu and the prophet Elisha**—a king overthrowing the wicked house of Ahab and eradicating Baal worship under prophetic guidance.

- **King David and the prophet Nathan**—a king seeking God's counsel and repenting after sinning with Bathsheba and orchestrating her husband Uriah's death.

Today's faith and political leaders are following this tradition, working to restore righteousness in America. During the National Day of Prayer, Pastor Paula White-Cain declared Trump "the greatest champion of faith we've ever had."[41]

But this movement is broader than Trump, faith leaders, and politicians. It is fueled by national prayer and repentance efforts—The Return, The Call, the National Day of Prayer, March for Life, and our own "40 Days to Save America" and "77 Days to Take Back America" campaigns—drawing millions to seek God's restoration for America and the world.

THE COST OF DISRUPTION

Being a disrupter comes at a price—cancel culture, legal battles, media attacks, and personal threats. Yet history remembers those who stand for truth in dark times, not the critics who tried to silence them. This is as much a spiritual battle as a political one, requiring daily prayer for Trump, his team, and all engaged in the fight to turn America and the world around.

A Gallup poll released in late August 2025 found President Trump's approval rating at 40 percent, down a few points from his first several months in office. "These numbers are largely driven by nearly-unanimous Republican support, overwhelming Democratic opposition and weakening levels of support from independents, further underlining the partisan nature of support for Trump and his second term," Kathryn Palmer wrote in her *USA Today* story.[42]

Given how close many elections are, this could spell trouble for Republicans in the 2026 midterm elections as well as the 2028 presidential election. This is why followers of Jesus must not become complacent during this time of God's mercy and revival. We must continue to fight the good fight of faith and vote, knowing the devil and his Deep State minions are going to use every trick up their sleeves to regain control of America and the world.

Since June 16, 2015, when Trump announced his candidacy for president, he has faced relentless attacks from political opponents and the global Deep State—media smears, indictments, censorship, harassment, and even assassination attempts. Anyone stepping into the fight for America's future faces similar risks. That's why prayer, fasting, and repentance are vital. As Ephesians 6:13–18 reminds believers, we must "put on the full armor of God" to be victorious in this battle.

CANCEL CULTURE AND THE SPIRIT OF JEZEBEL

Today's battle involves high-level spiritual warfare driven by Deep State psychological operations, scientific mind-control technologies, and coordinated efforts to confuse, deceive, and divide the populace. The devil knows his time is short, and he is deploying every weapon to hinder the revival now emerging. "But woe to the earth and the sea, because the devil has gone down to you! He is filled with fury, because he knows that his time is short" (Rev. 12:12).

What we see is the Jezebel spirit in action—intimidating leaders, silencing prophetic voices, and suppressing truth through fear, manipulation, and shame. This spirit operates as a system of control, seeking to dominate culture and keep the nation under spiritual oppression (Rev. 2:20).

Trump and other designated disrupters face twenty-first-century persecution: shadow bans, censorship, lawsuits, legal threats, financial targeting, de-banking, media hit pieces, public shaming, social isolation, and betrayal. It is the cost of standing for truth in a generation hostile to righteousness.

The biblical prophets understood the cost:

- **Jeremiah**—thrown into a mud-filled cistern for warning of judgment (Jer. 38:6).

- **Elijah**—fled for his life after confronting Jezebel (1 Kings 19).

- **Daniel**—cast into the lions' den for refusing to compromise (Dan. 6).

- **Jesus**—crucified for speaking truth to religious and political power (Matt. 27; Mark 15; Luke 23; John 19).

Jesus was clear: "If anyone desires to come after Me, let him deny himself, and take up his cross daily, and follow Me" (Luke 9:23, NKJV).

GOD'S SOVEREIGN STRATEGY

Despite relentless attacks and modern-day persecution, Trump and other disrupters continue to fight because they know reformation and revival always meet resistance. The question is not whether the attacks will stop—it is who will have the courage to keep standing, no matter how many "flaming arrows of the evil one" (Eph. 6:16) are fired.

This battle is bigger than America—it is about the future of freedom worldwide. Globalist elites are advancing the World Economic Forum's "Great Reset," pushing a technocratic system to control economies, currencies, speech, and even thought. Through central bank digital currencies, corporate-government alliances, and surveillance networks, they seek to replace national sovereignty with "global governance."

As I've written in *Designated Disrupter*, many prophetic voices have warned that America is the final firewall against these schemes. If America falls, the world will follow into the system of tyrannical control Daniel foresaw:

THIS BATTLE IS BIGGER THAN AMERICA—IT IS ABOUT THE FUTURE OF FREEDOM WORLDWIDE.

"The fourth beast shall be the fourth kingdom upon earth...[it] shall devour the whole earth...and shall wear out the saints of the most High, and think to change times and laws...." (Dan. 7:23–25, KJV).

Behind the scenes, the trajectory of human civilization is moving toward the rise of the "fourth beast"— a one-world government under the iron rule of the Antichrist and False Prophet.

Yet God is in control. Revival and shaking often come together. We are witnessing a Jehu moment, a Gideon hour, a David confronting the giant Goliath. At this prophetic crossroads, God is raising up unlikely leaders to root out corruption and prepare the way for revival.

The shaking will intensify. The question is, Will we recognize God's plan and join Him in the assignments He has for us?

PART III

BILLY GRAHAM'S NINEVEH MOMENT

CHAPTER 10

REVIVAL NATION

LORD, I have heard of your fame; I stand in awe of your deeds, LORD. Repeat them in our day, in our time make them known; in wrath remember mercy.
—HABAKKUK 3:2

O N JULY 4, 2025, my friend Paul McGuire had a vision in which God told him He wants a "biblical Great Awakening in America." He awoke from a deep sleep—a metaphor for how God desires to awaken His church from its lethargic state as revival breaks out in the last days. In the vision, the Lord warned that America has "one last chance."[1]

> God [said He] wants a biblical Great Awakening for America, but a biblical Great Awakening cannot happen in America unless we do it according to God's will and laws. God wants us to be responsible to take ownership for what's happening in our nation. God wants us to repent, wake up....God's not playing church. He's not playing games.
>
> And what He meant by that is the stakes are high....We obey Him by knowing what's going on, waking up theologically and intellectually...knowing what the threat is...knowing the Word of God, receiving the power of the Holy Spirit...and then...actually going into spiritual battle. It's a law abiding, peaceful spiritual battle, and we can overturn to whatever degree God will allow us the work of the enemy.[2]

In the vision, McGuire heard "worship in the heavenlies that was very loud"—the voices of angelic armies, saints, and the remnant church—rising above the clash between God's forces and demonic armies. "The battle was so fierce, but what overrode the...noises of Satan and the demonic armies was this wondrous celestial worship music, which was...a form of worship warfare. It was glorious," he said.[3]

The Lord showed him both the beauty of the angelic armies and the horrors on earth—nuclear blasts, biological attacks, and "one horror show after another."

> I saw forms of angelic armies, forms of God, forms of the angels in red hues and golden hues...confronting the demonic army....[This was]

the culmination of history…the triumph of…the Lordship of Christ.… Jesus Christ is returning not as a church mouse…[but as] Lord of lords and King of kings of multidimensional, quantum physics reality.

Jesus Christ, King of kings, Lord of lords, the Supreme Being, is coming quickly to the earth. No man knows the day or the hour, but when He comes it's going to be a resounding crash. When Jesus comes back…the armies of Armageddon will vibrationally shatter into a billion pieces. The demons will flee and scream in agony, and God will liberate those who are bought by the blood of Jesus Christ. It will be magnificent, glorious, and triumphant. Then God will rule and reign with [us] as His people…first in the Millennium for a thousand years—and then for all eternity.[4]

To hear Paul McGuire discuss this vision, scan the QR code or visit TroyAndersonBooks.com/mcguire.

A "BIBLICAL GREAT AWAKENING"

The message McGuire received revealed God's desire for a "biblical Great Awakening." This, along with his vision of the coming battle of Armageddon, is a prophetic wake-up call.

THIS PRESENT AWAKENING COULD RESTORE THE CHURCH TO ITS PROPHETIC ROLE— LEADING THE CULTURE INSTEAD OF FOLLOWING IT.

Throughout history God has used times of crisis to draw people into relationship with Him. In Scripture, revival begins with humility and prayer. When individuals and nations humbled themselves, repented, and sought His face, God often withheld judgment and ignited spiritual renewal.

"The Scriptures are very clear in 2 Chronicles 7:14 that 'If my people, who are called by my name, will humble themselves and pray and seek my face,' and basically cry out to God—that God will heal the land, that He'll transform not just individuals but a nation," said Rabbi Jonathan Bernis, host of *Jewish Voice with Jonathan Bernis*. "And we have that opportunity now.…This may, I believe, be our last chance as a nation, and we have to seize this opportunity as people of faith."[5]

From Nineveh to King Josiah, the biblical pattern is consistent: When God's people respond with prayer, fasting, and repentance, heaven responds with power. This present awakening could restore the church to its prophetic role—leading the culture instead of following it.

Unlike past awakenings that faded, I believe this move of the Holy Spirit is the last-days outpouring described in Acts 2. Yet, as prophetic voices warn, darkness will grow alongside the light. This fulfills Jesus' words in Matthew 13:30: "Let both grow together until the harvest. At that time I will tell the harvesters: First collect the weeds and tie them in bundles to be burned; then gather the wheat and bring it into my barn."

The late Kim Clement accurately prophesied many events in America, including that Donald Trump would serve two terms.

"God says, 'I will put at your helm for two terms a president that will pray, but he will not be a praying president when he starts. I will put him in office and then I will baptize him with the Holy Spirit and My power,'" Clement said.[6]

Clement also foresaw America's greatest days ahead, not as an empire, but as a prophetic voice declaring, "Prepare the way of the Lord." He likened Trump to Ronald Reagan, predicting Trump would survive assassination attempts and that his presidency would help trigger revival.

"He prays and [takes] the mantle of Ronald Reagan so that this nation may experience great revival," Clement said. "Great breakthrough, great, great, great, great breakthrough. But truly there shall be one that shall attempt to lead three others to his side to kill and to take out. But I am with you tonight where My warriors will stop an assassination because your prayers will make the difference."[7]

NINEVEH: HUMILITY BEFORE JUDGMENT

The story of Jonah and Nineveh shows how a nation on the brink of destruction can be transformed through humility and repentance.

Jonah, a reluctant prophet, was sent by God to the capital of Assyria—a ruthless, bloodthirsty kingdom. He carried a stark warning: "Forty more days and Nineveh will be overthrown" (Jon. 3:4).

What happened next was miraculous. From the king to the commoner, the people responded with brokenness, not defiance. The king left his throne, removed his royal garments, covered himself with sackcloth, and sat in ashes. He decreed national fasting and repentance: "Let everyone call urgently on God. Let them give up their evil ways and their violence" (Jon. 3:8).

This act revealed a timeless truth—no one is beyond God's mercy. The king's humility became the catalyst for national revival. And, "When God saw what they did and how they turned from their evil ways, he relented and did not bring on them the destruction he had threatened" (Jon. 3:10).

JOSIAH: REFORM ROOTED IN REVIVAL

Another powerful example of how prayer and humility can transform a nation is found in the story of King Josiah. Under Josiah's predecessors, Judah plunged into decadence. The temple was neglected, idolatry flourished, and God's Word was forgotten.

When Josiah became king at just eight years old, God raised up a young reformer whose heart burned with reverence and repentance. The turning point came when the Book of the Law (likely Deuteronomy) was rediscovered in the temple (2 Kings 22:8). Hearing its words, Josiah tore his robes in grief:

> Go and inquire of the LORD for me and for the people and for all Judah about what is written in this book that has been found. Great is the LORD's anger that burns against us because those who have gone before us have not obeyed the words of this book; they have not acted in accordance with all that is written there concerning us.
>
> —2 KINGS 22:13

Josiah sought guidance from the prophetess Huldah, who confirmed the scroll's authenticity and prophesied judgment for Judah's disobedience.

Josiah responded with sweeping reforms—tearing down idols, purging pagan altars, restoring temple worship, and reestablishing the Passover (2 Kings 23:1–25). Most significant was his humility:

> Your heart was responsive, and you humbled yourself before the LORD when you heard what I have spoken against this place and its people.
>
> —2 KINGS 22:19

These reforms brought a temporary revival and shielded Judah from judgment during Josiah's reign, though the people's repentance faded after his death.

Together, the stories of Nineveh and Josiah reveal a biblical road map for revival: When individuals or nations humble themselves, confess their sin, and seek God's mercy, He responds with spiritual awakening and renewal.

THE NATIONAL INVITATION: PRAYER, FASTING, AND REPENTANCE

In times of national crisis, God's invitation is clear:

> If my people, who are called by my name, will humble themselves and pray and seek my face and turn from their wicked ways, then I will hear from heaven, and I will forgive their sin and will heal their land.
>
> —2 CHRONICLES 7:14

Spoken at the dedication of Solomon's temple, this promise links God's forgiveness and healing to the humility, prayers, and repentance of His people.

Biblical repentance is more than asking for forgiveness. It is turning away from sin. Throughout Scripture, when Israel or Judah faced a crisis, the prophets called for national repentance. In response, God restored His blessings and protection.

Fasting has always been part of this process. In both the Old and New Testaments, fasting accompanied prayer and mourning as expressions of humility and sorrow for sin. The people of Nineveh (Jon. 3) and King Josiah's Judah (2 Kings 23) fasted as a public demonstration of repentance. Fasting humbles the body and soul, aligning us with God's will.

In the New Testament, Jesus fasted forty days in the wilderness (Matt. 4:1–11). When asked why His disciples did not fast, He replied that the time would come when they would (Matt. 9:15), showing fasting remains vital, especially in times of crisis or revival.

"'Even now,' declares the LORD, 'return to me with all your heart, with fasting and weeping and mourning'" (Joel 2:12).

This pattern is consistent: When God's people pray, fast, and repent, heaven responds with healing, protection, and revival. The same principle that saved Nineveh, preserved Josiah's Judah, and ignited Pentecost still applies today.

As America and the world face unprecedented dangers—natural disasters, debt crises, and moral collapse—God's invitation remains: "If My people…"

Sid Roth, host of *It's Supernatural!*, said God will use ordinary believers in extraordinary ways during this revival:

> [A] good preparation is [to] feed yourself every day with the Word of God. Another good preparation is, "You have not because you ask not" [Jas. 4:2–3]. Start asking God, "Send your Greater Glory. Send your Greater Glory to me." Pray and get excited. I pray that the joy of the Lord would overtake you.[8]

REVIVAL AMERICA

History shows that nations rise and fall not only by military or economic strength, but by the state of their moral and spiritual health.

In times of national crisis in America, political and faith leaders have often called for a return to the biblical principles that have long guided the country.

Many wonder if large-scale repentance and revival are possible in today's climate of skepticism, division, and moral confusion. As we've explored in *Designated Disrupter*, there are encouraging signs—especially among young people—but doubts remain about whether America is too far gone, too compromised and corrupt.

Faith leaders like Alveda King, niece of Martin Luther King Jr., believe authentic revival begins in the hearts of individuals and communities. Only by reclaiming our spiritual heritage, she says, can America experience lasting transformation.

"As my uncle, Dr. Martin Luther King Jr., said, 'I have a dream, and it is rooted in the American Dream,'" said Dr. King, chair of the Center for the American Dream, responding to President Trump's March 5, 2025, address to Congress. "Tonight, I stand with my friend, President Donald J. Trump, as he lays out his vision to renew that dream. And we're already seeing victories—empowering businesses, securing our border, defending women's sports, and protecting children from harmful agendas."[9]

AUTHENTIC REVIVAL BEGINS IN THE HEARTS OF INDIVIDUALS AND COMMUNITIES.

Today America stands at a tipping point. Revival is urgently needed—and possible. Each of us, whether a minister, parent, business owner, student, or public servant, has a sphere of influence. Through faith and perseverance we can become catalysts for change, helping usher in a new era of spiritual awakening.

One such unlikely catalyst is President Trump.

THE TRUMP REVIVAL

Few modern political figures have been as polarizing—or as inspirational—as Trump. To his critics, his defiance and rhetoric spark outrage.

But to millions, especially within the body of Christ, his leadership represents a long-awaited disruption of a Deep State-controlled political and economic system riddled with corruption and compromise.

Trump's first term stunned the establishment, igniting a geopolitical reset in America and beyond. For many, "The Trump Revolution" was more than a political movement; it was a divine intervention in human affairs.[10]

Now, in his second term, Trump's return to power is a "geopolitical shift of historic proportions," dismantling the "liberal-globalist order" and replacing it with an "Order of Great Powers"—a world in which "truly sovereign civilizations can assert themselves," as Russian philosopher Alexander Dugin writes.[11]

McGuire sees Trump as "kind of a combination of [King] Solomon before Solomon went astray...definitely a warrior, but also a manager of resources."[12]

Prophetically, McGuire connects Trump's role in the revival now underway to the Lord's appearance to Solomon in 2 Chronicles 7 where He told him that obedience brings blessing, disobedience brings judgment, and repentance brings awakening. McGuire believes the revival Trump helped ignite is connected spiritually to September 26, 2020, when he flew over the National Mall in Marine One and issued a proclamation for a "Day of Prayer and Return" during The Return: National and Global Day of Prayer and Repentance event.

"Your title [*Designated Disrupter: Trump and Other Unlikely Agents of Revival*] encapsulates the concept that the revival we're seeing...involves a release of knowledge of the Word of God that we talked about [in *The Babylon Code* and *Trumpocalypse*]," McGuire said. "It's gone all over the United States and the world....There's a massive shift in consciousness. The Deep State thought they had...their Great Reset on lockdown but...the God of the Bible is alive, the Infinite Personal Living God of the Universe is alive, but He's been artificially suppressed, He's been attacked."[13]

Beyond the headlines, Trump's leadership has become an inflection point for revival. He's governed unlike past Republicans, challenging the status quo and awakening a remnant of believers who have long prayed for righteous governance.

At the policy level, Trump's reforms have been seen by many faith leaders as direct answers to prayer. His 2017 executive order "Promoting Free Speech and Religious Liberty" and the "White House Faith and Opportunity Initiative" strengthened religious freedom.[14]

He's appointed over 230 federal judges, along with three Supreme Court justices, reshaping the judiciary for a generation.[15]

In his second term, Trump's disruption has accelerated. He created the Department of Government Efficiency (DOGE) to root out waste, fraud, and abuse; expanded immigration enforcement; granted clemency to hundreds of January 6 defendants; and restructured tariffs to protect US industry—rooted in the biblical principle of just weights and measures (Prov. 11:1).

"In his second term, President Donald Trump has reshaped US foreign policy, using tariffs not just as economic leverage but as a central tool of diplomacy," Emel

Akan wrote in *The Epoch Times.* "His administration has leveraged economic pressure to address global conflicts and secure concessions from other nations, marking one of the most significant shifts in U.S foreign policy in decades."[16]

He is also exploring cryptocurrency policy reforms that could fund the "wealth transfer" (Prov. 13:22) to pay for the spread of the gospel worldwide, and spearheading America's leading role in artificial intelligence.

But Trump's influence extends beyond policy; it is cultural, psychological, and spiritual. His courage has emboldened believers to reject political correctness, wokeness, and the complacency that has weakened the church.

Historian Victor Davis Hanson notes that Trump's blunt rhetoric awakened a part of America long silenced, although he faces enormous challenges:

> While Trump was successfully reelected in 2024…the changed conditions…[will] make implementing that agenda even more difficult.… Trump has now inherited an almost bankrupt country. The ratio of debt to annual GDP has reached a record high of nearly 125 percent— exceeding the worst years of World War II. The nation remains sharply divided.…Trump's own base demands that he address…unvetted illegal aliens; diversity, equity, and inclusion mandates…and enemies abroad.… And so often, when drastic remedies are proposed, their implementation may appear…as a cure worse than the disease.[17]

Yet through all of this, Trump has revived the church's prophetic voice. Like King Jehu, he has confronted entrenched corruption and stirred the nation to reconsider its Judeo-Christian foundations.

Trump does not claim sainthood, but his tenure has inspired a fresh urgency to pray, to speak truth, and to believe that—by God's mercy working through imperfect vessels—America's best days may yet be ahead.

THE "NINEVEH MOMENT" AND "GREAT HARVEST REVIVAL"

In 2013, I interviewed world-renowned evangelist Billy Graham for a WND. com series on the possibility of an end-times awakening—one of his final interviews on the Second Coming of Christ.

Graham, who preached to nearly 215 million people in over 185 countries and counseled every American president from Harry Truman to George H. W. Bush, died at age ninety-nine on February 21, 2018, just weeks after I joined a prayer gathering at The Billy Graham Training Center at The Cove in Asheville, North Carolina, to ask God for a national day of repentance.[18]

"There's a great deal to say in the Bible about the signs we're to watch for and when these signs all converge at one place we can be sure that we're close to the end of the age," Graham said. "And those signs, in my judgment, are converging now for the first time since Jesus made those predictions."[19]

Graham compared America to ancient Nineveh, the lone superpower of its time, noting that when Jonah proclaimed God's warning, the people repented and were spared judgment. He believed the same thing could happen again, this time in America.

"If ever there was a time this country needed the intervention of God, it is now," Graham said. "We can and should pray for America as a whole, but remember that when God sets out to change a nation, He begins by changing people. It starts with individuals."[20]

His words recall a statement he made to Los Angeles reporters during the 1949 Greater Los Angeles Revival: "When God gets ready to shake America, He may not take the Ph.D. and the D.D. God may choose a country boy....God may choose the man that no one knows, a little nobody, to shake America for Jesus Christ in this day, and I pray that He would!"[21]

Inspired by that interview, McGuire and I called for a day of national repentance in our 2018 book *Trumpocalypse*. By a miracle of the Holy Spirit, The Return took place on September 26, 2020, on the National Mall, drawing about 42 million viewers worldwide.[22]

In 2021, Pastor Paul Begley approached me to coauthor *Revelation 911: How the Book of Revelation Intersects with Today's Headlines*, based on a vision in which the Lord told him, "Revelation 9:11. It's about to happen. Warn the people."[23]

Revelation 9:11 says, "They had as king over them the angel of the Abyss, whose name in Hebrew is Abaddon and in Greek is Apollyon (that is, Destroyer)."

This often-overlooked chapter in the Book of Revelation tells the story of a key being given to an angel who uses it to open the Abyss—a bottomless pit in which the worst of the beings cast out of heaven alongside Lucifer have been kept imprisoned.

Begley believes the hour is near, with accelerating end-times signs leading toward economic collapse, a global conflagration, and the rise of the Antichrist. The book notes that by the time an angel blows the sixth trumpet in Revelation 9, about half the world's population will have perished in wars, plagues, and catastrophic natural disasters during the tribulation.

The book's final chapter, "The 'Great Harvest Revival' and You," envisions a brief end-times revival before the tribulation, calling believers to join the "army of God" and help "bring in the great harvest."[24]

In August 2025, Begley told me he believes we are "in the very beginning stages" of this revival:

There's been record baptisms in California and massive crowds gathering at stadiums....The Bible says..."Blessed are those who hunger and thirst for righteousness, for [they] will be filled" [Matt. 5:6]....We've seen...the Asbury [Revival] and...college campuses [baptizing thousands]...but it's still not even close to where it's going to get....

So I'm going to say on a scale of one to ten, we're almost a two.... This thing is going to blow sky high....[Another] sign of revival is you see athletes who score touchdowns, win Super Bowls, hit grand-slam home runs...and when asked how they did it...their answer is, "I want to thank my Lord and Savior Jesus Christ."...This is beginning sparks of the mighty revival.[25]

Begley calls this America's Nineveh moment:

We have fallen so far away from the truth that God is going to give us one last chance to make this thing right....You've got to start with repentance. That's what did it in Nineveh. I think that's what Billy Graham really meant when he said this could be America's Nineveh moment. He knew that if repentance didn't come to America, America would be destroyed.[26]

Jonah's message to Nineveh was simple: "You're going to be destroyed." Yet the people repented, fasted, and prayed, and God relented. God can change His mind and delay the fulfillment of prophecy.

What changed God's mind was they believed the preaching of Jonah, they fell on their knees and they began to fast and pray and cry out to God in repentance, and God saw their hearts and changed His mind. God can change His mind on the timing. He'll hold things back because He's a God that cannot lie. If you repent, He will bless you. If you don't, judgment will come. And so this is our [Nineveh] moment.[27]

To watch my interview with Paul Begley, scan the QR code or visit TroyAndersonBooks.com/begley.

THE TIPPING POINT

While God has used Trump's leadership to help spark the current revival, the real tipping point lies not in the Oval Office but in the church.

Historically, Great Awakenings have erupted in times of crisis. But what if the long-anticipated final Great Awakening is not just another revival but the culmination of God's destiny for America? Dutch Sheets, an internationally recognized teacher known for the "Appeal to Heaven" flag and movement, said:

> There's another level of intercession, prophetic declaration, kingly intercession—making decrees for Him—that is going to now launch us into what we've been asking for 25, 30 years—a third Great Awakening in America, another Great Awakening around the world, and I believe the greatest harvest of history begins now.
>
> Our Founders knew there was no way they could defeat the British unless God intervened....[They actually] put the phrase ["Appeal to Heaven"] in the Declaration [of Independence] at the end....[The Holy Spirit told me], "I need to use what I used to birth [the United States] to rebirth you because America needs a rebirth."...We're an apostate nation. We have rejected Him.[28]

Sheets emphasized that revival begins with a heart change: "It's a return to Him. It's a return to His Word. It's a return to His ways....I believe we'll see more people saved in the next 20 years than we have in the previous 2,000. I think in the billions....The best days of the church are not behind us; they're ahead of us."[29]

This awakening will not be limited to revival tents or Sunday services. It's already spreading into media, education, government, business, and the arts—a holy invasion of every sphere of influence, an Acts 2 outpouring on a global scale.

As McGuire foresaw in his July 4, 2012, vision,[30] California will play a key role. Kim Clement likewise prophesied on March 2, 2013, about "California, fire, and a coming spiritual revolution"—possibly connected to the January 2025 wildfires that burned over 50,000 acres, destroyed nearly 16,000 structures, and caused at least 440 deaths.[31]

"'That which I did in the '60s and the '70s, I have revealed this is that time again,'" Clement said. "'But it shall not be like then where it is restricted to just a few continents. This movement,' says the Lord, 'will begin again in California. And there shall be an economic boost in California. And they shall say, 'Why California? Is it not the hellhole of America?' God says, 'I don't care what it is; I will take the economy of California and show America that I will take the foolish things of this world to confound the wise. Then I will take the low things of this world to make my light shine.'"[32]

This is America's Nineveh moment—a brief window for repentance and alignment with God's destiny. If the church responds in humility, what follows could shake not just a nation, but the nations of the world.

THE CHURCH'S PROPHETIC CALL: RECONCILIATION, UNITY, AND REVIVAL

For revival to reach its full potential and healing to come to America, it must begin within the church. In times of national crisis, the church's mandate is not political triumph but unity, forgiveness, and reconciliation.

Too often the church has allowed the nation's politics to shape its theology rather than allowing its theology to shape the nation's politics. This inversion has weakened its witness and eroded its role as a moral and spiritual compass. Today, many believers remain divided by race, denomination, politics, and ideology.

THE CHURCH'S MANDATE IS NOT POLITICAL TRIUMPH BUT UNITY, FORGIVENESS, AND RECONCILIATION.

Before revival can fully unfold, the body of Christ must forgive past sins—slavery, division, polarization—and come together in unity. Scripture is clear: All are made in the image of God. Jesus condemned discrimination, urging wise judgment over superficial appearances:

- "Stop judging by mere appearances, but instead judge correctly" (John 7:24).

- "The LORD does not look at the things people look at. People look at the outward appearance, but the LORD looks at the heart" (1 Sam.16:7).

- "There is neither Jew nor Gentile...for you are all one in Christ Jesus" (Gal. 3:28).

- "But anyone who hates a brother or sister is in the darkness..." (1 John 2:11).

- "For we were all baptized by one Spirit...and we were all given the one Spirit to drink" (1 Cor. 12:13).

Jesus modeled radical forgiveness, dying so we could be reconciled to God and to one another. "Do not judge....Forgive, and you will be forgiven" (Luke 6:37).

Unity requires humility, compassion, and forgiveness. Offenses block the flow of the Holy Spirit, making unforgiveness one of Satan's most effective weapons.

Forgiveness is not weakness. It's spiritual leadership. The church must reclaim its identity as a "peculiar people" (1 Pet. 2:9, KJV), marked not by politics or denominational differences, but by love so radical it breaks barriers the world cannot.

Jesus prayed that they "may be one...so that the world may believe..." (John 17:21). Unity is not optional. It is the very soil in which revival grows.

As the body of Christ forgives, repents, and reconciles, it will regain its prophetic voice and lead in the next great move of the Holy Spirit.

GLOBAL REVIVAL: SIX STEPS TO AWAKENING

1. Organize prayer vigils and fasting campaigns

Join or create national efforts like our "40 Days to Save America" campaign of prayer, fasting, and repentance and mobilize local intercessory prayer groups calling for God's intervention. Focus prayer on family, friends, leaders, and revival. Engage in fasting, as encouraged in Joel 2:12: "'Even now,' declares the LORD, 'return to me with all your heart, with fasting and weeping and mourning.'" Prayer and fasting have preceded every great awakening in America.

2. Promote civic engagement with biblical values

Christians must redeem the public sphere—vote, encourage godly leaders to run for office, and speak truth to power. Matthew 5:13–16 says, "You are the salt of the earth....You are the light of the world....Let your light shine before others...." The silence of the church has let secularism and satanic evil dominate. Now is the time to speak graciously, courageously, and biblically.

3. Cultivate the next generation

Barna Group research shows most youth raised in the church leave the faith by adulthood.[33] The answer is discipleship, not entertainment. Prioritize mentorship, teaching biblical literacy, and worship. The next generation needs to witness the awesome power and presence of God.

4. Model revival in daily life

Revival starts in kitchens, classrooms, and conference rooms. Be a light in dark places. Host Bible studies, pray for coworkers, and live with integrity. Colossians 3:23 says, "Whatever you do, work at it with all your heart, as working for the Lord, not for human masters." When believers align with God's values, revival becomes visible.

5. Multiply leaders and movements

True revival reproduces. Invest in new leaders, empower Generation Alpha, Gen Z, and Millennial voices, and build unity across denominations and generations. Second Timothy 2:2 says, "And the things you have heard me say in the presence of many witnesses entrust to reliable people who will also be qualified to teach others."

6. Steward media and technology for the gospel

In a screen-driven world, revival must speak the digital language. Equip believers to use YouTube, TikTok, Instagram, podcasts, and live streams to spread the gospel. Romans 10:14 asks: "How, then, can they call on the one they have not believed in? And how can they believe in the one of whom they have not heard? And how can they hear without someone preaching to them?" The early church used Roman roads. We must use today's digital roads with authentic testimonies.

REVIVAL FLOURISHES WHEN HEARTS ARE BROKEN BEFORE GOD AND THE GOSPEL IS PROCLAIMED.

The spiritual fuel behind the road map

While these six steps offer a strategic blueprint, revival is not engineered by people—it is ignited by the Holy Spirit. History shows that moves of God are fueled by passionate prayer, sincere repentance, unapologetic evangelism, and radical obedience.

Revival flourishes when hearts are broken before God and the gospel is proclaimed. In this age, God is raising up messengers for a new frontier as Generation Z, Generation Alpha, and Millennials are scrolling for truth. Now is the time to fill the airwaves and algorithms with glory. Worship must invade the culture, evangelism must reclaim the lost, and the gospel must go viral.

Without the Spirit's power, even the best blueprint is just ink on paper. But when fueled by prayer and prophetic fire, these steps become a highway for a world-changing awakening.

PASSING THE TORCH TO THE NEXT GENERATION

Every move of God faces the same test: Will it last beyond the generation that birthed it?

Revival is not just about the first flame but about faithfully stewarding it and intentionally passing it on. Most revivals last only one or two generations unless sustained through discipleship.

If we want young people to carry this revival forward, they must witness God's miraculous power. Pastor Paul Begley said in an interview:

> Young people are disenchanted. You know what it is? They really want the real thing. They've been living in a pretend video…AI world. They've been looking and seeing things always polished.…I knew something was up when they started looking for…the old vinyl records [that]…have this…unbelievable sound. They want to go find an old record from the '70s and…listen to that original sound. They want original. They want people to be real. They want the pastors to be real. They want the message to be real. They want to be among each other and have a real feeling—a real relationship with God.…
>
> Everybody wants to go back to the original, and so I really believe that's the only way we're going to have revival.…We got to get back to the altar, back to the foundations of Christ, back to water baptism, back to the power of prayer, back to fasting, back to testifying, back to witnessing…and take it out there to the people who are hunting for something that's legitimate.[34]

As Deuteronomy 6:5–9 reminds us: "Love the LORD your God with all your heart and with all your soul and with all your strength. These commandments that I give you today are to be on your hearts. Impress them on your children. Talk about them when you sit at home and when you walk along the road, when you lie down and when you get up. Tie them as symbols on your hands and bind them on your foreheads. Write them on the doorframes of your houses and on your gates."

AMERICA'S AWAKENING AND THE GLOBAL RIPPLE EFFECT

From its earliest days America has carried a unique, though flawed, spiritual identity.

Despite failures, the prophetic mantle remains. If revival takes root here, it will not remain within our borders.

Historically, American revivals have sent shockwaves worldwide. The Azusa Street Revival of 1906 birthed modern Pentecostalism, now spanning the globe. Today, new revival centers are emerging in Brazil, Nigeria, Iran, and South Korea. Yet the United States still holds a crucial key because of its faith infrastructure:

mission networks, media platforms, theological training centers, and the global influence of the American church.

The end-time harvest will not be led by one nation alone, but America is called to be a spark—not because we are better, but because we are accountable. To whom much is given, much is required.

A CALL TO COURAGEOUS HOPE

Hope is not naïve optimism. It is the confident expectation that God will fulfill His promises. "It's time for us to take church seriously," wrote Flashpoint television show host Gene Bailey in *Flashpoint of Revival.* "The church is not a social club, a country club, or a motivational seminar....No more sitting on the sidelines. This fight for our faith in America is a marathon, not a sprint. Without perseverance and endurance, we won't survive. We need to get tough individually, and then we need to join together collectively as a force to be reckoned with! Evangelists need to evangelize. Prophets need to prophesy and not apologize. Pastors need to pastor. Leaders need to lead. And believers need to believe God for what seems to be impossible."[35]

AMERICA IS CALLED TO BE A SPARK—NOT BECAUSE WE ARE BETTER, BUT BECAUSE WE ARE ACCOUNTABLE.

God is not seeking perfect vessels but yielded ones. "Jesus is telling anyone who will listen that the harvest is now," evangelist Mario Murillo wrote in *It's Our Turn Now: God's Plan to Restore America Is Within Our Reach.* "Do not think more must happen before we harvest souls....Look with spiritual eyes to the fields."[36]

The fields are white, the harvest is here, and our call is clear.

The apostle Paul urged in Galatians 6:9, "Let us not become weary in doing good, for at the proper time we will reap a harvest if we do not give up."

Now is not the time for retreat or silence in the face of evil. It is the time for faithful courage, radical prayer, and unshakable hope.

The dream is alive. The hour is now. America and the world—revival awaits those who believe God can do the impossible.

THE REVIVAL GENERATION: FROM BAPTIZE CALIFORNIA TO "BAPTIZE THE WORLD"

Jesus came to the earth the first time on the heels of a national water baptism movement with a wild man named John the Baptist. Could it be that Jesus Christ returns to the earth the second time on the heels of a national water baptism movement?
—PASTOR MARK FRANCEY, FOUNDER OF BAPTIZE AMERICA[1]

ON JUNE 8, 2025, my wife, Irene, and I attended the Baptize America event at Pirate's Cove in Corona del Mar, California—the iconic birthplace of the Jesus movement. In the late 1960s and '70s, Calvary Chapel Costa Mesa Pastor Chuck Smith and hippie preacher Lonnie Frisbee baptized thousands of young people in the Pacific Ocean beneath these craggy cliffs.

After climbing over the rocks covered with hundreds of people gathered on Pentecost Sunday for this historic event, we took the stairs down to the secluded beach to watch the baptisms.

We interviewed Kandis McGee, a young woman preparing to be baptized. She described the hunger for Jesus among her generation.

> It's incredible. I just think the new generation is so hungry for something more and something different. I think they're tired of living with this anxiety and depression and [want to live] for something other than themselves....So many more people are more outspoken about their faith....In a funny way, it's become a trend to wear Christian clothing or to post about your faith and to pray for people....Pastor Mark called it kind of like the Great Awakening...Baptize America, and then eventually baptize the world. That's the hope.[2]

The 2025 Baptize America event became the largest synchronized baptism in US history: 650 churches hosted 1,080 events nationwide, baptizing 27,858 people, with 6,445 salvations.[3]

The inspiration came in 2022 while Oceans Church Pastor Mark Francey was praying and reading one of evangelist Mario Murillo's books on awakenings. He learned about the largest baptism in American history up to that point, in 1990 at Pirate's Cove, and heard "that internal whisper of the Holy Spirit."[4]

"He said, 'Mark, I want you to do this again. I want you to organize it....I want it to be a big 'C' church effort to fulfill the Great Commission.'"[5]

Francey described the revelation:

> I heard the heart of Jesus saying, "Mark, my lost kids only understand three days: They understand My birth at Christmas, they understand My resurrection at Easter, and they understand that water baptism is powerful....The church started in Acts 2 on the day of Pentecost—3,000 believed, 3,000 were baptized."...It's interesting that it's maybe one of the only doctrinal creeds that all of God's kids [agree on].[6]

To view my conversation with Mark Francey, scan the QR code or visit TroyAndersonBooks.com/francey.

In 2023, Baptize Southern California saw more than 4,100 baptisms. In 2024, the event expanded to Huntington Beach with over 12,000 baptisms at the beach and statewide. In May 2025, Baptize California baptized 7,752 more. By August 2025, over 50,000 had been baptized through more than 1,600 churches.[7]

Francey recalled God's challenge:

> He said, "Mark, if I could...revive Southern California, could I do it in all of California?" And I said, "Yes." And then I heard a whisper again saying, "If I could do it in California, could I do it in America?" And I'm like, "Yeah."...And then I heard a third question, "If I could do it in America, could this happen in other nations?" And I said, "Absolutely."... Our belief is that what starts on the shores of Southern California could go to the ends of the earth, and will.[8]

Looking ahead, Francey said President Trump wants to "make a very big deal about faith in America" as part of its 250th anniversary. As a part of this, Baptize America is beginning to plan a mass baptism event on the National Mall in Washington, D.C. around July 4, 2026.[9] Francey says:

I don't think that revival is coming. I think we're already in the shallow end of it and…it's going to get stronger.…We are in the middle of a great move of God in our nation.[10]

THE COURAGE TO DISRUPT

From the opening pages of *Designated Disrupter*, we've seen that we are living in a time of disruption of biblical proportions.

What began as whispers at The Return and the Asbury Revival is now a roar. From the Golden Gate Bridge to Pirate's Cove, from the National Mall to the streets of Los Angeles, from college campuses to TikTok feeds, the Holy Spirit is sweeping the nation.

This revolution is not led by the perfect or polished but by unlikely men and women—God's designated disrupters.

Trump, flawed yet Jehu-like, has been raised up to restrain the spirit of antichrist and a globalist takeover. Alongside him stand pastors, podcasters, celebrities, athletes, academics, and everyday believers courageous enough to step into the cultural hippodrome and point a generation back to God.

In the preface we declared how God uses the "foolish things of the world to shame the wise" (1 Cor. 1:27). Throughout this book we've traced how He is doing it again—shaking governments, disrupting the Deep State, and rattling globalist control systems. His purpose is greater than saving America. It is preparing the way for global revival.

Trump's reelection was a prophetic shooting star across the heavens: God is giving America and the world a reprieve, a Nineveh moment, an invitation to turn back before the last trumpet sounds.

The evidence is undeniable: prayer rising in public spaces, young people boldly wearing Christian apparel, worship flooding stadiums, and baptismal waters overflowing. Revival is here.

THE GREATEST REVIVAL IN HISTORY: THE STORY OF JONAH

In his classic 1971 sermon "The Greatest Revival in History," famed evangelist Billy Graham read from Matthew 12, recounting how the scribes and Pharisees asked Jesus for a sign. The only one He gave was the sign of Jonah. Graham described how God prepared a great fish to swallow the prophet, emphasizing that Jonah's primary mission was Nineveh's repentance. He said:

> The greatest miracle of all was the greatest revival in the history of the world—when one of the greatest cities of all of world history turned, from the king on down, to God in repentance of sin and faith in God.[11]

Nineveh stood on the brink of destruction, its wickedness so great that judgment was inevitable. Then one man obeyed the call of God, and a nation fell to its knees in repentance.

Today, America and the world are facing their own Nineveh moment. The storm clouds of war, moral collapse, and global turmoil are gathered over the nations. Yet the Bible reminds us: When people humble themselves, repent, and turn to God, He relents from judgment and pours out His Spirit.

Nineveh's dramatic transformation is an example of the unmatched scale of revival that can occur when a leader leads the population to turn toward God. It also provides a prophetic parallel for modern nations, including America, to heed God's warning before judgment falls. The revival in Nineveh is the prophetic blueprint for our time. Billy Graham said:

> When God saw their repentance, God changed his mind. He deferred judgment. The judgment was about to fall. They repented, and there's one thing God cannot do, and that's judge a man that's repenting or a man that's in Jesus Christ because you see, the word repentance means change. Change the direction of your life, change the pattern of your living. Change everything in your life because you see, Jesus Christ is a disturber. He comes to disturb. You can't be the same again when you've met Jesus, you are different. "Old things pass away and everything becomes new."[12]

If Nineveh could repent in forty days, America can repent today. But the call will not last forever. The question is, Will we answer before the window closes?

THE LEGACY OF REVIVAL

To grasp the weight of this moment, we must remember how God has moved before. We discussed America's legacy of revival and awakening in chapter 3.

Each of these awakenings seemed impossible at the time. Each disrupted the status quo, yet each was orchestrated by the Holy Spirit to call His people back and prepare them for what was coming.

Now we stand in that same stream. What God began in the colonies, rekindled on the frontier, unleashed on Azusa Street, and reignited in the Jesus movement is happening again. And once more He is using the unlikely—the disrupters, the broken, the willing—to carry His flame of revival to a new generation.

A GLOBAL AWAKENING IS UNDERWAY

Throughout this book we have chronicled the testimonies of faith leaders, disrupters, and everyday believers God is using to ignite a new spiritual awakening.

In a 2013 interview, Billy Graham foresaw a great awakening before Christ's return. Evangelist Reinhard Bonnke, who saw nearly 100 million people respond to the gospel, declared by the Holy Spirit that "All America shall be saved." Sid Roth has repeatedly proclaimed his conviction that "God's greater glory" is soon to manifest in the world. These prophetic witnesses laid a foundation, helping us recognize that a wave of revival is spreading worldwide.

The Baptize America movement is one of the most visible signs of this awakening. What began on the shores of Southern California is now sweeping across the nation and beyond as people publicly confess their faith in Christ and rise from baptismal waters with a fire to share "the hope that is in you" (1 Pet. 3:15, NKJV).

This movement is a visible sign of an outpouring of the Holy Spirit, a return to the power of the Book of Acts when three thousand people were baptized on the day of Pentecost. Through Baptize America, through Hollywood and through unexpected voices, the Holy Spirit is spreading revival in ways the world has never seen.

This awakening is not centralized or controlled by a single leader. It is springing up everywhere—across churches, campuses, cities, and nations. It is living proof that the Spirit of God is moving and the spiritual awakening millions have prayed for is no longer a distant hope. It is here.

THE BURNING HEARTS GENERATION

For years cultural commentators painted Generation Alpha, Generation Z, and Millennials as disillusioned, distracted, and even "lost."

Yet in an astonishingly short time, these are the very generations the Holy Spirit is using to ignite revival in America and beyond. With a hunger for authenticity, young people are rejecting lifeless religion. They want what is real, and many are experiencing life-changing encounters with Jesus.

We saw it in 2023 at Asbury University, where a routine chapel service turned into weeks of nonstop worship, prayer, and repentance, drawing tens of thousands from across the nation. Similar outpourings followed at Lee University, Baylor, Texas A&M, and many more institutions.

We see it at mass baptism events like Baptize SoCal, Baptize California, and Baptize America, where tens of thousands—mostly young people—step into oceans, lakes, and baptismal pools. Some grew up in church but never truly believed; others arrived as seekers or skeptics, only to leave as followers of Christ.

We see it on social media, where viral TikTok, Instagram, and YouTube videos capture students praying in classrooms, baptizing friends in bathtubs, and proclaiming the gospel on street corners.

This is not the image of a "lost" generation. This is the portrait of a chosen one. Far from being the weak link in the chain, Generation Alpha, Generation Z, and Millennials are the tip of the spear in the greatest awakening of our time.

What older generations feared might be the end of faith in America is becoming its rebirth.

CHARLIE KIRK AND THE CALL OF THE DISRUPTERS

Most every generation faces a time when the course of history cannot be left to politicians, institutions, and cultural elites. It's the moment when God raises up unlikely men and women, people willing to disrupt the status quo.

We have seen this in President Trump, who against all odds defied the globalist agenda and became a vessel for shaking America's foundations. We have seen it in pastors, evangelists, and prophetic leaders who continue to call the church to repentance. And now we have seen it in Charlie Kirk, a young man whose words stirred a generation and whose martyrdom has started a fire that no one can extinguish.

Kirk's death was not the end of a movement. His wife, Erika, has stepped into the prophetic role of a modern Esther, leading Turning Point USA and calling a generation to carry her husband's mission forward. Her voice is itself a sign that God multiplies what the enemy tries to destroy. Together, Charlie and Erika represent the torch now passed to Generations Z and Alpha to carry forward the revival underway.

Their courage testifies that God is raising up a new wave of designated disrupters.

During the emotional memorial service in Kirk's honor on September 21, 2025, in Glendale, Arizona, Erika recalled a speech her husband gave at AmericaFest 2023 in which he spoke of willingness to follow God's calling, quoting Isaiah 6:8: "Here I am, Lord. Send me."

"After Charlie finished, I met him backstage and told him there is so much power in those words, because when you say, 'Here I am, Lord, use me,' God will take you up on that," Erika said. "And He did with Charlie. Eleven days ago, God accepted that total surrender and called him to His side."[13]

When Erika saw her husband's body at the hospital, she took comfort in his final expression.

"Even in death, I could see the man that I love," she said. "I also saw on his lips the faintest smile, and that told me...Charlie didn't suffer....One moment Charlie was doing what he loved, arguing and debating on campus, fighting for the gospel and truth...and then he blinked—he blinked and saw his Savior in paradise....

"After Charlie's assassination, we didn't see violence, we didn't see rioting, we didn't see revolution. Instead...we saw revival. This past week, we saw people open a Bible for the first time in a decade. We saw people pray for the first time since they were children. We saw people go to a church service for the first time in their entire lives....That is what Charlie always prayed for in this country."[14]

And so, the charge remains for us all. This is not a time for silence. This is not a time for retreat. Like President Trump, like Charlie, like Erika, like the prophets of old, we are called to rise to the occasion in obedience to the Lord. We are called to speak truth without fear and to live out our faith without apology.

This is our time. This is our mission. And like the disrupters before us, we are called to stand, to speak out, and to never surrender.

THE GLOBAL RIPPLE EFFECT

Though much of this book has focused on America, the revival is far larger than one nation. The same Spirit stirring campuses, stadiums, and streets in America is moving with power worldwide—a global blaze preparing the bride of Christ for His return.

In Africa, mass baptisms are breaking records, continuing the legacy of evangelists like Reinhard Bonnke, who saw tens of millions come to Christ. Fields across the continent still fill with people hungry for salvation.

In China, despite fierce persecution and surveillance, the underground church is flourishing. House churches multiply in apartments, warehouses, and hidden places. By 2030, China is projected to be the world's largest Christian nation, with 247 million believers.[15]

"It is going to be less than a generation. Not many people are prepared for this dramatic change," said Fenggang Yang, a leading expert on religion in China. "Mao [Zedong] thought he could eliminate religion. He thought he had accomplished this. It's ironic—they didn't. They actually failed completely."[16]

In Latin America, revival is sweeping cities and towns where Pentecostal fire blends with Catholic traditions. Stadiums fill with worshippers, prayer marches flood streets, and reports of healings and conversions abound.

Even in Europe, long called "post-Christian," signs of awakening are emerging. In Germany, France, and the United Kingdom people march singing gospel songs, prayer movements are growing, and young people are rediscovering the faith of their ancestors. Missionaries are even being sent back to re-evangelize their homelands.

The Spirit of God is moving from continent to continent. What began in an upper room in Jerusalem two thousand years ago is reaching a worldwide crescendo.

This is not just America's Nineveh moment; it is the world's. As Jesus promised: "The gospel of the kingdom will be proclaimed throughout the whole world as a testimony to all nations, and then the end will come" (Matt. 24:14, ESV).

A SOLOMON WINDOW: THE "WEALTH TRANSFER" AND GLOBAL REVIVAL

What if we are entering a season of national blessing too? Just as King Solomon's reign ushered Israel into peace, prosperity, and influence, many see a similar "Solomon window" opening over America.

"The whole world sought audience with Solomon to hear the wisdom God had put in his heart" (1 Kings 10:24).

Trump's economic policies—reciprocal tariffs, AI investment, and efforts to make America the "crypto capital of the world"—are doing more than reshaping markets.[17]

In July 2025, he signed the GENIUS Act, making stablecoins more accessible by allowing banks to issue them, boosting trust in digital assets.[18]

Many faith leaders see this as part of a coming "wealth transfer" long prophesied in Scripture.

"The wealth of the sinner is stored up for the righteous" (Prov. 13:22, NKJV).

Joseph Z believes cryptocurrencies could be one vehicle for this transfer to help fund global revival. He pointed to Joseph's leadership during Egypt's famine (Gen. 47), when he strategically managed resources for a nation in crisis.

> When you think about Genesis 47, verse 15, it says when all the money failed in Egypt, the people came to Joseph....He was positioned... to be in the right place at the right time to manage the great wealth transfer, which often comes on the heels of a great crisis....I do believe God is preserving the wealth of the wicked to fund a last-days great

awakening....I think it involves crypto. I think it involves a number of things that are going to [be shaken] and it's going to be a change.[19]

Before the rise of the Antichrist and his "mark of the beast" system, Joseph Z said he believes digital currencies may serve the righteous:

> It says in Isaiah 45:3 [NKJV], He gives the hidden "treasures of darkness"...I believe that is coming....The only caveat is it's not going to be the way people have thought....When the people left Egypt... they left fully loaded....The wealth of the wicked [was prepared] for the righteous....But it will not come to those that are inactive, that are hiding and watching and not participating in the greatest move that God has launched on the earth in our generation...[but to those rightly aligned], positioned at the right place at the right time....If you obey God...I believe the wealth transfer is very real.[20]

Meanwhile, America's economy is rebounding—foreign investment is rising and manufacturing is returning.

But just as Solomon's reign depended on alignment with God's covenant, so too must America remember the source of her blessing. This window of opportunity is about fulfilling the nation's prophetic destiny to help fund and inspire global awakening.

"Arise, shine, for your light has come, and the glory of the LORD rises upon you" (Isa. 60:1).

STEP INTO THE ARENA

On April 23, 1910, in the Sorbonne in Paris, President Theodore Roosevelt delivered what would become one of the most quoted speeches of the twentieth century. Titled "Citizenship in a Republic," it contained a now-legendary passage known as "The Man in the Arena."

> It is not the critic who counts; not the man who points out how the strong man stumbles....The credit belongs to the man who is actually in the arena....[21]

As Roosevelt reminded us, it is not the critic who matters, but the one who dares—the man in the arena who risks, struggles, and gives his all for a cause greater than himself.

This book is a summons to that arena. A call to rise from the sidelines of history and step into the great story God is writing in our generation.

Like Noah, who built an ark when rain had never fallen; like Esther, who risked her life to intercede for her people; like Peter, who stepped onto the stormy waters of the Sea of Galilee; and like the apostle Paul, who proclaimed Christ before emperors and mobs, we may feel unqualified, unprepared, or overwhelmed. But God does not call the equipped; He equips the called. He qualifies the willing.

To be a designated disrupter is not to seek applause but to carry heaven's flame into dark places. It means daring greatly in prayer when others stay silent, witnessing boldly when culture demands compromise, sacrificing comfort for the gospel, and standing with courage when fear seeks to silence you.

The arena may not be a pulpit or stage. For some it is a classroom, a boardroom, a kitchen table, or the battlefield of ideas. Wherever God has placed you, He has positioned you to make an eternal difference. Your "yes" to Him—even in the smallest act of obedience—can ripple into eternity in ways unseen this side of heaven.

The world is watching, heaven is recording, and God is seeking those who will not shrink back but dare to live as His chosen disrupters in this critical hour.

"Therefore we make it our aim, whether present or absent, to be well pleasing to Him. For we must all appear before the judgment seat of Christ, that each one may receive the things done in the body, according to what he has done, whether good or bad" (2 Cor. 5:9–10, NKJV).

THE CALL TO HOLY DISRUPTION

As we conclude, remember this: Revival is not a spectator sport.

The Spirit of God is beckoning you—yes, you personally—to join the awakening shaking our generation. Revival begins in the home: in how you lead your family in prayer, in the courage with which you share the gospel, in your willingness to speak truth into a culture addicted to lies, and in the love you pour out as you serve your community.

It continues as you step into the arena God has placed before you—whether in politics, media, education, business, or the hidden places where few may ever see, but heaven takes note.

You may feel small, but so did David before Goliath. You may feel unworthy, but so did Peter before Pentecost. You may feel outnumbered, but so did Gideon when his army was reduced to three hundred. Yet in every case, history did not belong to the critics on the sidelines; it belonged to those who dared to believe God at His Word.

This is your moment. This is your call. Join the ranks of the great biblical heroes. Step into holy disruption.

RETURN OF THE KING OF KINGS AND LORD OF LORDS

Every revival in history—and the grand arc of redemption from Eden's Fall to Christ—has been pointing toward this moment.

In America's history, each awakening laid the foundation for a move of God. And now, this present revival is preparing the world for the greatest event in history: the return of the King of kings and Lord of lords.

The prophets and disciples foresaw this. Joel declared: "I will pour out my Spirit on all people" (Joel 2:28). At Pentecost, Peter proclaimed, "This is what was spoken by the prophet Joel" (Acts 2:16).

Yet Pentecost was only the beginning. The ultimate fulfillment is still to come, when the Spirit is poured out in unprecedented measure as signs in the heavens and wonders on earth point to Christ's return. Rabbi Jonathan Bernis said:

> I believe there [is] going to be a last, final revival....It's going to be massive. Now is the time to get in on it—to become a prayer warrior, to begin to step out and proclaim your faith, and not to allow the cancel culture to keep holding you back....
>
> It's time to break out of those restraints now and boldly proclaim our faith from the mountaintops. This is the opportunity, and yes, this is our last chance, and there is going to be a turnaround that's already blowing my mind, but it's going to be much, much greater than what we've seen so far, but it's happening before our very eyes.[22]

The outpouring we see today—on campuses and in stadiums, churches, and the digital world—is preparing the bride for the Bridegroom, the return of Jesus Christ.

This is why obedience matters. Every prayer at the family table, every choice of righteousness over compromise, every act of gospel witness prepares the way of the Lord. Jesus said, "Store up for yourselves treasures in heaven" (Matt. 6:20). What we do now will reverberate throughout eternity.

The revival before us is an act of mercy—a final call before the last trumpet sounds. The Holy Spirit is waking His end-times army of warriors, aligning the church with its prophetic destiny, and reminding us the time is short.

The gospel is going forth to the nations, the bride is being prepared, and soon the King of kings will return in great glory.

THE LAST TRUMPET

The Spirit is being poured out, the warriors of Christ are rising, and the King is coming soon.

Now is the time for all of us to step forward as God's disrupters.

May the history books—and more importantly, the scrolls of heaven—record that when the world teetered on the brink, we dared greatly, prayed fervently, lived faithfully, and helped usher in the last great awakening before the return of Christ.

"And behold, I am coming quickly, and My reward is with Me, to give to every one according to his work. I am the Alpha and the Omega, the Beginning and the End, the First and the Last" (Rev. 22:12–13, NKJV).

Maranatha! Come, Lord Jesus.

A PERSONAL INVITATION FROM THE AUTHOR

GOD LOVES YOU deeply. His Word is filled with promises that reveal His desire to bring healing, hope, and abundant life to every area of your being—body, mind, and spirit. More than anything, He wants a personal relationship with you through His Son, Jesus Christ.

If you've never invited Jesus into your life, you can do so right now. It's not about religion—it's about a relationship with the One who knows you completely and loves you unconditionally. If you're ready to take that step, simply pray this prayer with a sincere heart:

> *Lord Jesus, I want to know You as my Savior and Lord. I confess and believe that You are the Son of God and that You died for my sins. I believe You rose from the dead and are alive today. Please forgive me for my sins. I invite You into my heart and my life. Make me new. Help me to walk with You, grow in Your love, and live for You every day. In Jesus' name, amen.*

If you just prayed that prayer, you've made the most important decision of your life. All of heaven rejoices with you, and so do I! You are now a child of God, and your journey with Him has just begun.

To hear me personally share about what it means to follow Christ, scan the QR code on this page. I would be honored to guide you through the life-changing decision to accept Jesus and experience His love for yourself.

TroyAndersonBooks.com/author-note

If you accepted Jesus today—or if this book has encouraged or impacted your life in any way—please reach out to my publisher at pray4me@charisma-media.com. We'd love to celebrate with you and send you free materials to help strengthen your faith. We look forward to hearing from you!

ACKNOWLEDGMENTS

I AM PROFOUNDLY GRATEFUL to Stephen and Joy Strang, founders of Charisma Media, along with Chief Operating Officer Chad Dunlap, Director of Product Development Debbie Marrie, and the entire Charisma Media team for their vision and partnership in bringing this book to life.

I am deeply thankful to everyone at Charisma Media for recognizing the timeliness and importance of this book. Your support in helping chronicle the unfolding revival—and in encouraging readers to join in what the Holy Spirit is doing in our time—has been invaluable.

My sincere gratitude goes to Adrienne Gaines, developmental editor at Charisma Media, for her superb editorial insights, as well as to editor Tammy Fitzgerald and copy editor and copywriter Makena Song. I also want to thank Content Manager Robert Caggiano, Media Manager John Matarazzo, Director of Sales and Marketing Joshua Nolette, Publicity Coordinator Christian Lebron, and the entire Charisma team for their excellent work in bringing this book to readers.

Special gratitude goes to Pastor Paul Begley; his wife, Heidi; and the prayer team led by Chrystal Shields for their tireless prayers and steadfast encouragement. I am thankful as well to Paul McGuire for his enlightening foreword, and to McGuire, Begley, Sid Roth, Joseph Z, Sean Feucht, Rabbi Jonathan Bernis, Dr. Corné J. Bekker, Taylan Michael Seaman, Pastor Mark Francey, Dr. Bruce Oliver, Bishop Daniel Timotheos Yohannan, Sean Dunn, Tonya Prewitt, Pastor Caleb Cooper, Kandis McGee, and others for their insightful interviews, contributions, and prophetic voices featured in these pages.

I'd also like to express my gratitude to Pastor Paul Begley, Rabbi Jonathan Bernis, Dr. Robert Jeffress, Joseph Z, Jerry Moses, Michael Snyder, and others who graciously provided endorsements for *Designated Disrupter*. Your encouragement and affirmation mean more than words can convey.

Above all, I am profoundly grateful to God for my loving wife, Irene. Her prayers, encouragement, and unwavering partnership have been a constant source of strength and inspiration throughout this journey. *I'm also grateful for our beautiful, charming, and intelligent daughters, Marlee and Ashley, for their prayers and encouragement.*

To all who have contributed, supported, and inspired along the way—whether through prayer, counsel, collaboration, or encouragement—please know your involvement has been deeply appreciated. This book is as much yours as it is mine.

Thank you all for being part of this journey of faith and revival.

ABOUT THE AUTHOR

Troy Anderson is a Pulitzer Prize–nominated investigative journalist, best-selling author, founder and president of the Inspire Literary Group, vice president of Battle Ready Ministries, former executive editor of *Charisma* magazine and Charisma Media, speaker, and regular television and radio commentator. He spent two decades working as a reporter, bureau chief, and editorial writer at the *Los Angeles Daily News*, *The Press-Enterprise*, and other newspapers. He writes for *Newsmax*, Townhall, *Charisma*, Charisma News, *Human Events*, *The American Spectator*, *Outreach*, and other media outlets. He's the founder and editor-in-chief of Prophecy Investigators and cofounder of Revelation Watchers.

He appears regularly on Newsmax TV, CBN News, BlazeTV, GOD TV, Real America's Voice, Daystar Television Network's *Joni Table Talk* and *Ministry Now*, One America News Network, Salem News Channel, *Tipping Point With Jimmy Evans*, *The Jim Bakker Show*, *Jewish Voice With Jonathan Bernis*, SkyWatch TV, Cornerstone TV Network's *Real Life*, and many nationally syndicated radio programs and YouTube shows.

He's interviewed many prominent national figures, including Billy Graham, Pastor Rick Warren, Dr. Tim LaHaye, Hal Lindsey, Noam Chomsky, Dinesh D'Souza, and Rabbi Jonathan Cahn.

Anderson is a member of the American Society of Journalists and Authors and also a member of the Association of Ghostwriters, Investigative Reporters & Editors, and Gotham Ghostwriters. He is a graduate of the Act One and Movieguide screenwriting programs and graduated from the University of Oregon in 1991 with a bachelor's degree in news-editorial journalism and a minor in political science.

He is coauthor of *The Babylon Code, Trumpocalypse, The Military Guide to Armageddon, The Military Guide to Disarming Deception, Revelation 911, Your Mission in God's Army,* and *I've Been to Heaven.* He's author of *The Trump Code* and *Designated Disrupter.* Anderson lives with his family in Irvine, California. Learn more about him at troyanderson.us, or scan the QR code to connect with him.

linktr.ee/troyanderson.author

NOTES

PREFACE

1. Turning Point USA, "Charlie Kirk's beloved wife, Mrs. Erika Kirk addresses the Nation," September 12, 2025, YouTube, 30:50, https://www.youtube.com/watch?v=e5SHpvRYg_o.
2. Rhian Lubin, "Over 54,000 students have contacted Turning Point USA to sign up in the week after Charlie Kirk's death, organization claims," *The Independent*, September 17, 2025, https://www.the-independent.com/news/world/americas/us-politics/charlie-kirk-turning-point-students-sign-up-b2828294.html; CBN News, "Churches Overflowing After Charlie Kirk's Assassination," September 15, 2025, YouTube, 11:10, https://www.youtube.com/watch?v=qurMWL8EDww.
3. Jonathan Bernis, interview by the author, July 31, 2025.
4. Shannon Bond, "Trump Suspended From Facebook For 2 Years," NPR, June 4, 2021, https://www.npr.org/2021/06/04/1003284948/trump-suspended-from-facebook-for-2-years; Staff, "Weaponization Committee Exposes the Biden White House Censorship Regime in New Report," House Judiciary Committee, May 1, 2024, https://judiciary.house.gov/media/press-releases/weaponization-committee-exposes-biden-white-house-censorship-regime-new-report.
5. Troy Anderson, "94-year-old Billy Graham's warning for America," WND.com, August 4, 2013, https://www.wnd.com/2013/08/94-year-old-billy-grahams-warning-for-america.
6. Anderson, "94-year-old Billy Graham's warning for America"; Staff, "Evangelist Reinhard Bonnke Biography," Christ for All Nations, https://cfan.org/reinhard-bonnke.
7. Sid Roth, interview by the author, July 3, 2025.

INTRODUCTION

1. Lubin, "Over 54,000 students have contacted Turning Point USA to sign up in the week after Charlie Kirk's death"; Amanda Macias, "'This is the turning point:' TPUSA says campus chapter requests surge over 120,000 after Kirk's assassination," Fox News, updated September 17, 2025, https://www.foxnews.com/politics/this-turning-point-tpusa-says-campus-chapter-requests-surge-over-54000-after-kirks-assassination.
2. Leah Sarnoff and Katie Kindelan, "Erika Kirk delivers emotional remarks to the nation after killing of husband Charlie Kirk," ABC News, September 14, 2025, https://abcnews.go.com/US/charlie-kirks-widow-erika-set-deliver-1st-public/story?id=125528319.

3. The White House, "VP Vance Hosts the Charlie Kirk Show," September 17, 2025, YouTube, 1:38, https://www.youtube.com/watch?v=gy3GRvZNq_Q.
4. Abby Trivett, "Is Erika Kirk the Chosen 'Esther' Kim Clement Prophesied for America's Healing?" Charisma, September 15, 2025, https://mycharisma.com/propheticrevival/is-erika-kirk-the-chosen-esther-kim-clement-prophesied-for-americas-healing; Kim Clement, "Kim Clement Esther Prophecy | Prophetic Rewind," December 10, 2022, YouTube, 4:46, https://www.youtube.com/watch?v=s3r7acidxno.
5. Sid Roth, "There's Something BIG Coming...A Prophetic Vision That Will CHANGE EVERYTHING | The 700 Club," The 700 Club, April 26, 2025, https://www.youtube.com/watch?v=TbQJhdpZl48.

CHAPTER 1

1. Staff, "The Alternative Jesus: Psychedelic Christ," *TIME*, June 21, 1971, https://time.com/archive/6839039/the-alternative-jesus-psychedelic-christ.
2. "About Pastor Rick Warren," Pastor Rick's Daily Hope, accessed July 6, 2024, https://www.pastorrick.com/about.
3. Stacie Wood, "Saddleback Church Worship Service | Preparing for God to Move," Saddleback Church, January 18, 2025, https://youtu.be/30fjTbyeGdk?si=zc4lB8DOD9T72QRY.
4. James Lasher, "40 Days to Save America: A Call for National Repentance," Charisma News, October 1, 2024, https://charismanews.com/news/40-days-to-save-america-a-call-for-national-repentance/.
5. Troy Anderson, "Igniting a Final Great Awakening: 77 Days to Take Back America," Charisma Magazine Online, November 6, 2024, https://mycharisma.com/culture/igniting-a-final-great-awakening-77-days-to-take-back-america/.
6. Lasher, "40 Days to Save America"; Anderson, "Igniting a Final Great Awakening."
7. Staff, The Return: National and Global Day of Prayer and Repentance, The Return International, September 26, 2020, https://thereturn.org/thereturn-washingtondc.
8. Paul McGuire and Troy Anderson, *Trumpocalypse* (FaithWords/Hachette Book Group, 2018), 267–298.
9. "Hope for the Future: A Message from Billy Graham," The Billy Graham Evangelistic Association of Canada, accessed July 6, 2024, https://www.billygraham.ca/stories/hope-for-the-future-a-message-from-billy-graham/.
10. Encyclopaedia Britannica, "Mayflower Compact," accessed September 19, 2025, https://www.britannica.com/topic/Mayflower-Compact.
11. Statements & Releases, "Presidential Message on the National Day of Prayer and Return, 2020," September 26, 2020, https://trumpwhitehouse.archives.gov/briefings-statements/presidential-message-national-day-prayer-return-2020.

12. Staff, "The 500+ Best Writers of All Time," Ranker.com, May 16, 2025, https://www.ranker.com/list/best-writers-of-all-time/ranker-books; Gabriele Chaitkin, "'For He Was One of Us': Friedrich Schiller, the Poet of America," American Almanac, October 1996, https://members.tripod.com/american_almanac/schill96.htm; Friedrich von Schiller, "The man of courage thinks not of himself. Help the oppressed and put thy trust in God," Goodreads, accessed September 19, 2025, https://www.goodreads.com/work/quotes/6226707-wilhelm-tell; Schiller, "We shall be free, just as our fathers were," Goodreads, accessed September 19, 2025, https://www.goodreads.com/work/quotes/6226707-wilhelm-tell; Staff, "William Tell," IMDB.com, accessed September 19, 2025, https://www.imdb.com/title/tt22478818.

13. Dr. Corné J. Bekker, interview by the author, May 8, 2025.

14. Donald Trump, "The Inaugural Address," White House, January 20, 2025, https://www.whitehouse.gov/remarks/2025/01/the-inaugural-address.

15. Lily Rothman, "TIME's 'Is God Dead?' Cover Turns 50," *TIME*, April 8, 2016, https://time.com/isgoddead/.

16. TIME Magazine, "The Jesus Revolution," cover, June 21, 1971, https://content.time.com/time/covers/0,16641,19710621,00.html.

17. Jon Tyson, "The Return Gathering | Session 2 | Jon Tyson," Saddleback Church, February 21, 2025, https://www.youtube.com/watch?v=QUh40X1eKJs&list=PLvmupGaP47zSQqPKyjA0UukxpisB8UF9p&index=3.

18. Greg Laurie, "Is America On Brink Of Jesus Revolution 2.0?" Vision Christian Media, February 18, 2025, https://vision.org.au/read/articles/is-america-on-brink-of-jesus-revolution-20.

19. Staff, "New Research: Belief in Jesus Rises, Fueled by Younger Adults," Barna Group, April 7, 2025, https://www.barna.com/research/belief-in-jesus-rises.

20. Bekker, interview.

21. Bekker, interview.

22. Bekker, interview.

23. John Adams, "From John Adams to Massachusetts Militia, 11 October 1798," National Archives, accessed September 19, 2025, https://founders.archives.gov/documents/Adams/99-02-02-3102.

24. Jeffrey M. Jones, "Church Attendance Has Declined in Most U.S. Religious Groups," Gallup, March 25, 2024, https://news.gallup.com/poll/642548/church-attendance-declined-religious-groups.aspx.

25. Tracy Munsil, "Barna, CRC: Widespread Worldview Confusion Grows as Americans Redefine God," Arizona Christian University, February 18, 2025, https://www.arizonachristian.edu/2025/02/18/awvi-2025_01_most-americans-believe-in-a-supreme-power-but-not-the-god-of-the-bible.

26. Christian Life Magazine, *America's Great Revivals: The Story of Spiritual Revival in the United States, 1734–2000* (Baker Publishing Group, 2020), 9–28.
27. Christian Life Magazine, *America's Great Revivals*, 31–55.
28. Christian Life Magazine, *America's Great Revivals*, 59–78.
29. Christian Life Magazine, *America's Great Revivals*. 117–121.
30. Billy Hallowell, "Bible Sales Are Skyrocketing: What's Going On?" CBN News, December 27, 2024, https://cbn.com/news/us/bible-sales-are-skyrocketing-whats-going.
31. Maria Lencki, "Hallow CEO says a Christian 'revival' is happening as US sees boom in Bible sales," FoxNews.com, December 8, 2024, https://www.foxbusiness.com/media/hallow-ceo-says-christian-revival-happening-us-sees-boom-bible-sales.
32. Eric Mack, "Bible Sales Boom Amid 'Anxiety' as Things Go 'Off the Rails,'" Newsmax.com, December 1, 2024, https://www.newsmax.com/newsfront/bible-books-religious/2024/12/01/id/1189932.
33. Mack, "Bible Sales Boom Amid 'Anxiety' as Things Go 'Off the Rails.'"

CHAPTER 2

1. Jon Brown, "Franklin Graham Says Charlie Kirk Assassination 'Backfired,' Shows Left Wants to Silence Opponents,'" Christian Post, September 20, 2025, https://www.christianpost.com/news/franklin-graham-says-kirk-assassination-backfired.html.
2. Paul McGuire, interview by author, June 27, 2025.
3. McGuire, interview.
4. Anthony D. Romero, "ACLU Responds to Election of Donald Trump," American Civil Liberties Union, November 6, 2024, https://www.aclu.org/press-releases/aclu-responds-to-election-of-donald-trump.
5. Taylor Orth and Carl Bialik, "How Americans have reacted to Donald Trump's 2024 victory," YouGov, November 15, 2024, https://today.yougov.com/politics/articles/50960-how-americans-have-reacted-to-donald-trumps-2024-victory.
6. Brandon Livesay, "Donald Trump wins 2024 US election in historic comeback," BBC.com, November 5, 2024, https://www.bbc.com/news/live/czxrnw5qrprt; Staff, "2024," The American Presidency Project, December 31, 2024, https://www.presidency.ucsb.edu/statistics/elections/2024.
7. Sean Feucht, interview by the author, May 6, 2025.
8. Jonathan Cahn, "Trump's Win & What It Means | Jonathan Cahn Prophetic," posted November 7, 2024, by Jonathan Cahn Official, YouTube, 22:19, https://youtu.be/2bS0dYWWh0Q?si=_f0peZcm1m_sNN4p.

9. Staff, "Donald Trump: 'Americanism, Not Globalism, Will Be Our Credo,'" ABC News, July 21, 2016, https://abcnews.go.com/Politics/video/donald-trump-americanism-globalism-credo-40791714.

10. Joseph Z, "TRUMP PROPHECIES FULFILLED WHAT COMES NEXT!!," Joseph Z Ministries, 2024, https://video.josephz.com/channel/ZMinistries/video/1671.

11. Joseph Z, "PROPHETIC UPDATE—THE SHOT HEARD AROUND THE WORLD!!," YouTube video, July 14, 2024, https://www.youtube.com/watch?v=kS_BnuMJm3U&t=6s.

12. Troy Anderson, *The Trump Code: Exploring Time Travel, Nikola Tesla, the Trump Lineage, and America's Future* (CharismaHouse/FrontLine, 2024), xix.

13. Dutch Sheets, "About Dutch," Dutch Sheets Ministries, accessed September 19, 2025, https://dutchsheets.org/about.

14. Dutch Sheets, "Dutch Sheets: 'Trump's Assassination Attempt & the Power of Our Prayers,'" The Elijah List, July 22, 2024, https://www.elijahlist.com/words/display_word.html?ID=31267.

15. Sheets, "Trump's Assassination Attempt."

16. Sheets, "Trump's Assassination Attempt."

17. Dutch Sheets, "What America Desperately Needs," GiveHim15.com, September 20, 2024, https://www.givehim15.com/post/september-20-2024.

18. Sid Roth, interview by the author, August 29, 2024.

19. Troy Anderson, "An Open Letter to President Trump, Urging Him to Lead America in Prayer, Repentance and Revival!" Revelation Watchers, October 28, 2024, https://www.youtube.com/watch?v=4fHds9FRT3s.

20. Donald J. Trump, "Executive Order 13798—Promoting Free Speech and Religious Liberty," May 4, 2017, The American Presidency Project, https://www.presidency.ucsb.edu/documents/executive-order-13798-promoting-free-speech-and-religious-liberty.

21. Jeffrey Cimmino, "International Religious Freedom Policy in a Second Trump Term," Providence, January 13, 2025, https://providencemag.com/2025/01/international-religious-freedom-policy-in-a-second-trump-term.

22. Staff, "Abortion Statistics," National Right to Life, accessed September 19, 2025, https://www.nrlc.org/uploads/factsheets/FS01AbortionintheUS.pdf.

23. Donald J. Trump, "Fact Sheet: President Donald J. Trump Enforces Overwhelmingly Popular Demand to Stop Taxpayer Funding of Abortion," The White House, January 25, 2025, https://www.whitehouse.gov/fact-sheets/2025/01/fact-sheet-president-donald-j-trump-enforces-overwhelmingly-popular-demand-to-stop-taxpayer-funding-of-abortion.

24. Donald J. Trump, "Remarks by President Trump at the 47th Annual March for Life," Trump White House, January 24, 2020, https://

trumpwhitehouse.archives.gov/briefings-statements/remarks-president-trump-47th-annual-march-life.

25. Abby Trivett, "Chuck Pierce's Prophetic Word for Our New Season," *Charisma News*, November 11, 2024, https://charismanews.com/culture/chuck-pierces-prophetic-word-for-our-new-season.

26. Trivett, "Chuck Pierce's Prophetic Word for Our New Season."

27. Trivett, "Chuck Pierce's Prophetic Word for Our New Season."

28. Fred Markert, "The Rise & Fall of Civilization, Where Is America? Futurist Fred Markert Reveals Cautionary Pattern," Daystar TV, April 11, 2024, https://www.youtube.com/watch?v=SA59KeTbB6Y.

29. Staff, "Number of COVID-19 deaths reported to WHO (cumulative total)," World Health Organization, https://data.who.int/dashboards/covid19/deaths.

30. Markert, "The Rise & Fall of Civilization."

31. Trivett, "Chuck Pierce's Prophetic Word for Our New Season."

32. Strang Report, "The Next 100 Days Will Bring HUGE Changes To America with Chuck Pierce," February 13, 2025, YouTube, 45:10, https://www.youtube.com/watch?v=7kamgPhjVNc&t=7s.

CHAPTER 3

1. Riley Hoffman, "READ: Harris-Trump presidential debate transcript," ABC News, September 10, 2024, https://abcnews.go.com/Politics/harris-trump-presidential-debate-transcript/story?id=113560542.

2. Markert, "The Rise & Fall of Civilization."

3. Markert, "The Rise & Fall of Civilization."

4. Markert, "The Rise & Fall of Civilization."

5. Dutch Sheets, "Dutch & Tim Sheets Prophetic Word: Stay Focused! | FlashPoint Virginia Beach," The Victory Channel, April 30, 2024, YouTube, 5:33, https://www.youtube.com/watch?v=UzjO3L3E0BI&t=33s.

6. Dr. Robert Jeffress, "Trump friend and informal faith adviser: 'God is giving America another chance,'" FoxNews.com, January 19, 2025, https://www.foxnews.com/lifestyle/trump-friend-informal-faith-adviser-god-giving-america-another-chance.

7. The first book I proposed to write in 2011 was titled *The New Jesus Revolution* on this topic, although it was never published.

8. E. Michael and Sharon Rusten, "Five Key Revivals," Decision, May 5, 2005, https://decisionmagazine.com/five-key-revivals/.

9. Jonathan Edwards, *Sinners in the Hands of an Angry God* (P&R Publishing, 1992), 28–30.

10. Edwards, *Sinners in the Hands of an Angry God*, 28–30.

11. Diane Severance, PhD, "What was the Great Awakening? Key Figures and Events," Christianity.com, April 27, 2023, https://www.christianity.com/

church/church-history/timeline/1701-1800/the-great-awakening-11630212.
html.

12. Severance, "What was the Great Awakening?"

13. Michael and Rusten, "Five Key Revivals"; Staff, "1790 The Second Great Awakening in US," The Revival Library, https://revival-library.org/histories/1790-second-great-awakening-us; Mark Galli, "Revival at Cane Ridge," Christian History Institute, 1995, https://christianhistoryinstitute.org/magazine/article/revival-at-cane-ridge.

14. Christian Life Magazine, America's Great Revivals, 45.

15. Michael and Rusten, "Five Key Revivals."

16. Michael and Rusten, "Five Key Revivals."

17. Staff, "1790 The Second Great Awakening in US."; Charles Finney, How to Experience Revival (Whitaker House, 1984, 2017), 9–10, 15.

18. "God In America: People: Lyman Beecher," PBS, accessed August 6, 2025, https://www.pbs.org/wgbh/pages/frontline/godinamerica/people/lyman-beecher.html.

19. "The 1802 Yale College Revivals," Think Revival, accessed August 6, 2025, https://thinkrevival.org/the-1802-yale-college-revivals; Christian Life Magazine, America's Great Revivals, 38.

20. Staff, "3rd Great Awakening: 1830," The Revival Library, accessed September 19, 2025, https://revival-library.org/timelines/1830-3rd-great-awakening.

21. Charles Grandison Finney, Memoirs of Reverend Charles G. Finney (A. S. Barnes, 1876), 13–23, https://historymatters.gmu.edu/d/6374.

22. "3rd Great Awakening," The Revival Library.

23. "3rd Great Awakening," The Revival Library.

24. Staff, "The Time for Prayer: The Third Great Awakening," Christianity Today, 1989, https://www.christianitytoday.com/1989/07/time-for-prayer-third-great-awakening.

25. Charles Finney, "Lectures on Revivals of Religion," The Belknap Press of Harvard University Press, 1960, https://www.sas.upenn.edu/~cavitch/pdf-library/Finney_WhatARevivalOfReligionIs.pdf.

26. "3rd Great Awakening," The Revival Library.

27. Christian Life Magazine, America's Great Revivals, 88–89.

28. Alex McFarland, "JESUS REVOLUTION: It was real. It was historic. It is needed again," Alex McFarland Ministries, March 6, 2023, https://alexmcfarland.com/jesus-revolution-it-was-real-it-was-historic-it-is-needed-again.

29. R. Loren Sandford, The Last Great Outpouring: Preparing for an Unprecedented Move of God (Whitaker House, 2020), 56–58.

30. Taylan Michael Seaman, interview by the author, May 7, 2025.

31. Seaman, interview.

32. Aaron Earls, "9 Encouraging Trends for Global Christianity in 2025," Lifeway Research, February 11, 2025, https://research.lifeway.com/2025/02/11/9-encouraging-trends-for-global-christianity-in-2025/.

33. Chris Riches, "Why millions of young Gen Z Britons are flocking back to our churches," Daily Express, July 26, 2025, https://www.express.co.uk/news/uk/2087120/why-millions-young-gen-z.

34. Riches, "Why millions of young Gen Z Britons are flocking back to our churches."

35. Tim Keller, "The Decline and Renewal of the American Church: Part 3— The Path to Renewal," Gospel in Life, Spring 2022, https://gospelinlife.com/article/american-church-the-path-to-renewal.

36. Keller, "The Decline and Renewal of the American Church."

37. Tim Keller, "'Lord, Do It Again': Tim Keller on Revival," The Gospel Coalition, March 17, 2023, https://www.thegospelcoalition.org/article/tim-keller-revival.

CHAPTER 4

1. John Adams, "John Adams to Abigail Adams, 3 July 1776," Founders Online, National Archives, accessed September 19, 2025, https://founders.archives.gov/documents/Adams/04-02-02-0016.

2. Peter Marshal and David Manuel, *The Light and the Glory: Did God Have a Plan for America?* (Fleming H. Revell Company, 1977), 11.

3. The *Left Behind* series sold over 65 million copies, and Tim LaHaye graciously endorsed my first book, *The Babylon Code*.

4. Marshal and Manuel, *The Light and the Glory*, back cover.

5. John Winthrop, "A Model for Christian Charity," Winthrop Society, 1630, accessed September 19, 2025, https://www.winthropsociety.com/_files/ugd/9a2d3b_4d9f243ce4b34c0fad7f4f41df29d992.pdf.

6. Christopher Columbus, *The Book of Prophecies* (Wipf & Stock Publishers, 1997), 67–69.

7. Marshall and Manuel, *The Light and the Glory*, 17–18.

8. Richard "Little Bear" Wheeler, *God's Mighty Hand: Providential Occurrences in World History* (Mantle Ministries Press, 2014), 37–40.

9. William Bradford, *History of Plimoth Plantation* (Applewood Books, 2010), 32.

10. Daniel Webster, "Address on the 200 Year Anniversary of the Mayflower Landing at Plymouth Rock, December 22, 1820," Americanrhetoric.com, accessed September 19, 2025, https://www.americanrhetoric.com/speeches/danielwebsterplymouthorationcomplete.htm.

11. Webster, "Address on the 200 Year Anniversary."

12. Perry Miller, *Errand into the Wilderness* (Belknap Press of Harvard University Press, 1956), 11.

13. McGuire and Anderson, *Trumpocalypse*, 271–272.

14. Dr. Bruce Oliver, interview by the author, May 7, 2025.
15. Oliver, interview.
16. Marshall and Manuel, *The Light and the Glory*, 317–318.
17. John Adams, "From John Adams to Massachusetts Militia, 11 October 1798," National Archives, accessed September 19, 2025, https://founders.archives.gov/documents/Adams/99-02-02-3102.
18. Founding Fathers, "Declaration of Independence: A Transcription," National Archives, July 4, 1776, https://www.archives.gov/founding-docs/declaration-transcript.
19. Founding Fathers, "Declaration of Independence."
20. David Barton, Brad Cummings, and Lance Wubbels, *The Founders' Bible: The Origin of the Dream of Freedom* (Shiloh Road Publishers, 2012), 146–151.
21. Barton, Cummings, and Wubbels, *The Founders' Bible*, 146–151.
22. Barton, Cummings, and Wubbels, *The Founders' Bible*, 146–151.
23. Barton, Cummings, and Wubbels, *The Founders' Bible*, 146–151.
24. Barton, Cummings, and Wubbels, *The Founders' Bible*, 146–151.
25. Barton, Cummings, and Wubbels, *The Founders' Bible*, 146–151.
26. Founding Fathers, "Article IV Relationships Between the States," Congress.gov, accessed September 19, 2025, https://constitution.congress.gov/browse/article-4/section-4.
27. Barton, Cummings, and Wubbels, *The Founders' Bible*, 149.
28. Barton, Cummings, and Wubbels, *The Founders' Bible*, 149.
29. Barton, Cummings, and Wubbels, *The Founders' Bible*, 149–150.
30. John Adams, "From John Adams to Benjamin Rush, 2 February 1807," National Archives, accessed September 19, 2025, https://founders.archives.gov/documents/Adams/99-02-02-5166.
31. Noah Webster, *History of the United States* (Durrie & Peck, 1832), 307–308.
32. Frederick Douglass, "Northern Ballots and the Election of 1852: An Address Delivered in Ithaca, New York, on October 14, 1852," *The Frederick Douglass Papers*, digital edition, Frederick Douglass Papers Project, accessed September 19, 2025, https://frederickdouglasspapersproject.com/s/digitaledition/item/10316.
33. Staff, "The Bill of Rights: What Does it Say?" National Archives, April 27, 2023, https://www.archives.gov/founding-docs/bill-of-rights/what-does-it-say.
34. Bill of Rights, "First Amendment," Congress.gov, accessed September 19, 2025, https://constitution.congress.gov/constitution/amendment-1.
35. U.S. Constitution, "Article VI," Congress.gov, accessed September 19, 2025, https://constitution.congress.gov/constitution/article-6.

36. Eddie Hyatt, "Confronting 'Separation of Church and State' Myth," Charisma News, June 24, 2024, https://charismanews.com/news/confronting-separation-of-church-and-state-myth.

37. Dr. Robert Jeffress, "America Is a Christian Nation (Part 1) | Pathway To Victory with Dr. Robert Jeffress," Pathway to Victory with Dr. Robert Jeffress, July 3, 2025, YouTube, 27:30, https://www.youtube.com/watch?v=T-hIqyzDoPo.

38. Hyatt, "Confronting 'Separation of Church and State' Myth."

39. Hyatt, "Confronting 'Separation of Church and State' Myth."

40. Encyclopaedia Britannica, "John Locke," accessed September 19, 2025, https://www.britannica.com/biography/John-Locke.

41. Founding Fathers, "Declaration of Independence: A Transcription," National Archives, July 4, 1776, https://www.archives.gov/founding-docs/declaration-transcript.

42. Robert Shackleton, "Montesquieu," Encyclopaedia Britannica, last modified July 25, 2025, https://www.britannica.com/biography/Montesquieu.

43. The American Bible Society, "Bringing the Bible to Those Who Need It Most," accessed September 19, 2025, https://www.americanbible.org/the-mission/our-story.

44. Ronald Reagan, "Proclamation 5138-National Day of Prayer, 1984," Ronald Reagan Presidential Library & Museum, December 14, 1983, https://www.reaganlibrary.gov/archives/speech/proclamation-5138-national-day-prayer-1984.

45. Carl H. Esbeck, "Richard Neuhaus's The Naked Public Square: Religion and Democracy in America," *Missouri Law Review* 50, no. 1 (1985): 202.

46. Sameea Kamal, "Texas will require public school classrooms to display Ten Commandments under bill signed by governor," The Texas Tribune, May 24, 2025, https://www.texastribune.org/2025/05/24/ten-commandments-texas-schools-senate-bill-10.

47. Dr. Robert Jeffress, "America Is a Christian Nation (Part 2) | Pathway To Victory with Dr. Robert Jeffress," Pathway to Victory, July 3, 2025, YouTube, 27:30, https://www.youtube.com/watch?v=3Q6bS3uwL5Y.

48. Jeffress, "America Is a Christian Nation (Part 2)."

49. Jeffress, "America Is a Christian Nation (Part 2)."

CHAPTER 5

1. GODSPEED Magazine, "Will the World Turn Back to God?" September 4, 2020, YouTube, 20:24, https://www.youtube.com/watch?v=4M5nN2ezZSc.

2. GODSPEED Magazine, "Will the World Turn Back to God?"

3. Roth, interview.

4. Roth, interview.

5. Roth, interview.

6. Roth, interview.
7. Staff, "Status of Global Christianity, 2025, in the Context of 1900–2050," Center for the Study of Global Christianity at Gordon-Conwell Theological Seminary, February 2025, https://www.gordonconwell.edu/wp-content/uploads/sites/13/2025/01/Status-of-Global-Christianity-2025.pdf.
8. Staff, "Pentecostalism: William Seymour," Christianity Today, 2000, accessed September 19, 2025, https://www.christianitytoday.com/2000/01/pentecostalism-william-seymour.
9. "Pentecostalism: William Seymour," Christianity Today.
10. "Pentecostalism: William Seymour," Christianity Today.
11. Jennifer A. Miskov, PhD, *Ignite Azusa: Positioning for a New Jesus Revolution* (Silver to Gold, 2016), 39–41.
12. "Pentecostalism: William Seymour," Christianity Today.
13. Gary Dauphin, "#blackhistory: On April 9, 1906, the Azusa Street Revival begins in Los Angeles," California African American Museum, April 9, 2018, https://caamuseum.org/learn/600state/black-history/blackhistory-on-april-9-1906-the-azusa-street-revival-begins-in-los-angeles.
14. Caleb Cooper, "Is the Azusa Street Revival Prophecy Coming to Pass?" Prophecy Investigators' News, May 13, 2025, https://www.prophecyinvestigators.com/p/is-the-azusa-street-revival-prophecy.
15. Staff, "The Great 1906 San Francisco Earthquake," U.S. Geological Survey, 1990, https://earthquake.usgs.gov/earthquakes/events/1906calif/18april; Encyclopaedia Britannica, "San Francisco earthquake of 1906," accessed September 19, 2025, https://www.britannica.com/event/San-Francisco-earthquake-of-1906.
16. Jeff Oliver, *Pentecost to the Present: The Holy Spirit's Enduring Work in the Church—Book 3: Worldwide Revivals and Renewal* (Bridge-Logos Publishers, 2017), 32, 34.
17. Jeff Oliver and Rick Joyner, *Keys to Experiencing Azusa Fire* (Destiny Image Publishers, 2024), 98.
18. "Pentecostalism: William Seymour," Christianity Today.
19. Oliver and Joyner, *Keys to Experiencing Azusa Fire*, 82.
20. Cooper, "Is the Azusa Street Revival Prophecy Coming to Pass?"
21. Cooper, interview by the author, April 22, 2025.
22. Paul McGuire, email interview by the author, April 8, 2025.
23. McGuire, email interview.
24. Michael Dorstewitz, "Newsmax Rising Bestsellers—Week of April 29, 2024," Newsmax.com, April 29, 2024, https://www.newsmax.com/books/books-newsmax-bestsellers/2024/05/03/id/1163423.
25. McGuire, interview.
26. GODSPEED Magazine, "Will the World Turn Back to God?"; Roth, interview; Markert, "The Rise & Fall of Civilization."

27. Patrick Murray, "National: Most Say Fundamental Rights Under Threat," Monmouth University, June 23, 2023, https://www.monmouth.edu/polling-institute/documents/monmouthpoll_us_062023.pdf.

28. Adam Shaw, "Homan takes victory lap after illegal immigrant crossings plummet during Trump admin: 'He is delivering,'" Fox News, February 17, 2025, https://www.foxnews.com/politics/homan-victory-lap-after-illegal-immigrant-crossings-plummet-during-trump-admin-delivering.

29. Roth, interview.

30. Roth, interview.

31. Roth, interview.

32. Roth, interview.

33. Roth, interview.

34. Daniel Timotheos Yohannan, interview by the author, July 16, 2025.

CHAPTER 6

1. Becka A. Alper, "How Religion Intersects With Americans' Views on the Environment," Pew Research Center, November 17, 2022, https://www.pewresearch.org/religion/2022/11/17/how-religion-intersects-with-americans-views-on-the-environment; Aaron Earls, "Vast Majority of Pastors See Signs of End Times in Current Events," Lifeway Research, April 7, 2020, https://research.lifeway.com/2020/04/07/vast-majority-of-pastors-see-signs-of-end-times-in-current-events.

2. Beth Bogucki and Linda Klosterman, "Jonathan Cahn delivers urgent prophetic message to Donald Trump," Charisma Media, November 4, 2024, https://mycharismashop.com/blogs/press-releases/jonathan-cahn-delivers-urgent-prophetic-message-to-donald-trump?srsltid=AfmBOopvW1Xe8sXZhkchtSRrTfs5plBiU6PFoak962-C5vKpBTW1RJAM.

3. Lance Wallnau, *God's Chaos Candidate: Donald J. Trump and the American Unraveling* (Killer Sheep Media, 2016), 30.

4. Joseph Z, interview by the author, August 27, 2024.

5. Joseph Z, interview.

6. Joseph Z, interview.

7. Joseph Z, interview.

8. Abby Trivett, "Joseph Z: This is the Year to Storm Babylon," Charisma News, January 2, 2025, https://charismanews.com/news/joseph-z-this-is-the-year-to-storm-babylon.

9. Trivett, "Joseph Z."

10. Troy Anderson, "Judgment or Revival–Great Awakening or Great Reset?" Prophecy Investigators, July 28, 2024, https://x.com/ProphecyInvest1/status/1817770962206834903.

11. Joseph Z, interview.

12. Jordan Peterson, "Lecture: Biblical Series I: Introduction to the Idea of God," Jordan B. Peterson, May 20, 2017, YouTube, 2:38:28, https://www.youtube.com/watch?v=f-wWBGo6a2w.

13. Peterson, "Lecture: Biblical Series I."

14. Abby Trivett, "Russell Brand is 'Grateful' to be in Christ After Baptism," Charisma, April 29, 2024, https://mycharisma.com/culture/russell-brand-is-grateful-to-be-in-christ-after-baptism.

15. James Lasher, "Tucker Carlson: Demons Are Here but Revival is Coming," Charisma News, June 6, 2024, https://charismanews.com/culture/tucker-carlson-demons-are-here-but-revival-is-coming.

16. PowerfulJRE, "Joe Rogan Experience #2219-Donald Trump," October 25, 2024, YouTube, 2:58:49, https://www.youtube.com/watch?v=hBMoPUAeLnY.

17. James Marriot, "How Joe Rogan helped Donald Trump to win America," The Times, November 6, 2024, https://www.thetimes.com/life-style/celebrity/article/donald-trump-joe-rogan-8grmztcjn.

18. Joe Rogan, "Richard Dawkins: Outgrowing God and Debunking Religion," The Joe Rogan Experience, October 22, 2019, https://podcastnotes.org/joe-rogan-experience/richard-dawkins-god-religion/?utm_source=chatgpt.com.

19. Ryan Teague Beckwith, "Read President Trump's Remarks at the National Prayer Breakfast," Time, February 2, 2017, https://time.com/4658012/donald-trump-national-prayer-breakfast-transcript/?utm_source=chatgpt.com.

20. Dr. Hugh Ross, "Fulfilled Prophecy: Evidence for the Reliability of the Bible," Reasons to Believe, April 22, 2003, https://reasons.org/explore/publications/articles/fulfilled-prophecy-evidence-for-the-reliability-of-the-bible; Encyclopaedia Britannica, "Eschatology," accessed September 19, 2025, https://www.britannica.com/topic/eschatology.

21. McGuire, interview, June 27, 2025.

22. Staff, World Health Organization, "Number of COVID-19 deaths reported to WHO (cumulative total)," June 29, 2025, https://data.who.int/dashboards/covid19/deaths.

23. Alec Tyson, Michael Lipka, and Claudia Deane, "5 Years Later: America Looks Back at the Impact of COVID-19," Pew Research Center, February 12, 2025, https://www.pewresearch.org/politics/2025/02/12/5-years-later-america-looks-back-at-the-impact-of-covid-19.

24. Jonathan Cahn Official, "Jonathan Cahn: Prophecy for Washington DC," February 17, 2025, YouTube, 17:34, https://www.youtube.com/watch?v=0UmZTt-FbQw.

25. Klaus Scwabb, "Now is the time for a 'great reset,'" World Economic Forum, June 3, 2020, https://www.weforum.org/stories/2020/06/now-is-the-time-for-a-great-reset.

26. Staff, "What is the National Debt today?" Peter G. Peterson Foundation, https://www.pgpf.org/national-debt-clock.

27. Caitlin Yilek, "Politics: House passes historic crypto bill, the GENIUS Act, after right-wing rebellion," CBS News, July 17, 2025, https://www.cbsnews.com/news/house-vote-crypto-genius-act-stablecoin-regulations; Rob Wile, "Investors cheer new crypto law while critics warn of potential for crisis," NBC News, July 18, 2025, https://www.nbcnews.com/tech/crypto/genius-act-new-crypto-law-stablecoins-explained-rcna219658.

28. Ronald Reagan, "A Time for Choosing Speech, October 27, 1964," Ronald Reagan Presidential Library & Museum, October 27, 1964, https://www.reaganlibrary.gov/reagans/ronald-reagan/time-choosing-speech-october-27-1964.

29. Cecily Hilleary, "1620: Dreams of a 'New' Jerusalem," Voice of America, December 21, 2020, https://www.voanews.com/a/usa_hilleary-1620-plymouth-pilgrims/6199721.html.

30. Paul McGuire and Troy Anderson, *The Babylon Code: Solving the Bible's Greatest End-Times Mystery* (FaithWords/Hachette Book Group, 2015), 141.

31. Staff, "President Trump: We have a true golden age for America," Fox News, July 15, 2025, https://www.foxnews.com/video/6375687275112.

32. Chris Mitchell, "'We're Seeing Prophecy Unfold': Trump's Jerusalem Embassy Sends a Message to Israel's Enemies," CBN News, May 15, 2018, https://cbn.com/news/news/were-seeing-prophecy-unfold-trumps-jerusalem-embassy-sends-message-israels-enemies?utm_source=chatgpt.com.

33. Bernis, interview.

34. Bernis, interview.

35. Bernis, interview.

36. Zeke Miller, Josh Boak, and Jamey Keaten, "Trump tells Davos elite to invest in US or face tariffs," Associated Press, January 23, 2025, https://www.wfla.com/news/politics/ap-politics/ap-trump-tells-davos-elite-to-invest-in-us-or-face-tariffs/?utm_source=chatgpt.com.

37. The Last Watch, "Paul McGuire the Man Who Changed My Life. Wow," The Last Watch with Mike Kerr, July 10, 2025, YouTube, 1:14:23, https://www.youtube.com/watch?v=g4vwtnSLlBc.

38. The Last Watch, "Paul McGuire the Man Who Changed My Life."

39. The Last Watch, "Paul McGuire the Man Who Changed My Life."

40. The Last Watch, "Paul McGuire the Man Who Changed My Life."

41. Troy Anderson, "Trump's Return and America's Divine Reprieve," Charisma News, November 13, 2024, https://charismanews.com/news/trumps-return-and-americas-divine-reprieve/?utm_source=chatgpt.com.

42. The Last Watch, "Paul McGuire the Man Who Changed My Life."

43. McGuire and Anderson, *The Babylon Code*.

44. McGuire and Anderson, *The Babylon Code*, 313–316.

45. The Last Watch, "Paul McGuire the Man Who Changed My Life."

46. The Last Watch, "Paul McGuire the Man Who Changed My Life."

47. Staff, "Full text: Donald Trump 2016 RNC draft speech transcript," Politico, July 21, 2016, https://www.politico.com/story/2016/07/full-transcript-donald-trump-nomination-acceptance-speech-at-rnc-225974.

CHAPTER 7

1. Wendy Griffith, "Greg and Cathe Laurie on 'Jesus Revolution', Their Love Story, and a New Jesus Revival," CBN.com, April 17, 2023, https://cbn.com/news/us/greg-and-cathe-laurie-jesus-revolution-their-love-story-and-new-jesus-revival.

2. Feucht, interview.

3. Troy Anderson and Anne Mount, "Hollywood, Jesus & The Holy Spirit," Charisma, March 2024, https://mycharisma.com/wp-content/uploads/2024/03/CMO-Special-Edition-March-2024.pdf.

4. Michael Foust, "Jonathan Roumie: Hollywood Is Undergoing a 'Revival Moment' of Faith Content," Crosswalk.com, July 28, 2023, https://www.crosswalk.com/headlines/contributors/michael-foust/jonathan-roumie-hollywood-is-undergoing-a-revival-moment-of-faith-content.html.

5. Jonathan Roumie (@jonathanroumieofficial), 2023, "Pretty sweet feature in this Friday's @newsweek issue," Instagram, July 27, 2023, https://www.instagram.com/p/CvMBvSUstQD/?hl=en.

6. Matt Grobar, "Mel Gibson's 'The Resurrection Of The Christ' Split Into Two Movies; Release Dates Set For Both," Deadline, August 5, 2025, https://deadline.com/2025/08/the-resurrection-of-the-christ-release-dates-lionsgate-1236479264.

7. Staff, "God is Using the 'JESUS' Film to Transform Lives!," Jesus Film Project, accessed September 19, 2025, https://www.jesusfilm.org/give/see-the-impact/#:~:text=Since%20its%20release%20in%201979,Praise%20the%20Lord!.

8. Donald Trump (@realDonaldTrump), 2025, "It is my honor to announce Jon Voight, Mel Gibson, and Sylvester Stallone," Truth Social, January 16, 2025, https://truthsocial.com/@realDonaldTrump/posts/113839243472952784.

9. Troy Anderson, "Golden Age: Hollywood Revival | 77 Days to Take Back America: Igniting A Final Great Awakening | Day 75," Prophecy Investigators' News, January 18, 2025, https://www.prophecyinvestigators.com/p/golden-age-hollywood-revival-77-days.

10. Staff, "The Passion of the Christ," Box Office Mojo, https://www.boxofficemojo.com/release/rl3781789185; Staff, "The Passion of the Christ," Box Office Mojo by IMDbPro, https://web.archive.org/web/20190204065734/http://www.boxofficemojo.com/movies/?id=passionofthechrist.htm&adjust_yr=1&p=.htm.

11. PowerfulJRE, "Joe Rogan Experience #2254-Mel Gibson," Joe Rogan Experience, January 9, 2025, YouTube, 2:20:58, https://www.youtube.com/watch?v=1rYtrS5IbrQ.
12. PowerfulJRE, "Joe Rogan Experience #2254-Mel Gibson."
13. PowerfulJRE, "Joe Rogan Experience #2254-Mel Gibson."
14. PowerfulJRE, "Joe Rogan Experience #2254-Mel Gibson."
15. Abid Rahman, "Mel Gibson's Malibu House Burned Down While He Was in Austin for Joe Rogan Interview: 'My Place Looked Like Dresden,'" The Hollywood Reporter, January 9, 2025, https://www.hollywoodreporter.com/news/general-news/mel-gibson-wildfires-malibu-house-burned-down-joe-rogan-1236106022.
16. Staff, "God is Using the 'JESUS' Film to Transform Lives!"
17. Staff, "The JESUS Film Reaches Its 2,200th Language Translation," Jesus Film Project, March 28, 2025, https://www.jesusfilm.org/press.
18. Kate O'Hare, "'Jesus Revolution': Jonathan Roumie Connects With Playing Hippie Preacher Lonnie Frisbee," Family Theater Productions, February 21, 2023, https://www.familytheater.org/blog/jesus-revolution-jonathan-roumie-lonnie-frisbee.
19. O'Hare, "Jesus Revolution."
20. Staff, "Capacity Crowd of 45,000 Attends Greg Laurie's Evangelistic Crusade, Packing Out Angel Stadium in California," Newswire, July 21, 2025, https://www.newswire.com/news/capacity-crowd-of-45-000-attends-greg-lauries-evangelistic-crusade-22613418.
21. Talia Wise, "45,000 Believers Worship God During Greg Laurie's Harvest Crusade: 'Truly A Holy Moment,'" CBN News, July 21, 2025, https://cbn.com/news/us/45000-believers-worship-god-during-greg-lauries-harvest-crusade-truly-holy-moment.
22. Staff, "BY THE NUMBERS: 'THE CHOSEN' REACHES #1 IN APPLE TV APP STORE AS SEASON 4 DEBUTS," The Chosen, June 6, 2024, https://www.thechosen.tv/en-us/explore/by-the-numbers-the-chosen-reaches-1-in-apple-tv-app-store-as-season-4-debuts.
23. Paul J. Pastor, "Dallas Jenkins: Seeing in the Dark," Outreach, July 11, 2023, https://outreachmagazine.com/features/76824-dallas-jenkins-seeing-in-the-dark.html.
24. Rachel Sterzer Gibson, "Lessons in loaves and fishes: How failure fueled Dallas Jenkins' success with 'The Chosen,'" Church News, October 30, 2024, https://www.thechurchnews.com/living-faith/2024/10/30/the-chosen-creator-dallas-jenkins-byu-forum-surrender-god.
25. Gibson, "Lessons in loaves and fishes."
26. Gibson, "Lessons in loaves and fishes."

27. Ben Child, "Jim Caviezel claims The Passion of the Christ made him a Hollywood outcast," The Guardian, May 3, 2011, https://www.theguardian.com/film/2011/may/03/jim-caviezel-passion-of-the-christ.

28. Mel Gibson, "Quotes," IMDB.com, accessed September 19, 2025, https://www.imdb.com/name/nm0000154/quotes.

29. Tucker Carlson Network, "'This Feels Wrong'—The Moment Jonathan Roumie Stopped Production on the Set of The Chosen," March 5, 2025, YouTube, 10:23, https://www.youtube.com/watch?v=Vn-OGYc-i-0.

30. Roma Downey, "Interview with Writing Mom Roma Downey and Giveaway," Gina Conroy, January 12, 2012, https://ginaconroy.com/2012/01/12/interview-with-roma-downey-and-giveaway.

31. Staff, "Mark Burnett Reveals Story Behind THE BIBLE Docudrama: 'God's Hands Were On This Series,'" Movieguide, March 27, 2023, https://www.movieguide.org/news-articles/mark-burnett-reveals-story-behind-the-bible-docudrama-gods-hands-were-on-this-series.html.

32. Benjamin Gill, "Hollywood Icon Sylvester Stallone Reveals His Mom Tried to Abort Him Several Times," CBN.com, August 30, 2024, https://cbn.com/news/entertainment/hollywood-icon-sylvester-stallone-reveals-his-mom-tried-abort-him-several-times.

33. Ree Hines, "Mark Wahlberg explains why it's important to him not to 'deny' his faith," Today.com, February 22, 2023, https://www.today.com/life/inspiration/mark-wahlberg-explains-important-not-deny-faith-rcna71761.

34. Denzel Washington, "Denzel Washington: 'Number one: Put God first', Dillard University—2015," Dillard University, May 7, 2015, https://speakola.com/grad/denzel-washington-everything-i-have-is-by-the-grace-of-god-full-2015.

35. Dave Carlin, "Legendary actor Denzel Washington gets minister's license at New York City church," CBS News, December 23, 2024, https://www.cbsnews.com/newyork/news/denzel-washington-ministers-license-kelly-temple-church-of-god-in-christ.

36. Oscars, "Matthew McConaughey winning Best Actor | 86th Oscars (2014)," YouTube, March 2, 2014, YouTube, 4:30, https://www.youtube.com/watch?v=wD2cVhC-63I.

37. Staff, "Matthew McConaughey Is Figuring Out His Faith," Relevant, May 26, 2025, https://relevantmagazine.com/culture/matthew-mcconaughey-on-how-faith-impacts-his-life.

38. Andrea Morris, "'God is Real, He Knows Us': Actor Jon Voight Says a Divine Encounter Got His Life Back on Track," CBN.com, July 18, 2021, https://cbn.com/news/news/god-real-he-knows-us-actor-jon-voight-says-divine-encounter-got-his-life-back-track.

39. Nia Noelle, "Chris Tucker Talks About How Good God Has Been to Him and His New Projects," Get Up! Mornings with Erica Campbell, March 13,

2024, https://getuperica.com/1299521/chris-tucker-tour-info-and-upcoming-projects.

40. Alice Cooper, Goodreads, accessed September 19, 2025, https://www.goodreads.com/quotes/386796-drinking-beer-is-easy-trashing-your-hotel-room-is-easy.

41. Marissa Mayer, "It's Not 'Things that Fill the Voids': Hailey Bieber Shares Wise Words on Faith and Marriage," Pure Flix, February 8, 2022, https://www.pureflix.com/insider/hailey-bieber-on-faith-marriage.

42. Norwegian War Cry, "Q&A with Candace Cameron Bure," The War Cry, accessed September 19, 2025, https://www.thewarcry.org/articles/qa-with-candace-cameron-bure.

43. Staff, "Dennis Quaid: 'I Have a Personal Relationship With' Jesus," Movieguide, July 24, 2024, https://www.movieguide.org/news-articles/dennis-quaid-i-have-a-personal-relationship-with-jesus.html.

44. Will Dawson, "'Not Ashamed of the Gospel': Coach Deion Sanders Stands Firm in His Faith Despite Opposition," CBN News, November 22, 2024, https://cbn.com/news/entertainment/not-ashamed-gospel-coach-deion-sanders-stands-firm-his-faith-despite-opposition.

45. Staff, "Tebow: 'I don't know what my future holds,'" Sports Illustrated, January 15, 2013, https://www.si.com/nfl/2013/01/15/tim-tebow-future-uncertain.

46. Benjamin Gill, "'The Holy Spirit Is Never Confused': Great Christian Wisdom from 10 Top NFL Quarterbacks," CBN News, September 3, 2019, https://cbn.com/news/news/holy-spirit-never-confused-great-christian-wisdom-10-top-nfl-quarterbacks.

47. Joseph Z, interview.

48. Seaman, interview.

CHAPTER 8

1. Sean Feucht, interview.

2. Soren Kierkegaard, *The Journals of Kierkegaard*, accessed September 25, 2025, https://www.goodreads.com/quotes/38371-the-tyrant-dies-and-his-rule-is-over-the-martyr.

3. Staff, "New Barna Data: Young Adults Lead a Resurgence in Church Attendance," Barna Group, September 2, 2025, https://www.barna.com/research/young-adults-lead-resurgence-in-church-attendance.

4. Greg Laurie, "Gen Z Is Growing Hungry for Jesus and It Shows," Harvest, July 26, 2025, https://harvest.org/resources/gregs-blog/post/gen-z-is-growing-hungry-for-jesus-and-it-shows.

5. Charlie Kirk, "Turning Point USA Announces 'The American Comeback Tour,'" Turning Point USA, February 11, 2025, https://tpusa.com/wp-content/

uploads/2025/04/Press-Release-The-American-Comeback-Tour-Spring-2025-.
pdf.

6. Michael Katz, "Rev. Graham: 'Devil Overplayed His Hand' With Kirk's Death," Newsmax, September 12, 2025, https://www.newsmax.com/politics/ franklin-graham-charlie-kirk-erika-kirk/2025/09/12/id/1226272.

7. Turning Point USA, "Charlie Kirk's beloved wife, Mrs. Erika Kirk addresses the Nation."

8. Steven Vago and Chris Nesi, "Charlie Kirk funeral hits capacity as 200K people turn out—with President Trump, widow Erika speak of 'patriot,'" New York Post, September 21, 2025, https://nypost.com/2025/09/21/us-news/ charlie-kirk-funeral-hits-capacity-as-200k-people-turn-out/; Amanda Macias, "Charlie Kirk honored by 90K in one of the largest memorials for a private citizen," Fox News, September 21, 2025, https://www.foxnews.com/politics/ charlie-kirk-honored-90k-one-largest-memorials-private-citizen.

9. Eric Mack, "Dr. Ben Carson: 'Get on Board of the Revival That Is Coming,'" Newsmax, September 21, 2025, https://www.newsmax.com/newsmax-tv/ memorial-charlie-kirk-dr-ben-carson/2025/09/21/id/1227261.

10. Sandy Fitzgerald, "Kirk Producer Kolvet: Slain Leader Was a 'Modern-Day Prophet,'" Newsmax, September 21, 2025, https://www.newsmax.com/ politics/charlie-kirk-andrew-kolvet-turningpointusa/2025/09/21/ id/1227241.

11. Piper Hudspeth Blackburn, "Erika Kirk says husband's mission is now her mission, will continue campus events," CNN, September 21, 2025, https://edition.cnn.com/politics/live-news/charlie-kirk-funeral-09-21- 25?t=1758490592991; Charlie Kirk, "LIVE NOW: Building A Legacy, Remembering Charlie Kirk," September 21, 2025, YouTube, 9:13:13, https://www.youtube.com/watch?v=zkX2rIn_q8o.

12. Sandy Fitzgerald, "Erika Kirk Forgives Husband's Alleged Killer, Vows to Continue TPUSA Mission," Newsmax, September 21, 2025, https://www. newsmax.com/newsmax-tv/erika-kirk-charlie-kirk-tpusa/2025/09/21/ id/1227280; Charlie Kirk, "LIVE NOW: Building A Legacy, Remembering Charlie Kirk."

13. Chris Williams, "Read President Donald Trump's full speech at Charlie Kirk's funeral," LiveNowFox.com, September 21, 2025, https://www. livenowfox.com/news/donald-trumps-full-speech-charlie-kirks-funeral; Charlie Kirk, "LIVE NOW: Building A Legacy, Remembering Charlie Kirk."

14. Sandy Fitzgerald, "Trump: Charlie Kirk Changed History With His Life, Faith," Newsmax, September 21, 2025, https://www.newsmax.com/us/ charlie-kirk-donald-trump-memorial-service/2025/09/21/id/1227283; Charlie Kirk, "LIVE NOW: Building A Legacy, Remembering Charlie Kirk."

15. Charlie Kirk, "LIVE NOW: Building A Legacy, Remembering Charlie Kirk."

16. Bekker, interview.

17. Staff, "100 DAYS OF HOAXES: Cutting Through the Fake News," The White House, April 29, 2025, https://www.whitehouse.gov/articles/2025/04/100-days-of-hoaxes-cutting-through-the-fake-news; Staff, "Trump: Third of Americans see fake news media as 'enemy of the people,'" BBC, November 1, 2018, https://www.bbc.com/news/world-us-canada-46053036.

18. Joseph Z, interview by the author, July 23, 2025.

19. Joseph Z, interview.

20. Joseph Z, interview.

21. Staff, "How to Help Gen Z Connect Spiritually Online at Church," The Barna Group, October 22, 2024, https://www.barna.com/trends/how-to-help-gen-z-connect-spiritually-online-and-at-church.

22. Staff, "How to Help Gen Z Connect Spiritually."

23. Sean Dunn, interview by the author, May 5, 2025.

24. Dunn, interview.

25. Dunn, interview.

26. Taylan Michael Seaman, interview by the author, May 7, 2025.

27. Seaman, interview.

28. Seaman, interview.

29. Seaman, interview.

30. Greg Laurie, "Gen Z Is Growing Hungry for Jesus and It Shows," Harvest.org, July 26, 2025, https://harvest.org/resources/gregs-blog/post/gen-z-is-growing-hungry-for-jesus-and-it-shows.

31. James Lasher, "Digital Evangelism is Reaching the Next Generation and Changing Lives," Charisma, January 30, 2025, https://mycharisma.com/culture/digital-evangelism-is-reaching-the-next-generation-and-changing-lives.

32. Isaiah Saldivar, "About Me," IsaiahSaldivar.com, https://www.isaiahsaldivar.com.

33. Jenny Weaver, "Meet Jenny," JennyWeaverWorships.com, https://www.jennyweaverworships.com.

34. Staff, "The Gen Z Audio Report," Edison Research, June 25, 2025, https://www.edisonresearch.com/the-gen-z-audio-report.

35. Staff, "The Gen Z Audio Report."

36. Ruslan KD, "About," YouTube, https://www.youtube.com/@RuslanKD/videos.

37. Tim Ross, "About Us," Upset the World, https://www.upsettheworld.com/about-us.

38. Allie Beth Stuckey, "About," Allie Beth Stuckey.com, https://www. alliebethstuckey.com/about.

39. Zach Hrynowski and Stephanie Marken," Gen Z Voices Lackluster Trust in Major U.S. Institutions," Gallup, September 14, 2023, https:// news.gallup.com/opinion/gallup/510395/gen-voices-lackluster-trust-major-institutions.aspx.

40. Sean Feucht, Facebook, July 11, 2025, https://www.facebook.com/reel/1082294593877226.

41. Mike Signorelli, "About Mike," MikeSignorelli.com, https://mikesignorelli.com/about.

42. Joseph Z, interview by the author, July 23, 2025.

43. Tovares Grey, YouTube, https://www.youtube.com/@GodlyDating101/featured.

44. Emily Wilson Hussem, "About," Emily Wilson Ministries, https://emilywilsonministries.com/about.

45. Nick Yeh, "Jesus and Joysticks: How Playing Games Shaped My Faith," InterVarsity Christian Fellowship/USA, September 7, 2023, https://intervarsity.org/blog/jesus-and-joysticks-how-playing-games-shaped-my-faith.

46. Yeh, "Jesus and Joysticks."

47. Billy Hallowell, "New Video Game Aims to Help Young People 'Experience Jesus,'" CBN, July 24, 2023, https://cbn.com/news/entertainment/new-video-game-aims-help-young-people-experience-jesus.

48. Staff, "Reach Millions of Youth With The Ultimate Bible Video Game!" NextGen Bible Media, https://nextgenbiblemedia.org/donate.

49. Staff," GATE ZERO by Bible X–Press kit," Gate Zero, https://biblex. notion.site/gate-zero-press-kit.

50. Hallowell, "New Video Game Aims to Help Young People."

51. Joseph Z, interview by the author, July 23, 2025.

CHAPTER 9

1. Brandon Biggs, "Going over what the Lord showed me about the asteroid that's coming," July 26, 2025, Last Days, YouTube, 53:28, https://www.youtube.com/watch?v=xUTlHLlBy_g.

2. Biggs, "Going over what the Lord showed me about the asteroid that's coming."

3. Biggs, "Going over what the Lord showed me about the asteroid that's coming."

4. Troy Anderson, "Revelation 911: Q & A with Pastor Paul Begley and Troy Anderson," *Prophecy Investigators*, January 27, 2024, https://www.prophecyinvestigators.com/p/revelation-911-q-and-a-with-pastor.

5. Joseph Z, interview.

6. Abby Trivett, "Prophecy in Action? What Kim Clement Saw for 2025," *Charisma*, May 6, 2025, https://mycharisma.com/propheticrevival/prophecy-in-action-what-kim-clement-saw-for-2025/.

7. Donald Trump, "National Day of Prayer, 2025," The White House, May 1, 2025, https://www.whitehouse.gov/presidential-actions/2025/05/national-day-of-prayer-2025.

8. Trump, "National Day of Prayer."

9. Staff, "6 Months of Power: President Trump's Comeback. America's Revival," The White House, July 20, 2025, https://www.youtube.com/watch?v=HiFMCVdv1to.

10. Staff, "President Trump Marks Six Months in Office with Historic Successes," The White House, July 20, 2025, https://www.whitehouse.gov/articles/2025/07/president-trump-marks-six-months-in-office-with-historic-successes/?utm_source=chatgpt.com.

11. "President Trump Marks Six Months in Office with Historic Successes," The White House.

12. Committee for a Responsible Federal Budget, "Tariffs Are Generating Meaningful New Revenue," August 11, 2025, https://www.crfb.org/blogs/tariffs-are-generating-meaningful-new-revenue; Danielle Kurtzleben, "Trump's tariff revenue has skyrocketed. But how big is it, really?" NPR, August 11, 2025, https://www.npr.org/2025/08/11/g-s1-81934/trump-tariffs-record-revenue.

13. "President Trump Marks Six Months in Office with Historic Successes," The White House.

14. Molly Olmstead, "J.D. Vance Used to Be an Atheist. What He Believes Now Is Telling," Slate, August 8, 2024, https://slate.com/life/2024/08/jd-vance-tim-walz-trump-kamala-religion.html.

15. Sarah Beth Hensley, "What role Speaker Mike Johnson's religious views play in his politics," ABC News, October 27, 2023, https://abcnews.go.com/Politics/role-speaker-mike-johnsons-religious-views-play-politics/story?id=104366347.

16. Brendan Duke and Bobby Kogan, "Scott Bessent's 3 Percent Deficit Target Would Require Massive Cuts to Anti-Poverty Programs and Middle-Class Tax Increases," Center for American Progress, January 15, 2025, https://www.americanprogress.org/article/scott-bessents-3-percent-deficit-target-would-require-massive-cuts-to-anti-poverty-programs-and-middle-class-tax-increases.

17. Larry Kudlow, "LARRY KUDLOW: Howard Lutnick will keep America first as Commerce Secretary," Fox Business, November 19, 2024, https://www.foxbusiness.com/media/larry-kudlow-howard-lutnick-keep-america-first-commerce-secretary.

18. Robert Tait, "The rise of Stephen Miller, the architect of Trump's hardline immigration policy," The Guardian, June 15, 2025, https://www.theguardian.com/us-news/2025/jun/15/trump-immigration-stephen-miller-influence.

19. C. Todd Lopez, "'Historically Successful' Strike on Iranian Nuclear Site Was 15 Years in the Making," U.S. Department of Defense, June 26, 2025, https://www.defense.gov/News/News-Stories/Article/Article/4227082/historically-successful-strike-on-iranian-nuclear-site-was-15-years-in-the-maki.

20. Staff, "Director Kash Patel," Federal Bureau of Investigation, https://www.fbi.gov/about/leadership-and-structure/director-patel.

21. Encyclopaedia Britannica, "Susie Wiles," accessed September 19, 2025, https://www.britannica.com/biography/Susie-Wiles.

22. Hannah Rabinowitz, "Attorney General Bondi orders prosecutors to start grand jury probe into Obama officials over Russia investigation," CNN, August 4, 2025, https://www.cnn.com/2025/08/04/politics/justice-department-russia-grand-jury.

23. Staff, "Ambassador Mike Huckabee," U.S. Embassy Jerusalem, https://il.usembassy.gov/our-relationship/our-ambassador.

24. Encyclopaedia Britannica, "Tulsi Gabbard," accessed September 19, 2025, https://www.britannica.com/biography/Tulsi-Gabbard.

25. Jim Reed, "Is RFK Jr's divisive plan to Make America Healthy Again fearmongering—or revolutionary?" BBC, June 30, 2025, https://www.bbc.com/news/articles/ceq7jx3dlj9o.

26. Encyclopaedia Britannica, "Karoline Leavitt," accessed September 19, 2025, https://www.britannica.com/biography/Karoline-Leavitt.

27. Morgan Phillips, "Trump to sign executive order establishing White House faith office," Fox News, February 7, 2025, https://www.foxnews.com/politics/trump-executive-order-white-house-faith-office.

28. Danielle Wallace and Brooke Singman, "Trump announces executive order creating task force to 'eradicate anti-Christian bias,'" Fox News, February 6, 2025, https://www.foxnews.com/politics/trump-announces-executive-order-creating-task-force-eradicate-anti-christian-bias.

29. Wallace and Singman, "Trump announces executive order."

30. Staff, "President Trump Announces Appointments to the White House Faith Office," The White House, February 7, 2025, https://www.whitehouse.gov/presidential-actions/2025/02/president-trump-announces-appointments-to-the-white-house-faith-office.

31. Franklin Graham, "Franklin Graham Participates in White House Easter Celebration," Billy Graham Evangelistic Association, April 17, 2025, https://billygraham.org/articles/franklin-graham-participates-in-white-house-easter-celebration; Franklin Graham, "Franklin Graham: Proclaiming Christ in

the Nation's Capital," Decision, June 1, 2025, https://decisionmagazine.com/franklin-graham-proclaiming-christ-in-the-nations-capital.

32. Eric Killelea, "Texas megachurch pastor echoes GOP talking points after White House prayer meeting," *Houston Chronicle*, March 24, 2025, https://www.chron.com/culture/religion/article/texas-pastor-prays-for-trump-20238571.php.

33. Greg Laurie, "Are we seeing another spiritual awakening?" The Christian Post, August 5, 2025,https://www.christianpost.com/voices/are-we-seeing-another-spiritual-awakening.html.

34. Ryan Foley, "Evangelical leaders pray over Trump in Oval Office: 'Faith is more important than ever before,'" The Christian Post, March 21, 2025, https://www.christianpost.com/news/evangelical-leaders-pray-over-trump-in-oval-office.html.

35. Milton Quintanilla, "Alveda King Calls for Unity as MLK Day and Trump Inauguration Align," Crosswalk.com, January 21, 2025, https://www.crosswalk.com/headlines/contributors/milton-quintanilla/alveda-king-calls-for-unity-as-mlk-day-and-trump-inauguration-align.html.

36. Alan DiDio, "The Next 18 Months Will Change EVERYTHING | Lance Wallnau," Encounter Today, February 28, 2025, YouTube, 17:56, https://www.youtube.com/live/USRzpL5hG5w.

37. Che Ahn, "Called to Serve: Why I'm Running for Governor of California," Che Ahn for Governor, accessed September 19, 2025, https://che4ca.com/called-to-serve-why-im-running-for-governor-of-california.

38. James Lasher, "Mario Murillo Issues a Prophetic Warning, a Spiritual Showdown Coming to America," Charisma, May 26, 2025, https://mycharisma.com/propheticrevival/mario-murillo-issues-a-prophetic-warning-a-spiritual-showdown-coming-to-america.

39. Bernis, interview.

40. Staff, "The State of Church Attendance: Trends and Statistics [2025]," ChurchTrac, https://www.churchtrac.com/articles/the-state-of-church-attendance-trends-and-statistics-2023.

41. John Fea, "From Prosperity Televangelism to the White House," Christianity Today, May 29, 2025, https://www.christianitytoday.com/2025/05/paula-white-cain-trump-faith-office-leader/?utm_source=chatgpt.com.

42. Kathryn Palmer, "Partisanship hits peak in Gallup's new Trump approval rating poll. See results," *USA Today*, August 27, 2025, https://www.usatoday.com/story/news/politics/2025/08/27/trump-approval-rating-poll/85847255007.

CHAPTER 10

1. The Last Watch, "Paul McGuire the Man Who Changed My Life."

2. The Last Watch, "Paul McGuire the Man Who Changed My Life."
3. The Last Watch, "Paul McGuire the Man Who Changed My Life."
4. The Last Watch, "Paul McGuire the Man Who Changed My Life."
5. Jonathan Bernis, interview.
6. Abby Trivett, "8 Kim Clement Prophecies Fulfilled in 2024," Charisma, December 13, 2024, https://mycharisma.com/news/8-kim-clement-prophecies-fulfilled-in-2024.
7. Trivett, "8 Kim Clement Prophecies Fulfilled in 2024."
8. Roth, interview.
9. Dr. Alveda King, "AFPI Salutes President Trump's Renewal of the American Dream," America First Policy Institute, March 5, 2025, https://www.americafirstpolicy.com/issues/afpi-salutes-president-dtrumps-renewal-of-the-american-dream.
10. Stephen Collinson, "The Trump revolution is being slowed by its own political debris field," CNN, March 7, 2025, https://www.cnn.com/2025/03/07/politics/trump-revolution-slowed-down-analysis.
11. Alexander Dugin, *The Trump Revolution: A New Order of Great Powers* (Arktos Media Ltd., 2025), Back Cover, https://www.barnesandnoble.com/w/the-trump-revolution-alexander-dugin/1147072863.
12. Paul McGuire, interview on The Inspire Show with Troy Anderson, July 27, 2025.
13. McGuire, interview.
14. Trump, "Presidential Executive Order Promoting Free Speech and Religious Liberty," Trump White House, May 4, 2017, https://trumpwhitehouse.archives.gov/presidential-actions/presidential-executive-order-promoting-free-speech-religious-liberty; Donald Trump, "Executive Order on the Establishment of a White House Faith and Opportunity Initiative," Trump White House, May 3, 2018, https://trumpwhitehouse.archives.gov/presidential-actions/executive-order-establishment-white-house-faith-opportunity-initiative.
15. Russell Wheeler, "How much will Trump's second-term judicial appointments shift court balance?" Brookings Institute, May 12, 2025, https://www.brookings.edu/articles/how-much-will-trumps-second-term-judicial-appointments-shift-court-balance.
16. Emel Akan, "Trump Reshapes Foreign Policy With Tariff Diplomacy," The Epoch Times, August 4, 2025, https://www.theepochtimes.com/article/trump-reshapes-foreign-policy-with-tariff-diplomacy-5896587.
17. Victor Davis Hanson, "Victor Davis Hanson: Can Trump Revolutionize America?" The Free Press, March 4, 2025, https://www.thefp.com/p/victor-davis-hanson-can-trump-reset.
18. Staff, "Billy Graham," The Billy Graham Library, accessed September 19, 2025, https://billygrahamlibrary.org/billy-graham.

19. Troy Anderson, "Billy Graham sounds alarm for 2nd Coming," WND.com, October 20, 2013, https://www.wnd.com/2013/10/billy-graham-sounds-alarm-for-2nd-coming.

20. Troy Anderson, "Billy Graham: Now is time for 'fresh awakening,'" WND.com, September 22, 2013, https://www.wnd.com/2013/09/billy-graham-now-is-time-for-fresh-awakening.

21. William Martin, "The Riptide of Revival," Christian History Institute, Fall 2006, https://christianhistoryinstitute.org/magazine/article/the-riptide-of-revival.

22. Staff, "The Return USA 2020," The Return International, accessed September 19, 2025, https://thereturn.org/thereturn-washingtondc.

23. Paul Begley and Troy Anderson, *Revelation 911: How the Book of Revelation Intersects with Today's Headlines* (Salem Books, 2024), xiii–xiv.

24. Begley and Anderson, *Revelation 911*, 179–182.

25. Begley, interview with the author, August 11, 2025.

26. Begley, interview.

27. Begley, interview.

28. Dutch Sheets, "Dutch Sheets Says Turnaround's Coming That Will Save Billions of Souls," CBN News, February 23, 2018, https://www.youtube.com/watch?v=dXFmd2Y3rL0.

29. Sheets, "Dutch Sheets Says Turnaround's Coming."

30. McGuire and Anderson, *The Babylon Code*.

31. Staff, "Morning Rundown: Kim Clement Prophecy: From Fire to Revival," Charisma, January 15, 2025, https://mycharisma.com/news/morning-rundown-kim-clement-prophecy-from-fire-to-revival; Jillian McKoy, "Wildfires Death Count for 2025 LA County Wildfires Likely Higher than Records Show, BU Research Finds," Boston University, August 12, 2025, https://www.bu.edu/articles/2025/death-count-california-wildfires-higher-than-recorded.

32. Staff, "Morning Rundown: Kim Clement Prophecy."

33. "Church Dropouts Have Risen to 64%—But What About Those Who Stay?" Barna, September 4, 2019, https://www.barna.com/research/resilient-disciples/.

34. Begley, interview.

35. Gene Bailey, *Flashpoint of Revival* (Harrison House Publishers, 2021), 9.

36. Mario Murillo, *It's Our Turn Now* (Charisma House, 2023), 2.

CONCLUSION

1. Troy Anderson, "Baptize America: The Prophetic Outpouring Sweeping a Nation Back to God," *Charisma*, June 7, 2025, https://mycharisma.com/propheticrevival/baptize-america-the-prophetic-outpouring-sweeping-a-nation-back-to-god.

2. Kandis McGee, interview by the author, June 8, 2025.
3. Michael Foust, "26,000 Baptized across U.S. in Historic One-Day Event," Crosswalk.com, June 9, 2025, https://www.crosswalk.com/headlines/contributors/michael-foust/26000-baptized-across-us-in-historic-one-day-event.html; Staff, "The Movement," Baptize.org, accessed September 19, 2025, https://baptize.org.
4. Mark Francey, interview by the author, May 13, 2025.
5. Francey, interview.
6. Francey, interview.
7. "The Movement," Baptize.org.
8. Francey, interview.
9. Francey, interview.
10. Francey, interview.
11. Billy Graham, "The Greatest Revival in History | Billy Graham Classic Sermon," Billy Graham Evangelistic Association, December 21, 2020, YouTube, 27:31, https://www.youtube.com/watch?v=D6PMmVydhgQ.
12. Graham, "The Greatest Revival in History."
13. Fitzgerald, "Erika Kirk Forgives Husband's Alleged Killer."
14. Charlie Kirk, "LIVE NOW: Building A Legacy, Remembering Charlie Kirk."
15. Staff, "China Set to Be 'Most Christian Nation' by 2030," CBN, December 31, 1969, https://cbn.com/news/world/china-set-be-most-christian-nation-2030.
16. "China Set to Be 'Most Christian Nation' by 2030," CBN.
17. Staff, "Fact Sheet: President Donald J. Trump Signs GENIUS Act into Law," The White House, July 18, 2025, https://www.whitehouse.gov/fact-sheets/2025/07/fact-sheet-president-donald-j-trump-signs-genius-act-into-law.
18. Jay O'Brien, Allison Pecorin, Ivan Pereira, and John Parkinson, "Trump signs 1st major federal cryptocurrency bill into law," ABC News, July 18, 2025, https://abcnews.go.com/Politics/trump-sign-1st-major-federal-cryptocurrency-bill-law/story?id=123862419.
19. Joseph Z, interview.
20. Joseph Z, interview.
21. Theodore Roosevelt, "Address at the Sorbonne in Paris, France: 'Citizenship in a Republic,'" The American Presidency Project, April 23, 1910, https://www.presidency.ucsb.edu/documents/address-the-sorbonne-paris-france-citizenship-republic.
22. Jonathan Bernis, interview.